Literature and Legal Problem Solving

Literature and Legal Problem Solving

Law and Literature as Ethical Discourse

EDITED BY
Paul J. Heald

CAROLINA ACADEMIC PRESS
Durham, North Carolina

Library of Congress Cataloging-in-Publication

Literature and legal problem solving : law and literature as ethical
discourse / edited by Paul J. Heald.
    p.   cm.
    Includes bibliographical references.
    ISBN 0-89089-791-3 (cloth)
    1. Law and literature. 2. Law in literature. 3. Literature—History
and criticism.   I. Heald, Paul J., 1959– .
PN56.L33L57 1998
809'.93355—dc21   97-50391
                                                CIP

CAROLINA ACADEMIC PRESS
700 Kent Street
Durham, North Carolina
Telephone (919) 489-7486
Fax (919) 493-5668
E-mail: cap@cap-press.com
www.cap-press.com

Printed in the United States of America

Contents

Acknowledgments

I would like to thank the University of Georgia School of Law for providing the financial support that made writing this book possible and Kelly Casey for her editorial help. The Humanities Center at the University of Georgia provided financial support for the conference that underlies much of the work presented here.

The following copyright holders granted permission for their works, or portions thereof, to be reprinted in this volume:

Princeton University Press: Martha C. Nussbaum, "Equity and Mercy," 22 *Philosophy and Public Affairs* 83–125 (New Jersey: 1993).

Beacon Press: Martha C. Nussbaum, "Rational Emotions," in *Poetic Justice* 53–78 (Boston: 1995).

Bantam Books: Elizabeth George, *Playing for the Ashes* (New York: 1994) (three pages).

Literature and Legal Problem Solving

Introduction

Law and Literature as Ethical Discourse

Paul J. Heald

Malraux told me to drop out of graduate school. When asked to render a second opinion, Pascal, Sartre, Camus, Koestler, Brecht, and Gunter Grass concurred. Tired of classroom theorizing and frustrated by my professors' unwillingness to focus on the fascinating ethical content of the required readings, I found Malraux's advice irresistible. Taking my favorite books with me, I left school and eventually found myself making a career in law. From my first encounter with it, law promised to be a place of engagement, where theory was inevitably connected in important ways to the lives of real people. As Robert Cover bluntly reminded us, "[l]egal interpretation is . . . played out on the field of pain and death."[1] Decisions made by lawyers and judges in both criminal and civil disputes can radically rearrange human relationships. They are directly relevant to human lives in ways that decisions made about literature by graduate students and their professors seldom seem to be. Literary critics appear merely to form opinions — legal actors take part in a palpable drama.

The bite and weight of law stems inevitably from its source in community determinations as to what is good and bad, what is true and false. Society's value choices are embodied in law, rendering its practice primarily a series of ethical exercises. The community speaks of legal decisions as right or wrong, of the content of laws as good or bad, and of legal voices as speaking truthfully or falsely. One does not have to accept any *a priori* assumptions about natural legal foundations to understand the reality of the "rightness" or "wrongness" of decisions made by legal actors. Legal decisions are inescapably ethical decisions.

Legal discourse is not, however, inevitably ethical discourse. Legal language often obscures the value-laden nature of legal choices. In fact, law talk is seldom concerned with overtly separating good from bad. On occasion, judges discuss the comparative desirability of the worlds we might inhabit and why the shape of one world is preferable to another. For example, the transformation of products liability and negligence law over the last eighty

---

1. Robert Cover, "Violence and the Word," 95 *Yale L. J.* 1601, 1606 (1986).

years from *McPherson* to *Li* rests expressly on transformed notions of human responsibility and the right relationship of communities to individuals. But this is the exception. More often, legal opinions pretend to do something other than identify how we should constitute ourselves as a community. Nonetheless, whether judges admit it or not, most implementation of legal rules revolves around questions of "should."

On the other hand, ethics is the formal and express practice of stumbling toward the answers to "should" questions. What should I do? How should a community constitute itself? How should I treat another? Who should be responsible for a loss? The intersection of law and ethics — this fundamental preoccupation with questions of should — is what brought me back to the study of literature.

The essential connection of law to the question of how we should live, even when legal discourse obscures the connection, makes the study of literature relevant to law. Why? Because fiction is an undeniably rich collection of studies in the appropriateness of human action. In fact, literature in its various forms may be a unique repository for information capable of enriching legal decision making. In *Love's Knowledge*, Martha Nussbaum argues forcefully that "certain truths about human life can only be fittingly and accurately stated in the language and forms characteristic of the narrative artist."[2] For her, and probably for most of us who take literature seriously, the linear rhetoric of the logician cannot adequately describe nor convey the knowledge necessary to address the question of how one should make decisions. Although Nussbaum does not set forth as a foundationalist prescription any particular "truths" she has found, she eloquently seeks to reestablish an ethical dimension to literary criticism. And, to the extent that the law involves making ethical judgments, she has made an important point about jurisprudence as well by implying that some knowledge essential to seeking justice has been most perfectly articulated by artists.

In other words, relevant raw materials for solving some legal problems may be found in novels, drama, and mythology. So far, most "law and literature" efforts have not sought to bring art to bear on specific legal questions.[3] Most academics have been content to apply their legal expertise to interpret literary texts or to rehash postmodern debates over foundationalism and moral relativism in the legal context.[4] If we internalize literary lessons, however, we may find that a poem may be as relevant a guide to

---

2. Martha C. Nussbaum, *Love's Knowledge* 5 (New York: Oxford Univ. Press, 1992).

3. But see Richard H. Weisberg, *Poethics* (New York: Columbia Univ. Press, 1992); David Luban, "Some Greek Trials," 54 *Tenn. L. Rev.* 279, 321–22 (1987).

4. For a host of abstractions, see Symposium, "Beyond Critique: Law, Culture, and the Politics of Form," 69 *Tex. L. Rev.* 1595 (1991). By stressing the violent implications of all legal discourse, Robert Cover has pointedly criticized the high level of abstraction of Law

the interpretation of a statute as a congressional committee report (those who have read many committee reports will not find this surprising).

Taking the relevance of literature as a given, all of the essays in this volume attempt to address a specific legal problem in light of particular literary works. The essays are notable both in their deemphasis of meta-theory and abstraction and in the seriousness with which they approach the ethical dimension of the interdisciplinary study of law and literature. To introduce fully the approach to law and literature explored herein, a preliminary comparison of Nussbaum's approach to literature with that of other prominent scholars should help to place the essayists' claims into context.

Although Martha Nussbaum's *Love's Knowledge* does not target directly the relationship between law and literature, she refocuses the debate as framed in recent years by commentators such as James Boyd White, Stanley Fish, and Lief Carter. White writes that "law is best regarded not as a kind of social science but as one of the humanities... [T]he life of the law is thus a life of art, the art of making meaning in language with others."[5] Law and art are both processes through which we constitute ourselves in community with others—languages through which we create meaning in our lives. They are not identical, of course, the language of law often entailing the violence of the state. In spite of the differences in the direct political impact of legal and literary discourse, the rhetoric and substance of each are equally important to creating and maintaining community. The institutional separation of law and the humanities is, therefore, artificial and potentially impoverishing to both disciplines. For White, breaking down distinctions between the two should be the main goal of a law and literature movement.

White focuses on both law and literature as processes and finds that studying them together facilitates our understanding and recognition of the legitimacy of the multitude of voices in our community. The importance of his work lies in his examination of the functions of legal and literary discourse and their connection to the virtues of tolerance, pluralism, and constitutive rhetoric. He does not, however, make clear the justification for privileging these values.

By contrast, although Stanley Fish applauds White's process-oriented integrationist approach to both literature and law, he finds fault with "White's hopes for the law [that] are not rhetorical, but transcendental."[6]

---

and Literature scholarship. See Robert M. Cover, "Violence and the Word," 95 *Yale L.J.* 1601, 1601–02 & n.2 (1986).

5. James B. White, *Heracles' Bow: Essays on the Rhetoric and Poetics of the Law* xii (Madison: Univ. of Wisconsin Press, 1985).

6. Stanley Fish, "The Law Wishes to Have a Formal Existence," in Austin Sarat & Thomas R. Kearns, Jr. (eds.) *The Fate of Law* 159, 201 (Ann Arbor: Univ. of Mich. Press, 1991).

Like White, he recognizes doctrinal inconsistency and linguistic indeterminacy, but nonetheless appreciates the pragmatic success of the law and the constraints of professionalism. Fish does not, however, as he accuses White of doing, "look forward to a time when all parties will lay down their forensic arms and join together in the effort to build a new and more rational community."[7] An appreciation of the artistic nature of the legal endeavor will not improve the law nor nurture a better community. As an objective matter, Fish would deny that the word "justice" itself has any fixed, noncontextual meaning. White would also deny a fixed content for justice, in the sense that a bicameral legislature might be called the "most just"; however, he clearly privileges peace, tolerance and pluralism to such an extent that a consistent vision of justice might be implied. This hint of objectivism leads Fish to admonish White to cease having progressive hopes for the interesting relationship he has described.

In a slightly different vein, Lief Carter suggests that recognizing law as an art form implicates another possible standard by which to measure justice.[8] Although he does not offer an absolute objective standard, he notes that judicial opinions productively bear aesthetic scrutiny. The legal aesthetic examines the "fit" between the "raw experiences" of the community and "common pattern[s] in the way we think."[9] Some judicial decisions fit better than others, for the same reasons that some artistic performances please the audience more than others: "The good performance creates in that audience a belief that it shares a communal experience.... 'Doing justice' is a subset of this phenomenon."[10] Even though our politics may be offended by a particular decision—Justice Harlan himself clearly disapproved of the protester he vindicated in Cohen[11]—or our moral sense may be at odds with the message of a particular work of art—some of my atheist friends love Brahms' Requiem—our aesthetic sense may nonetheless be able to appreciate voices in conflict with our own.

Carter echoes White in his call for a peaceful turf on which to argue and recognize our unique positions. Our differences make consensus unlikely, but a move toward an aesthetics of decision making and away from fixation on pure ideological or technological correctness (ends discourse) will improve the quality of legal discourse. Like White, however, Carter fails to explain adequately his privileging of plural voices and peaceful discourse

---

7. Id.

8. Lief H. Carter, *Contemporary Constitutional Lawmaking: The Supreme Court and the Art of Politics* 13 (New York: Pergamon, 1985).

9. Id. at 162.

10. Id. at 151.

11. See *Cohen v. California*, 403 U.S. 15 (1971) (upholding a protestor's First Amendment right to wear a jacket emblazoned with the slogan "Fuck the Draft").

as the core of his aesthetics. He would reject the suggestion that the Nuremberg rallies in any sense "did justice," and yet they were undoubtedly a profoundly "share[d]...communal experience."[12] Aesthetic considerations, as opposed to ethical ones, do not obviously demand the inclusion of plural (non-racist) voices.

White, Fish, and Carter are representative of many who integrate law and literature.[13] They focus on process and function—how law works, how literature works. Although White and Carter might be interpreted as hinting at external substantive norms (plurality, tolerance, and peaceful discourse) that could be used to judge when law or literature is "working" well, all three avoid traditional ethical language. Of recent commentators, Richard Weisberg and David Luban are noteworthy for expressly considering the ethical dimension of law and literature.[14] Most theorists are not expressly engaged in an Aristotelian search for "justice" or "the good." They are wary of any projects tainted with objectivist notions because projects claiming to have the "truth" or to know what "justice" demands have too frequently justified political and moral atrocities. The current goal of legal philosophy seems to be the establishment of a jurisprudence that denies validity to atrocity and nihilism, while avoiding ethical discourse.

In *Love's Knowledge,* Nussbaum describes an ethics of reading and the possibility of ethical discourse that makes no grand, oppressive (or monopolistic) claim to the truth. She asserts that literature is worth studying for reasons other than to scrutinize the literary process or the art of rhetoric. Every work of art contains clues as to how we should live. We read not primarily to find out something about the process of writing but to decide how to act and think, to encounter "certain truths" available nowhere else. We read to become wiser. Her position, of course, is as old as Aristotle (on whom she frequently relies), but it establishes her as a leading voice in opposition to postmodern skepticism.

---

12. See Carter, supra note 10, at 151.

13. See, e.g., Richard H. Weisberg, *Poethics* 3–47 (New York: Columbia Univ. Press, 1992) (noting similarities between metaphors and other literary devices used in poetry and those used in law, including the personification of abstractions); Owen Barfield, "Poetic Diction and Legal Fiction," in *Essays Presented to Charles Williams* 106, 121 (Grand Rapids: Eerdmans, 1966) (formalizing the relationship as: "metaphor: language: meaning [as] legal fiction: law: social life"); Thomas D. Eisele, "The Activity of Being a Lawyer: The Imaginative Pursuit of Implications and Possibilities," 54 *Tenn. L. Rev.* 345, 360–61 (1987) (examining, as one way of understanding the activity of lawyering, the implications of a paradigm that "imagines the...lawyer...to be a worker in words, an author and a reader" whose activities are fundamentally linguistic).

14. See supra note 3.

Following her lead, the essays in this volume comprise the first concerted attempt to establish law and literature as traditional ethical discourse.

The first essay, Nussbaum's "Equity and Mercy," serves as the paradigm. Dissenting in *Walton v. Arizona*,[15] Justice Scalia argues that the inquiry conducted by courts in the punishment phase of capital murder trials is seriously flawed. Defendants facing the death penalty can offer whatever mitigating evidence is available, but prosecutors are constrained by specific statutory aggravating factors. Nussbaum responds that although this state of affairs seems unbalanced, it is quite consistent with classical notions of retribution, equity, and mercy. Notions of retribution embodied in the statutory aggravating factors — basically a legislated list of what we as society find to be particularly evil acts — render a murderer eligible for the death penalty, but the appropriateness of execution can only be judged in light of the individual characteristics of the accused. Death is an extreme penalty; those doing the sentencing should be authorized to examine the inner-life of the murderer.

While avoiding justifying capital punishment in general, Nussbaum finds support in ancient Greek and Roman literature for heavily criticized recent case law on mitigating circumstances. Although some pre-Socratic Greeks advocated a pure *lex talionis* — punishment based purely on deed and not motivation, intent, or character — most classical literature, and later western works building upon it, considers individuation of the criminal actor to be a critical part of the process of judgment. This individuation, authorized now by the Court, can be justified historically and also from a moral perspective. Standing in place of the community as a whole and charged with carrying out its will, the sentencing authority must be able to learn as precisely as possible upon whom it is passing judgment. A sentence that is deliberately based on inadequate information is immoral, and Nussbaum's resort to literature suggests why the Court considers full information in this context to be critical. Scalia makes a superficially appealing and logical point in *Walton*; Nussbaum uses literature to demolish it and improve our understanding of death penalty procedure.

In the second essay, "Medea and the Un-Man," I apply Nussbaum's approach to another difficult question involving capital sentencing. In *Maynard v. Cartwright*,[16] the Supreme Court struck down one of the aggravating factors in Oklahoma's death penalty scheme. It held that the term "especially heinous murder," as used in Oklahoma, was unconstitutionally vague and provided inadequate guidance to juries. Interestingly, the Court did not hold that a state could not use heinousness as a justifica-

---

15. 497 U.S. 639 (1990).
16. 486 U.S. 356 (1988).

tion for inflicting the death penalty, but rather demanded that state courts explain more clearly to their juries what "especially heinous" means.

Literature, of course, provides many illustrations of what is heinous and what is merely pathetic. By comparing Euripides' version of the Medea myth to Dante's portrayal of Friar Alberigo in the Inferno and C.S. Lewis's depiction of the "Un-Man" in Perelandra, my essay tries to respond to the mandate of *Cartwright* and evaluates the states' attempts to comply with the opinion. One issue with which state courts have grappled is whether the definition of heinous should focus on the circumstances of the crime or the mental state of the murderer during the commission of the crime. The literature explored in the essay suggests that the primary focus should be on mental state and concludes specifically that murderers fitting the Medea archetype should not be labeled heinous. Given that Medea is a multiple infanticide, this conclusion may be somewhat startling. The essay argues that Dante and Lewis provide better examples of who might be properly classified by the state as eligible for the death penalty.

Pursuing the topic of infanticide further, Susan Sage Heinzelman examines two Texas cases involving mothers accused of murdering their children. She illustrates the critical role of stories and folklore in mediating the legal consequences of the mothers' crimes. In one actual case, a prosecutor was persuaded, in light of the Mexican myth of "La Llorona" (the weeping woman), to reduce drastically charges against an Hispanic mother who intentionally drowned two of her children. Heinzelman demonstrates that sometimes literature, folklore, and mythology provide the best access for the outsider (judge, prosecutor, professor, jury, student) to the seemingly incomprehensible actions of another. She not only provides an example of literature in action, but also expands our notions of how literature might impact law. If a literary sensibility can inform the decision making of not only judges and juries, but also prosecutors, why should fiction not be directly relevant to the choices made by private attorneys, law students, and legislators too?

Although the subsequent essay, Nussbaum's "Rational Emotions," expressly focuses on judges and juries, her discussion of the role of emotion in legal decision making is widely applicable. Her essay directly addresses two issues raised in the first three essays: What can literature tell us about good judgment and what use of literature should the good judge make? The particular problem she deals with is raised by *California v. Brown*,[17] in which the Court approved of "anti-sympathy" instructions given to juries in capital sentencing proceedings in some states. Her discussion of Dickens, Seneca, and Adam Smith casts serious doubt on the

---

17. 479 U.S. 538 (1986).

Court's approach and sets forth the proper role for emotions in legal decision making. Her observations about the nature of good judgment create a nice bridge to the issues discussed in the final three essays.

In "Elizabeth George, Cantor's Theorem, and the Admissibility of Scientific Evidence," Lief Carter explores the ethical dimension of his approach to the aesthetics of legal decision making. In *Daubert v. Merrell Dow Pharmaceuticals, Inc.,*[18] the Court set forth new criteria for determining the admissibility of scientific evidence under the Federal Rules of Evidence. Carter defends the new standard from charges that it permits the admission of "junk science" into the courtroom by examining the new test in light of the novels of master mystery writer Elizabeth George. Carter argues that our conception of scientific truth has changed significantly since *Frye v. U.S.* articulated a standard that excluded evidence not "generally accepted" in the scientific community.[19] The new standard forces judges to evaluate directly the quality of the scientific "story" being offered as evidence. *Deus ex machina*, in the form of acceptance by scientific authority, no longer suffices.

According to Carter, the experience of writers (and readers) of the best mystery novels suggests that we need not be overly worried about the competency of judges to evaluate independently the evidentiary stories they are told. *Daubert* does not offer judges carte blanche to admit or deny whatever they want. The interpretive constraints within the relevant legal community are analogous to the cultural constraints (literary conventions) under which the writer of a good mystery operates. Carter demonstrates how the mystery genre done well provides not just a critical stance on *Daubert*, but also a model for how any appellate opinion might avoid the legal equivalent of *deus ex machina*. In a compelling attempt to merge form and content to make his point, Carter structures his essay "to present mysteries to solve so that readers can participate in the construction of its truth. Just like jurors at a trial."

In the following essay, "Saul and David, and Corporate Takeover Law," David Skeel also examines the nature of judicial performance. Recent decisions of the Delaware Supreme Court in critical cases involving corporate governance have been attacked as completely contradictory and as providing little guidance to corporate directors. Skeel finds in the biblical story of Saul and David in First Samuel a useful illustration of the sort of coherent story that the Delaware court may be telling. God punishes the sinful actions of Saul and David differently for much the same reason that the Delaware court distinguishes between the legitimacy of superficially similar reactions of corporate directors to takeover threats. Viewed in light of First Samuel, recent Delaware takeover decisions become coherent and instructive.

---

18. 509 U.S. 579 (1993).
19. 293 F. 1013 (1921).

The final essay, "Don Juan and the Tort of Seduction," inserts itself into the debate that is currently raging over the extent to which misrepresentations made to obtain sexual consent should be actionable in a civil suit. It explores the fascinating history of Don Juan as a literary archetype from his first appearance in Tirso de Molina's *El Burlador de Sevilla* (1636) to Max Frisch's *Don Juan oder die Liebe zu Geometrie* (1956). Surprisingly, a survey of the many manifestations of Don Juan teaches one little about the essence of sex or seduction. What Don Juan fiction reveals about the differences between masculine and feminine archetypes, however, suggests that a focus on unconscionability principles as developed in contract law, rather than the law of fraud, best identifies the sort of seduction that should be considered tortious.

Each essayist addresses a particular legal problem in light of specific literary texts and answers the question: What should the rule be? Although the ultimate test of this approach to law and literature should be the persuasiveness of the individual arguments made by the authors, one might nonetheless indulge the current rage for theory and examine what sort of theoretical claims might be made for this sort of incorporation of literature into law.

One claim, easily recast as criticism, might be that literature provides a ready source of metaphor and, for the crafty lawyer, an effective rhetorical weapon. This volume's response, however, is that considering the works of artists like Dickens, Dante, and Seneca is a distinctly ethical exercise, part of the constant re-examination of how one should live. If James Boyd White is right about the closeness of the relationship between law and art, then this rigor naturally extends beyond our own discrete selves to the world and, more concretely, to the question of how we should constitute ourselves in community with others. Not only the works discussed herein, but the whole corpus of literature, and indeed all art, is potentially relevant to making ethical choices, including legal decisions. They are particularly fertile sources of wisdom available to shape legal rules, not mere tools of persuasion.

The claim that literature is highly relevant to law, however, must be separated from the potential claim that exposure to literature will ultimately render the law just or even enable us to articulate a clear definition of justice. Nussbaum's explanation of the ethics of reading does not include a set of behavioral prescriptions for us, nor a tidy list of truths she has found. By the same token, although an ethical conception of law demands the incorporation of literature, such an incorporation will not enable us to construct a comprehensive list of just legal rules. Justice is out there, but we cannot often be very sure of its particulars. To paraphrase Lief Carter, at best we dance around the truth.

The ethical conception suggested here might be best illustrated with yet another literary example. The simultaneous embracing of objective truth and the rejection of grand claims about its content is the core of Blaise Pascal's conception of God. Pascal's notion of a "hidden God" emerges from his extending "paradox to God himself," and making Him "both certain and uncertain, present and absent" and thus opening a new chapter in the history of philosophical thought.[20] According to Pascal, God exists—and so therefore does truth in an objective sense—but he is mostly hidden. Human rationality, although evidence of the divine spark, is incapable of fully realizing justice or truth. We can meditate, read, pray, and make intelligent guesses as to the nature of the cosmos, but we are far too fragmented and broken to put the puzzle together. According to Pascal, "[w]e possess truth and goodness only in part, and mingled with falsehood and evil."[21]

Pascal suggests that justice exists—that natural law contains right and wrong answers to legal questions. The hidden nature of God, however prevents us from perceiving justice clearly. A combination of intuition, reason, and experience reveals some things with relative certainty—for example, that murder is bad—but mostly we grope for the truth. Like Plato's cave dwellers, we can only make guesses from the shadows we see playing on the walls of our cave. Literature provides many shadows for us to scrutinize and discuss. We may misapply our learning, but we are at least proceeding in good faith.

Any claims made in the essays are similarly modest: We pursue wisdom when we read. What we ultimately find is another matter. We can, however, remain faithful to the ethics of the pursuit. The existential nature of our journey is not a denial of an ultimate reality, but a recognition of human frailty.

This frailty must be recognized when we look to literature for help in making legal decisions, especially when the legal pronouncement may be death. In some well-known contexts—for example, the Spanish Inquisition—what is called "truthseeking" becomes synonymous with dehumanization. Only the constant recognition of the frailty of human judgment can forestall the dangerous confluence of intellectual arrogance and claims of truth. If we remember our frailty, literature may help us humanize even violent legal moments. After all, even an inquisition has a hard time surviving *The Brothers Karamazov*.

Literature may help us approximate a just legal rule, but human nature stands in the way of the establishment of justice. That nature, however, is not entirely base. We are at least capable of embarking on the Aristotelian inquiry, and literature can be a valuable part of the ethical grop-

---

20. Lucien Goldmann, *The Hidden God* 198 (Philip Thody trans., Humanities Press 1964) (1955).

21. Blaise Pascal, *Pensées*, Fragment 385 at 104 (W.F. Trotter trans., E.P. Dutton & Co. 1931) (1670).

ing we call legal decision making. The predominant view of law and literature as exemplified by James Boyd White or Stanley Fish can only partially be reconciled with the essays presented here. For White, both law and literature are processes through which we constitute ourselves and generate community values. Fish shares this view to the extent that value and meaning arise organically from the community, and not from on high. For them, law is not truthseeking, but truthmaking.

The contribution of these essays is their illustration of an approach that enables us to make ethical choices without setting ourselves up as gods, arrogantly ready to impose our perceptions of truth upon all dissenters. We incorporate literature into law in the hope of better defining the shadows that play on the wall of our cave. Because we cannot avoid living in community, we extend to the law itself our personal ethical inquiry into the nature of the good.

Chapter One

Equity and Mercy

Martha C. Nussbaum

> We stomp on the rape magazines or we invade where they prostitute us,
> where we are herded and sold, we ruin their theatres where they have sex
> on us, we face them, we scream in their fucking faces, we are the women
> they have made scream when they choose...We're all the same, cunt is cunt
> is cunt, we're facsimiles of the ones they done it to, or we are the ones
> they done it to, and I can't tell him from him from him...so at night,
> ghosts, we convene; to spread justice, which stands in for law, which has
> always been merciless, which is by its nature, cruel.
>
> Andrea Dworkin, Mercy

> This second doctrine [of mercy]—counter-doctrine would be a better word—
> has completely exploded whatever coherence the notion of 'guided discretion'
> once had...The requirement [of mitigation] destroys whatever rationality
> and predictability the...requirement [of aggravation] was designed to achieve.
>
> Justice Scalia, in Walton v. Arizona

> O child...do not cure evil with evil. Many people have preferred the more
> equitable to the more just.
>
> Herodotus, History

I.

I begin with the plot of a novel whose title is *Mercy*.[1] By the author's
deliberate design, it is not really a novel, and there is no mercy in it. These

---

This paper was delivered as a Dewey Lecture at the University of Chicago Law School,
as a Boutwood Lecture at Cambridge University, as a Whitehall-Linn Lecture at Bryn
Mawr College, and at a Legal Humanities conference at Stanford University. I am grateful
to these audiences for their questions and comments, and especially to Ronald Allen,
Albert Alschuler, Allen Boegehold, Daniel Brudney, Myles Burnyeat, Scott Crider, John
Lawless, Richard Posner, John Roemer, Cass Sunstein, and the Editors of *Philosophy &
Public Affairs* for comments that have been very helpful to me in revising an earlier draft,
and to Susan Wolf and Joyce Carol Oates for valuable discussions.
1. Andrea Dworkin, *Mercy* (New York: Four Walls, Eight Windows, 1991); see my
review in *The Boston Review* (May–June 1992). In the September–October issue I reply
to letters defending Dworkin's position.

facts are connected. My plan is to pursue this connection. The author of this "novel" is the feminist writer and antipornography activist Andrea Dworkin. Its narrator is also named Andrea—a name that, as she tells us, means "courage" or "manhood." At the age of nine, Andrea is molested by an anonymous man in a movie theater. At fourteen, she is cut with a knife by a sadistic teenage lover. At eighteen she sleeps with many men for money; she finds a tender black lover, but is brutally raped by his roommate. Jailed for antiwar activity, she is assaulted and tortured by prison doctors. She goes to Crete and has a passionate loving relationship with a Greek bartender, but when he discovers that she has been making love casually with many men he rapes her and gives her up. Returning to New York, she lives a marginal life of sex, drink, and drugs. Threatened by a gang one night, she tries to make peace with its leader. He holds her hostage at knifepoint in her own bed. Apparently rescued by a man who turns up at her door, she finds herself raped by her rescuer.

At twenty-two she marries a tender young revolutionary. As soon as they are husband and wife, he finds himself unable to make love without tying her up and hitting her. She leaves him for street life. Some years later, after many other abuses, she takes karate lessons and becomes adept at kicking drunken homeless men to death. We encounter at this point the passage that I have quoted as an epigraph to this article; it expresses Andrea's angry refusal of mercy, her determination to exact retribution without concern for the identity of the particulars. ("I can't tell him from him from him.") Although one might wonder whether the point is that terrible experiences have corrupted Andrea's perception, it appears that her refusal of mercy is endorsed by the novel as a whole.

This novel does not read like a traditional novel, because its form express-es the retributive idea that its message preaches. That is, it refuses to per-ceive any of the male offenders—or any other male—as a particular indi-vidual, and it refuses to invite the reader into the story of their lives. Like Andrea, it can't tell him from him from him. The reader hears only the solitary voice of the narrator; others exist for her only as sources of her pain. Like the women in the male pornography that Dworkin decries, her males have no history, no psychology, no concrete reasons for action. They are just knives that cut, arms that beat, penises that maim by the very act of penetration. Dworkin's refusal of the traditional novelist's attention to the stories of particular lives seems closely connected with her heroine's refusal to be merciful to any of those lives, with her doctrine that justice is cruel and hard.[2] But the nature of the connection between mercy and a vision of the particular is not yet evident; my hope is to make it evi-

---

2. I note that we do not find this refusal in some of Dworkin's best essays on sexuality, in particular the essays on Tennessee Williams and James Baldwin in *Intercourse*.

dent—and, in the process, to make a case for the moral and legal importance of the novelist's art.

In order to do this, however, I must begin with a historical inquiry into the origins, in the Western tradition, of the close connection between equitable judgment—judgment that attends to the particulars and mercy, defined by Seneca as "the inclination of the mind toward leniency in exacting punishment." I begin with a puzzle in ancient Greek thought about law and justice. Solving this puzzle requires understanding some features of the archaic idea of justice that turn out to be highly pertinent to Andrea Dworkin's project. This sort of justice is soon criticized, with appeal to both equity and mercy. After following the arguments of Aristotle and Seneca on this question, I shall return to contemporary issues, using these ideas to make a case for the moral and legal importance of narrative art in several areas of contemporary law and politics, defending the equity/mercy tradition as an alternative both to retributive views of punishment and to some modern deterrence-based views.

II.

There is a puzzle in the evidence for ancient Greek thought about legal and moral reasoning. Two concepts that do not appear to be at all the same are treated as so closely linked as to be aspects of the same concept and are introduced together by one and the same moral term. The moral term is *epieikeia*.[3] The concepts are the two that I have already identified as my theme: the ability to judge in such a way as to respond with sensitivity to all the particulars of a person and situation and the "inclination of the mind" toward leniency in punishing—equity and mercy.[4] From the beginning, the idea of flexible particularized judgment is linked with leniency. *Epieikeia*, which originally designated the former, is therefore said to be accompanied by the latter; it is something mild and gentle, something

---

3. For an excellent discussion of the term and its philosophical and legal history in Greece and Rome, see Francesco D'Agostino, *Epieikeia: Il Tema Dell'Equità nell'Antichita Greca* (Milan: A Giuffre, 1973). An excellent study that focuses on fourth-century B.C. oratory and its relationship to Aristotle is John Lawless, *Law, Argument and Equity in the Speeches of Isaeus*, Ph.D. diss., Brown University, 1991. Both D'Agostino and Lawless have extensive bibliographies. *Epieikeia* is usually translated into Latin by *clementia*. Modern scholars generally render it into German with *Billigkeit*, Italian by *equità*, French by *équité* or (translating the Latin) *clémence*.

4. Both equity and mercy can be spoken of as attributes of persons, as features of judgments rendered by a person, or as moral abstractions in their own right. Thus a person may be praised as *epieikês*; his or her judgments or decisions to display *epieikes*, or show a respect for *epieikes*.

contrasted to the rigid or harsh. The Herodotean father, in my epigraph, contrasts the notion of strict retributive justice with *epieikeia*, at a time when that word was already clearly associated with situational appropriateness.[5] The orator Gorgias, praising the civic character of soldiers fallen in battle, says of them that "on many occasions they preferred the gentle equitable (*to praon epieikes*) to the harshly stubborn just (*tou authadous dikaiou*), and appropriateness of reasoning to the precision of the law, thinking that this is the most divine and most common law, namely to say and not say, to do and to leave undone, the thing required by the situation at the time required by the situation."[6] He too, then, links the ability to do and say the right thing in the situation with a certain mildness or softness; opposed to both is the stubborn and inflexible harshness of law. By this time, the original and real etymology of the *epieikeia*—from *eikos*, the "plausible" or appropriate,"[7]—is being supplemented by a popular derivation of the term from *eikô*, "yield," "give way." Thus even in writing the history of their term, Greek thinkers discover a connection between appropriate judgment and leniency.[8]

The puzzle lies, as I have said, in the unexplained connection between appropriate situational judgment and mercy. One might well suppose that a judgment that gets all the situational particulars correct will set the level of fault sometimes high up, sometimes low down, as the situation demands. If the judgment is a penalty-setting judgment, it will sometimes set a heavy penalty and sometimes a light one, again as the situation demands. If the equitable judgment or penalty is being contrasted with a general principle designed beforehand to fit a large number of situations—as is usually the case—then we might expect that the equitable will sometimes be more

---

5. Hdt. III.53; for discussion, see D'Agostino, *Epieikeia* p. 7. See also Soph fr. 770 (Pearson), which contrasts "simple justice" (*tên haplôs dikên*) with both equity and grace (*charis*). All translations from the Greek are my own.

6. Gorgias, *Epitaphios*, fragment Diels-Kranz 82B6. The passage has occasioned much comment and controversy: see D'Agostino, *Epieikeia*, p. 28ff. for some examples. It seems crucial to understand the passage as pertaining to the civic virtue of the fallen, not their military attributes.

7. See P. Chantraine, *Dictionnaire étymologique de la langue grecque: Histoire des mots*, vol. 2 (Paris: Klinsieck, 1970), p. 355. For other references, see D'Agostino, *Epieikeia*, pp. 1–2, n. 3. *Eikos* is the participle of *eoika*, "seems." (The English word "seemly" is an instructive parallel.) In early poetry, the opposite of *epieikes* is *aeikes*, "outrageous," "totally inappropriate," "horrible."

8. In addition to the passages discussed below, see Pseudo-Plato, *Definitions* 412A, the first known definition of *epieikeia*, which defines it as "good order of the reasoning soul with respect to the fine and shameful," as "the ability to hit on what is appropriate in contracts," and also as "mitigation of that which is just and advantageous."

lenient than the generality of the law, but sometimes harsher. For, as that not-very-merciful philosopher Plato puts it in the *Laws*, sometimes the offender turns out to be unusually good for an offender of that sort, but sometimes, too, unusually bad.[9] Plato has a modern ally in Justice Scalia, who feels that it is absurd that aggravation and mitigation should be treated asymmetrically in the law. The very same requirements should hold for both; presumably, once we begin looking at the specific circumstances, we will be about as likely to find grounds for the one as for the other.[10]

But this is not what many Greek and Roman thinkers seem to think. They think that the decision to concern oneself with the particulars is connected with taking up a gentle and lenient cast of mind toward human wrongdoing. They endorse the asymmetry that Justice Scalia finds absurd and incoherent. We must now ask on what grounds, and with what rationality and coherence of their own, they do so.

III.

We can make some progress by looking at what *epieikeia* opposes or corrects. We see in our passages a contrast between *epieikeia* as flexible situational judgment and the exceptionless and inflexible mandates of law or rule. We also find these laws or rules described as "harsh," "harshly stubborn," a "cure of evil with evil." This goes to the heart of our puzzle, clearly, for what we need to know is how that sort of justice comes to be seen as harsh in its lack of fit to the particulars, rather than as simply imprecise.

Let us think, then, of the archaic conception of justice. And let us examine the first surviving philosophical text to use the notion of justice, for in its metaphorical application of *dikê* to cosmic process it illustrates very vividly what *dikê*, in human legal and moral matters, was taken to involve. Writing about the cyclical changes of the basic elements into one another — as the hot, the cold, the wet, and the dry succeed one another in varying combinations that make up the seasons of the year — the sixth-century B.C. philosopher Anaximander writes, "They pay penalty and

---

9. Plato, *Laws* 867d. on regulations concerning the recall of an exiled homicide.

10. See *Walton v. Arizona*, 479 U.S. 639, 362 (1993) ("Our cases proudly announce that the Constitution effectively prohibits the States from excluding from the sentencing decision an aspect of a defendant's character or record or any circumstance surrounding the crime: [for example] that the defendant had a poor and deprived childhood, or that he had a rich and spoiled childhood.") (Scalia, J., dissenting).

retribution (*dikén kai tisin*) to one another in accordance with the assessment of time."[11]

Anaximander describes a process in which "encroachments" by one element are made up in exact proportion, over time, by compensatory "encroachments" of the corresponding opposite element. We are, it seems, to imagine as neutral a state of balance in which each element has, so to speak, its own — its due sphere, its due representation in the sphere of things. Next the balance is thrown off, in that one or more of the elements goes too far, trespasses on the preserve of the other — as, for example, winter is an invasion by the cold and the wet into the due preserve of the warm and the dry. (Thus the root notion of injustice, already in the sixth century, is the notion of *pleonexia*, grasping more than one's due share, the very notion that Plato exploits in the *Republic*, trying to capture its opposite with the notion of "having and doing one's own.")[12] Winter is in imbalance, and in order for justice or *dikê* to be restored, retribution (*tisis*) must take place; the elements that encroached must "pay justice and retribution" to the ones they squeezed out. What this seems to mean is that a corresponding encroachment in the other direction must take place, in order that "the doer should suffer."[13] Summer is the due retribution for the imbalance of winter; mere springtime would not right the balance, because cold and wet would not be duly squeezed out in their turn.

In short, this cosmology works with an intuitive idea that derives from the legal and moral sphere. It is the idea that for encroachment and pain inflicted a compensating pain and encroachment must be performed. The primitive sense of the just — remarkably constant from several ancient cultures to modern intuitions such as those illustrated in our Andrea Dworkin passage — starts from the notion that a human life (or, here, the life of the cosmos) is a vulnerable thing, a thing that can be invaded, wounded, or violated by another's act in many ways. For this penetration, the only remedy that seems appropriate is a counterinvasion, equally deliberate, equally grave. And to right the balance truly, the retribution must be exactly,

---

11. Anaximander DK fragment B1, the first surviving verbatim fragment of ancient Greek philosophy. (We know it to be verbatim because Simplicus, who reports it, also comments with some embarrassment about its language, saying "as he said using rather poetic terms.") For an excellent account of Anaximander's idea and its connection with ideas of justice and equality in law and morals see Gregory Vlastos, "Equality and Justice in Early Greek Cosmologies," in *Studies in Presocratic Philosophy*, ed. David Furley and Reginald Allen, vol. 1 (London: Routledge, 1970), 56–91.

12. See G. Vlastos, "Plato's Theory of Social Justice," in *Interpretations of Plato: A Swarthmore Symposium*, ed. H. North (Leiden: Brill 1977).

13. *Ton drasanta pathein*, Aeschylus, *Choephoroi*, l. 313. A similar idea is expressed in many other places; see for example, Aes., *Agamemnon* 249, 1564.

strictly proportional to the original encroachment. It differs from the original act only in the sequence of time and in the fact that it is a response rather than an original act—a fact frequently obscured if there is a long sequence of acts and counteracts.

This retributive idea is committed to a certain neglect of the particulars. For Anaximander, it hardly matters whether the snow and rain that get evaporated are in any sense "the same" snow and rain that did the original aggressing. The very question is odd, and Anaximander seems altogether uninterested in the issues of individuation and identity that would enable us to go further with it. Nor are things terribly different in the human legal and moral applications of retributive *dikê*. Very often the original offender is no longer on the scene, or is inaccessible to the victim, and yet the balance still remains to be righted. What then happens is that a substitute target must be found, usually some member of the offender's family. The crimes of Atreus are avenged against Agamemnon, Agamemenon's offense burdens Orestes. The law that "the doer must suffer" becomes, in this conception of justice as balanced retribution, the law that for every bad action some surrogate for the doer must suffer; and, like Andrea Dworkin's narrator, the ancient concept of *dikê* can't "tell him from him from him." A male has raped Andrea; then another male will get a karate kick. The substitution is usually justified through an intuitive notion that the real offender is "the line of X" or "the house of X," or, in Dworkin, "the gender of X." But this alleged justification entails neglect of the particularity of the so-called offender; it neglects, too, questions of motive and intention that one might think crucial in just sentencing.

A closely related sort of neglect can arise even if the original offender is around to receive the punishment. For suppose that the offender committed an act that is in some sense heinous, but did so with extenuating circumstances. (Oedipus committed both parricide and incest, but with an excusable ignorance of crucial information.) *Dikê* says that parricide and incest have occurred here, and the balance must be righted. The eyes that saw their mother's naked body must be blinded. Now in this case the doer and sufferer are the same individual, but notice that Oedipus's particularity is still in a significant sense neglected for he is being treated the same way, by *dikê*, as a true or voluntary parricide would be treated, and crucial facts about him, about his good character, innocent motives, and fine intentions, are neglected. But to neglect all this is to neglect him: substitution again, though of a more subtle sort, neglecting crucial elements of the person's individual identity.[14]

---

14. One might wonder whether parricide and incest have actually been committed, for one might argue that intention is relevant to the categorization of the act.

If we start thinking this way, the asymmetry we asked about begins to arise naturally. For looked at in this way, *dikê* is always harsh and unyielding. Sometimes the harshness is merited, sometimes excessive. But it is rarely too soft, for it begins from the assumption that the doer should suffer, that any wrong should be "made up" by a penalty that befits a deliberate wrong. The particulars of the case, more closely inspected, lead toward extenuation or mitigation far more frequently than in the opposite direction. If *dikê* has got the right person, well and good; nothing more need be added. If, however, *dikê* has got hold of the wrong person, a more flexible and particularized judgment will let that person off. So too in the Oedipus case: for *dikê* assumes that Oedipus is a parricide; there is nothing more we can find out about him that will aggravate his offense. We can and do, on the other hand, find out that in a most relevant sense he is not a parricide, because the act that he intended and chose was not the act that we have judged him to have performed. Once again, the more flexible judgment of *epieikeia* steps in to say, be gentle with this man, for we cannot assume without looking further that he really did the awful thing for which strict justice holds him responsible. Getting the right life and getting the life right are not two separate issues but two aspects of a single process of appropriate scrutiny.

In effect, the asymmetry arises from the fact that the circumstances of human life throw up many and various obstacles to meeting the tough standards of justice; if we set a high standard of good action, the very course of life will often make it difficult for mere human beings to measure up. To put it another way, the asymmetry arises from a certain view about the common or likely causes of wrongdoing: the asymmetrist claims that a certain number of wrongful acts are fully deliberate wrongs and that a certain number are produced by obstacles such as failure of knowledge, mistaken identification, bad education, or the presence of a competing moral claim. There may be some cases of parricide and incest that are produced by an especially or unusually blameworthy degree of hatred or wickedness, going beyond the responsible deliberateness assumed by the law, but the claim is that this is likely to be a smaller class than the Oedipus-type class, given the character of human life and the nature of human motivation.

The world of strict *dikê* is a harsh and symmetrical world, in which order and design are preserved with exceptionless clarity. After summer comes fall, after fall comes winter, after day comes the night; the fact that Agamemnon was not the killer of Thyestes' children is as irrelevant to *dikê* as the fact that the night did not deliberately aggress against the day; the fact that Oedipus acted in ignorance is as irrelevant to *dikê* as the fact that the winter came in ignorance of its crimes against the summer. It is a world in which gods are at home, and in which morals often fare badly. As a fragment of Sophocles puts it, "The god before whom you come...knows neither equity nor grace (*oute toupieikes oute tên charin*), but only cares for strict and simple justice (*tên haplôs dikên*)."[15] The world of *epieikeia* or equity, by contrast, is a world of imperfect human efforts and of complex obstacles to doing well, a world in which humans sometimes deliberately do wrong, but sometimes also get tripped up by ignorance, passion, poverty, bad education, or circumstantial constraints of various sorts. It is a world in which bad things are sometimes simply bad, sometimes extremely bad, but sometimes — and more often, when one goes into them — somewhat less bad, given the obstacles the person faced on the way to acting properly. *Epieikeia* is a gentle art of particular perception, a temper of mind that refuses to demand retribution without understanding the whole story; it responds to Oedipus's demand to be seen for the person he is.

IV.

So far we have been dealing only with a contrast between the equitable and the just. Justice itself is still understood as strict retribution, and therefore the equitable, insofar as it recognizes features of the particular case that the strict law does not cover, stands in opposition to the just. But justice or *dikê* is by the fifth century a venerated moral norm, associated in general with the idea of giving to each his or her due. We would expect, then, as the conflict between equity and strict retributive justice assumed prominence, an attempt to forge a new conception of justice, one that incorporated the insights of equity. This project was pursued to some extent by Plato, in his late works the *Statesman* and the *Laws*.[16] Even more significant for our purposes, it was pursued, albeit unsystematically, by the Attic

---

15. Sophocles fr. 770 (Pearson). See D'Agostino, *Epieikeia*, p. 8ff. for other related passages.

16. See *Statesman* 294A–95A, *Laws* 757E, 867D, 876A–E, 925D–26D. Like Aristotle, Plato recognizes the importance of *epieikeia* both in the judgment of whether a certain offense was committed and in the assessment of penalties. He suggests that laws are written deliberately in such a way as to leave gaps to be filled in by the judgment of judges or juries. He compares the prescriptions of law to the general instructions that an athletic trainer has to give when he cannot deal with each pupil one by one and also to a trainer or a medical doctor who has to go out of town and therefore leaves instructions that cannot anticipate all the circumstances that may arise. This being so, it is in the spirit of law that when one does look into the particular case, one will modify the prescription to suit the differing conditions.

orators in their arguments over particular cases in front of citizen juries.[17] But it was Aristotle who made the major contribution.

Aristotle's discussion of the equitable in the *Nicomachean Ethics* occurs within his account of justice. It begins with an apparent dilemma. The *epieikes*, he says, is neither strictly the same as the just nor altogether different in kind (EN 1137a33–4). On the one hand, it looks as if it would be strange to separate *epieikeia* from justice, for we praise both people and their judgments for the quality of *epieikeia*, recognizing it as a normatively good thing. But in that case it will be odd if *epieikeia* turns out to be altogether opposed to the just. Then we would either have to say that justice is not a normatively good quality, or withdraw our normative claims for *epieikeia* (1137a34).[18] Aristotle's solution to the dilemma is to define equity as a kind of justice, but a kind that is superior to and frequently opposed to another sort, namely strict legal justice (1137b68ff). Equity may be regarded as a "correcting" and "completing" of legal justice.[19]

The reason for this opposition, he continues, is that the law must speak in general terms, and therefore must err in two ways, both leaving gaps that must be filled up by particular judgments, and sometimes even getting things wrong. Aristotle says that this is not the fault of the lawgiver, but is in the very nature of human ethical life; the "matter of the practical" can be grasped only crudely by rules given in advance and adequately only by a flexible judgment suited to the complexities of the case. He uses the famous image of the good architect who does not measure a complicated structure (for example a fluted column) with a straightedge. If he did, he would get a woefully inadequate measurement. Instead he uses a flexible strip of metal that "bends to the shape of the stone and is not fixed" (1137b30–32). Exactly in this way, particular judgments, superior in flexibility to the general dictates of law, should bend round to suit the case.[20]

---

17. See Lawless, *Law, Argument and Equity*, supra note 3, with comprehensive bibliography.

18. Strictly speaking, there is another possibility: that they are both valuable norms that pervasively conflict in their requirements. Aristotle does recognize contingent conflicts of obligation, but not this more deep-seated value conflict.

19. *Epanorthôma* suggests both things: the image is of straightening up something that has fallen over or gone crooked a bit. Equity is putting law into the condition to which it aspires in the first place.

20. On the role of this passage in Aristotle's ethical theory generally, see my essay "The Discernment of Perception: An Aristotelian Model for Public and Private Rationality," in *Love's Knowledge: Essays on Philosophy and Literature* (New York: Oxford University Press, 1990). There I discuss in greater detail Aristotle's reasons for thinking that general rules cannot be sufficient for the complexities of particular cases.

Aristotle ends the discussion with some remarks that seem ill-suited to the context, but by now we should be prepared to understand how they fit in:

> It is also clear from this [account of the equitable] what sort of person the equitable person is. For a person who chooses and does such things, and who is not zealous for strict judgment in the direction of the worse, but is inclined to mitigation, even though he can invoke the law on his side — such a person is equitable, and this trait of character is equity, being a kind of justice and not a distinct trait of character (1137b34–1138a3).

Here Aristotle alludes to and endorses the tradition that links perception of the particular with mitigation, and by now we can see on what grounds he does so. But Aristotle makes a new contribution, for he insists that this is the way a truly just person is. In keeping with his insistence throughout his ethical and political writings that justice, as a virtue of character, is a peculiarly human virtue, one that gods neither possess nor comprehend, and indeed would think "ridiculous" (EN 1178b11), he now gives the just a definition suited to an imperfect human life.[21]

In the *Rhetoric* discussion of *epieikeia*, having given a very similar account of the equitable as that which corrects or supplements — and thereby fulfills — the written law, Aristotle adds a somewhat more detailed account of equitable assessment, telling us that the equitable person is characterized by a sympathetic understanding of "human things." He uses the word *suggnômê*, "judging with." He links this ability with particular perception, and both of these with the ability to classify actions in accordance with the agent's motives and intentions (1374b2–10).[22]

The logic of these connections seems to be as follows. To perceive the particular accurately, one must "judge with" the agent who has done the alleged wrong. One must, that is, see things from that person's point of view, for only then will one begin to comprehend what obstacles that person faced as he or she acted. In this sense, it takes *suggnômê* to deliver a "correct discrimination" of the equitable. When one looks at the person's case with *suggnômê*, certain distinctions that do not play a part in the archaic conception of *dikê* assume a remarkable salience. Equity, like the sympathetic spectatorship of the tragic audience, accepts Oedipus's plea that the ignorant and nonvoluntary nature of his act be acknowledged; it acknowledges, too, the terrible dilemmas faced by characters such as Agamemnon, Antigone, and Creon, and the terrible moral defectiveness of all their options. Recognizing the burdens of these "human things," the

---

21. See EN VII.1 on ethical excellence in general; Pol. I.1 on the social excellences and EN X.8, 1178a9–b18 on virtue and justice as purely human and not divine.

22. Cf. also EN 1143a19–20, connecting *suggnômê* and equity, and both with perception of the particular; cf. also EN 1110a24–2.1, 1111a1–2, on *suggnômê* in tragic situations.

equitable judge is inclined not to be zealous for strict judgment in the direction of the worse, but to prefer merciful mitigation.

I have already illustrated Aristotle's argument by alluding to tragedy and tragic spectatorship. And since I shall go on to develop my own account of the equitable with reference to literature, it seems well worth pointing out that Aristotle's account of *suggnômê* and *epieikeia* in these passages has close links with his theory of tragedy. For in his theory the spectator forms bonds of both sympathy and identification with the tragic hero.[23] This means that "judging with" is built into the drama itself, into the way in which the form solicits attention. If I see Oedipus as one whom I might be, I will be concerned with understanding how and why his predicament came about; I will focus on all those features of motive and agency, those aspects of the unfortunate operations of chance, that I would judge important were I in a similar plight myself. I would ask how and why all this came about, and ask not from a vantage point of lofty superiority, but by seeing his tragedy as something "such as might happen" in my own life.[24] Tragedy is thus a school of equity, and therefore of mercy. If I prove unable to occupy the equitable attitude, I will not even enjoy tragedy, for its proper pleasure requires emotions of pity and fear that only *suggnômê* makes possible.

Aristotle's attitude to law and equity was not simply a theoretical fiction. There is evidence that it both shaped legal practice and even more clearly, built upon an already developed and developing tradition of Athenian legal thought.[25] We have, of course, almost no records of the actual outcomes of jury trials, and no record at all of the deliberations of jurors. The process did not encourage lengthy or communal deliberation, as each juror cast a separate vote after hearing the various arguments, apparently without much mutual consultation.[26] We do, however have many examples of persuasive speeches delivered to such juries. Since the orator's reputation

---

23. See Stephen Halliwell, *Aristotle's Poetics* (London: Duckworth, 1986) and "Pleasure, Understanding, and Emotion in Aristotle's *Poetics*," in *Essays on Aristotle's Poetics*, ed. A. Rorty (Princeton: Princeton University Press, 1992), 241–60.

24. See *Poetics*, ch. 9, and the excellent discussion in Halliwell, "Pleasure." Aristotle remarks that neither pity nor fear will be experienced by a person who believes that he or she is above the uncertainties of life and can suffer no serious reversal. See *Rhet.* 1382b3off., 1385b21–22, 31: he calls this state of mind a *hubristikê diathesis*, an "overweening disposition."

25. Among the legal and rhetorical figures mentioned, Lysias predates Aristotle and is active in the late fifth century, while both Isaeus and Isocrates are contemporaries of Aristotle; their period of activity overlaps with the likely period of composition of Aristotle's *Rhetoric*, which is prior to Aristotle's first departure from Athens in 347. Isaeus's earliest and latest works, for example, can be dated approximately to 389 and 344/3 B.C.

26. On all this, see Lawless, *Law, Argument and Equity*, supra note 3, with copious references to sources ancient and modern.

rested on his ability to persuade a jury of average citizens chosen by lot, we can rely on these speeches for evidence of widespread popular beliefs about legal and ethical concepts. These speeches show the orators relying on a concept of law and even of justice that is very much like the one that Aristotle renders explicit and systematic. Thus litigants frequently call for a justice tailored to the circumstances of their own case, and frequently use the expression *ta dikaia* ("those things that are just) in that sense.[27] They often proceed as if the written law is understood to be a set of guidelines with gaps to be filled in or corrected by arguments appealing to the notion of equity.[28] In this process, frequent appeal is made to the jurors' sense of fairness, as if, once the particular circumstances of the case are understood, they can be expected to see that justice consists in an equitable determination.

This is a deep insight, one that I support. For it seems wrong to make a simple contrast between justice and equity, suggesting that we have to choose between the one and the other.[29] Nor, in a deep sense, do we have to choose between equity and the rule of law as understandings of what justice demands. The point of the rule of law is to bring us as close as possible to what equity would discern in a variety of cases, given the dangers of carelessness, bias, and arbitrariness endemic to any totally discretionary procedure. But no such rules can be precise or sensitive enough, and when they have manifestly erred, it is justice itself, not a departure from justice, to use equity's flexible standard.

V.

We are still not all the way to a doctrine of mercy. For what Aristotle recommends is precise attention to the circumstances of offense and offend-

---

27. See Michael Hillgruber, *Die zehnte Rede des Lysias: Einleitung, Text und Kommentar mit einem Anhang über die Gesetzesinterpretation bei den attischen Rednern* (Berlin and New York: Walter de Gruyter, 1988), 116–17. Hillgruber cites passages in the orators where an appeal to *ta dikaia* is used to persuade the jurors that obedience to the letter of the law is not required by their oath. These passages are : Andocides 1.31, Lysias 15.8, Demosthenes 21.4, 21.212, 23.194, 24.175, [Dem.] 58.61. Lawless, *Law, Argument and Equity*, supra note 3, at 78, discusses this material and adds Isaeus 1.40 to the list.

28. See K. Seeliger, "Zur Charackteristik des Isaios," *Jahrb. für Philologie* 113 (1876): 673–79, translated in Lawless, *Law, Argument and Equity*, supra note 3, "The principle of equity is almost always maintained, while the letter of the law is not infrequently circumvented, however much the orator is accustomed to holding his opponents to it."

29. For examples of such contrasts, see Richard Posner, *Law and Literature* (Cambridge, Mass.: Harvard University Press, 1988), 108ff.

er, both in ascertaining whether or not there is any guilt and in assessing the penalty if there is. He is prepared to let people off the hook if it can be shown that their wrongdoing is unintentional, or to judge them more lightly if it is the result of something less than fully deliberate badness. But the point of this is to separate out the fully and truly guilty from those who superficially resemble them. In effect, we are given a more precise classification of offenses, a classification that takes intention and motive into account. But once a particular offense is correctly classified, the offender is punished exactly in proportion to the actual offense.

By contrast to the archaic conception of justice, this is indeed merciful, but it does not suffice, I think, for all that we mean by mercy, which seems to involve a gentleness going beyond due proportion, even to the deliberate offender. With his emphasis on sympathetic understanding, Aristotle is on his way to this idea. And he insists that the virtuous disposition in the area of retributive anger is best named "gentleness" (using the same word that Gorgias had used in connection with *epieikeia*). He stresses that "the gentle person is not given to retribution [*timôrêtikos*], but is rather inclined to sympathetic understanding [*suggnômonikos*]" (EN 1126a2–3). But retribution will still play an important role, where the circumstances demand it. For "people who do not get retributively angry[30] at those at whom they should look like fools... For they seem to have no perception and no feeling of pain... and to allow oneself and one's loved ones to be kicked around and overlook it, is slavish" (1126a4–8). The demand to avoid the slavish is certain to play a role in the public world of the law, as well as in the private world of the family. This demand makes Aristotelian *suggnômê* stop short of mercy. For the full development of that idea, we must wait for Roman Stoicism and for Seneca.[31]

Stoic moral theory accepts and builds on the Aristotelian insight that rules and precepts are useful only as guidelines in both private and public thought. Any fully adequate moral or legal judgment must be built upon a full grasp of all the particular circumstances of the situation, including the motives and intentions of the agent. Like Aristotle, Stoics are fond of using an analogy between medicine and ethics to illustrate this point: general ethical or legal rules are about as useful as medical rules and precepts — which is to say, useful as outlines, but no substitute for a resourceful confrontation with all the circumstances of the case. Both the Greek and the later Roman Stoics stress that an act is fully correct and moral,

---

30. I am translating *orgizesthai* this way because Aristotle defines *orgê* as a desire for retribution, on account of the pain of a believed slight.

31. I have discussed Seneca's views on mercy in "Seneca on Anger in Public Life," Chapter 11 of *The Therapy of Desire: Theory and Practice in Hellenistic Ethics* (Princeton: Princeton University Press, 1994).

what they call a *katorthôma*, only if it is done with the appropriate motives and the appropriate knowledge; *a kathêkon* or (in Latin) *officium* is an act of (merely) the right general type, without consideration of the agent's thoughts and motivations. Rules can tell you what the *kathêkonta* are, but to get all the way to a full *katorthôma* you need to become a certain sort of person. The same goes in reverse for bad actions. This means that the Aristotelian idea of justice as equity is already built into the moral schema from the beginning, and it will automatically influence the classification of offenses in public reasoning and in the law.[32]

The Greek Stoics stop there, and in their moral rigor they explicitly reject any application of *epieikeia* that goes beyond the careful classification of offenses. The soul of the good Stoic judge is a hard soul that protects itself from all impulses that might sway it from the strict path of virtue and duty. "All wise men," they announce, "are harshly rigorous [*austêroi*]."[33] They "never permit their soul to give way or to be caught by any pleasure or pain."[34] This hardness cordons them off from any yielding response to the defects of another person. The wise man, they announce, does not forgive those who err, and he never waives the punishment required in the law. An unyielding judge, the Stoic will do exactly what strict justice requires. In this connection, *epieikeia* is explicitly rejected: the Stoic will never waive the punishment that is mandated for that particular type of offense.[35]

Many Greek Stoic texts show us this attitude of detachment and hardness to offenders, an attitude far removed from the Aristotelian norm of *suggnômê*. One can see this emerge with particular clarity in the treatment of tragedy, which Stoics are permitted to watch, so long as they watch it from a vantage point of secure critical detachment (like Odysseus, they say, lashed to the mast so that he can hear, but not be swayed by, the sirens' song).[36] From this secure vantage point they view the disasters and vul-

---

32. One possible difference: Aristotle's ethical schema makes a big distinction between *adikêmata*, for which it is necessary to have a bad character, and lesser wrongdoings that will be classified as among the blameworthy *hamartêmata*. The latter class will include bad acts done from weakness of will with respect to some passion. Stoic moral theory is harsher toward the passions, treating them as types of false judgment that are always in an agent's power to refuse. Thus the distinction between *akrasia* and wrongdoing from bad character is significantly weakened, if not altogether eroded.

33. Diogenes Laertius VII. 17 = *Stoicorum Veterum Fragmenta* (SVF) III.637.

34. Clement, *Strom.* VII.7 = SVF III.639.

35. SVF III, 640.

36. Plutarch, *On How the Young Person Should Listen to Poetry* 15CD. I argue that this work represents some of the contents of Chrysipus's lost work of the same title, in my "Poetry and the Passions: Two Stoic Views," in *Passions & Perceptions*, ed., J. Brunschwig and M. Nussbaum (Cambridge: Cambridge University Press, 1993), 97–149.

nerabilities of ordinary mortals with amusement and even scorn, defining tragedy as what happens "when chance events befall fools."[37] To Oedipus, the wise man says, "Slave, where are your crowns, where your diadem?" To Medea, the wise man says, "Stop wanting your husband, and there is not one of the things you want that will fail to happen."[38] There is no inevitability in tragedy, for if one has the proper moral views there is no contingency in the world that can bring one low.[39]

Here Seneca steps in, perceiving a serious tension in the Greek Stoic position. On the one hand, Stoicism is deeply committed to the Aristotelian position that good moral assessment, like good medical assessment, is searchingly particular, devoted to a deep and internal understanding of each concrete case. On the other hand, the Stoic norm of critical detachment withholds psychological understanding, treating deep and complex predicaments as easily avoidable mistakes, simply refusing to see the obstacles to good action from the erring agent's own viewpoint.

Seneca opts for the medical side of this dilemma, offering a complex account of the origins of human wrongdoing that leads to a new view of the proper response to it. Seneca begins his argument in the *De Ira* as an Aristotelian would, asking the judge to look at all the circumstances of the offense (1.19.5–8). At this point he still seems to be a symmetrist, urging that sometimes a closer look makes the person appear better, sometimes worse. But he then continues his reflections, in the second book, in a manner that makes our asymmetry open up. People who do bad things—even when they act from bad motives—are not, he insists, simply making a foolish and easily corrigible error. They are yielding to pressures—many of them social—that lie deep in the fabric of human life. Before a child is capable of the critical exercise of reason, he or she has internalized a socially taught scheme of values that is in many ways diseased, giving rise to similarly diseased passions: the excessive love of money and honor, angers connected with slights to one's honor, excessive attachment to sex (especially to romanticized conceptions of the sexual act and the sexual partner), anger and violence connected with sexual jealousy; the list goes on and on.[40]

These cultural forces are in error, and in that sense someone who is in their grip is indeed a "fool," as Epictetus holds. But there is not much point in giving a little sermon to Medea as to a docile child; such errors,

---

37. Epictetus, *Diss.* 2.26.31. Though a Roman Stoic, Epictetus is loyal to the original views of the Greek Stoics.

38. Epictetus 1.24.16–18, 2.17.19–22.

39. The proper view is that virtue by itself is sufficient for *eudaimonia*.

40. Most of my argument in this passage is based on the *De ira* (*On Anger*), though there are many similar passages in other works.

taught from an early age, take over the soul and can be eradicated, if at all, only by a lifetime of zealous and obsessive self-examination. And, furthermore, Seneca suggests that anger and the desire to inflict pain—the worst, in his opinion, of the errors of the soul—are not in any simple way just the result of a corrigible error, even at the social level. He repeatedly commits himself to the view that they do not result from innate instinct. On the other hand, they "omit no time of life, exempt no race of human beings" (*De ira* III.22).

In a crucial passage, Seneca says that the wise person is not surprised at the omnipresence of aggression and injustice, "since he has examined thoroughly the circumstances of human life" (*Condicio humanae vitae*, II.10). Circumstances, then, and not innate propensities, are at the origins of vice. And when the wise person looks at these circumstances clearly, he finds that they make it extremely difficult not to err. The world into which human beings are born is a rough place, one that confronts them with threats to their safety on every side. If they remain attached to their safety and to the resources that are necessary to protect it—as is natural and rational—that very attachment to the world will almost certainly, in time, lead to competitive or retaliatory aggression. For when goods are in short supply and people are attached to them, they compete for them. Thus aggression and violence grow not so much inside us as from an interaction between our nature and external conditions that is prior to and more deeply rooted than any specific form of society.

Seneca now uses this view as the basis for his argument against retributive anger and in favor of mercy. Given the omnipresence of aggression and wrongdoing, he now argues, if we look at the lives of others with the attitudes typical of the retributive tradition of justice—even in its modified particularist form—if, that is, we are determined to fix a penalty precisely proportionate to the nature of the particular wrongdoing, then we will never cease to be retributive and to inflict punishment, for everything we see will upset us. But this retributive attitude, even when in some sense justified, is not without its consequences for the human spirit. A person who notes and reacts to every injustice, and who becomes preoccupied with assigning just punishments, becomes, in the end, oddly similar to the raging ungentle people against whom he reacts. Retributive anger hardens the spirit, turning it against the humanity it sees. And in turning against humanity, in evincing the rage and hardness of the angry, one then becomes perilously close to the callous wrongdoers who arouse rage in the first place. Thus in Seneca's examples we find acts of horrifying vindictiveness and cruelty committed by people whose anger is initially justified, according to a precise assessment of the nature of the crime. Sulla's acts of retribution were first directed against legitimate enemies; they ended in the murder of innocent children (II.34). Caligula was justified in his anger over the imprisonment of his mother, and yet this led him to cruelty and destruction. Cambyses had just cause of battle against the Ethiopians, but in his obsession with revenge he led his men on a fatal campaign that ended in cannibalism (III.20). Andrea Dworkin's heroine would be right at home here, for she reacts in some sense appropriately to real wrongs, but becomes in the process an engine of revenge, indifferent to the face of humanity.[41]

Seneca's famous counterproposal, announced at the very end of the *De ira* is that we should "cultivate humanity" (*colamus humanitatem* III.43). He elsewhere describes this as the proposal to "give a pardon to the human species" (II.10). It is this attitude that he now calls by the name of mercy, translating Greek *epieikeia* with the Latin word *clementia*. Rejecting the austerity and rigor of the Greek Stoic, he makes a sympathetic participatory attitude central to the norm of good judging. Senecan *clementia* does not fail to pass judgment on wrongdoing; this is continually stressed. Seneca does not hold that the circumstances of human life remove moral and legal responsibility for bad acts. We may still convict defendants who fulfill some basic conditions of rationality in action. But, looking at the circumstances of human life, one comes to understand how such things have happened, and this "medical" understanding leads to mercy.

Clementia, mercy, is even defined in a manner that makes its difference from Greek Stoic harshness evident: it is an "inclination of the soul to mildness in exacting penalties," and also, "that which turns its course away this side of that which could be justly determined" (*De clem.* II.3). The Greek Stoic soul, by contrast, never bends aside, never inclines away from hardness. The somewhat more gentle Aristotelian soul does bend, but inconstantly, conscious always that it is slavish to allow oneself and one's loved ones to be kicked around. Given that Seneca defines mercy as the opposite of cruelty, and given that cruelty is held to be a frequent outgrowth of retributive anger, we can say, putting all this together, that mercy, *clementia*, is opposed at one and the same time both to strictness in exacting penalties and also to retributive anger, as if that strictness does indeed lie very close to anger in the heart. As Seneca says, "It is a fault to punish a fault in full" (*Culpa est totamm perseui culpam, De clem.* II.7, fr.).[42]

---

41. Insofar as she punishes people who are totally innocent of crime, she is not even a good Greek Stoic judge, for whom the particulars of the crime and offender must be correct. But the Greek Stoic would say that once some basic criteria of responsibility are met, a tough punishment is in order without a search for mitigating factors, and here her judicial procedure is like theirs.

42. Unlike Aristotle, Seneca does not endorse pity or compassion as a correct response to the misfortunes of human life. In his view, to do so would be to give too little credit to the person's own will and dignity and, frequently, too much importance to external events.

One might, of course, adopt this attitude as a practical strategy to keep the self pure from anger without endorsing it as just or correct toward the offender. Seneca sometimes appears to oscillate between those two positions, since he can commend the practical strategy even to those who do not accept his position about correctness. But in the end his position is clearly that it is right and correct to assign punishments in accordance with mercy, both because of what it means for oneself and because of what it says about and to the offender.

The merciful attitude, as Seneca develops it, entails regarding each particular case as a complex narrative of human effort in a world full of obstacles. The merciful judge will not fail to judge the guilt of the offender, but she will also see the many obstacles this offender faced as a member of a culture, a gender, a city or country, and, above all, as a member of the human species, facing the obstacles characteristic of human life in a world of scarcity and accident. The starting point is a general view of human life and its difficulties, but the search for mitigating factors must at every point be searchingly particular. The narrative-medical attitude asks the judge to imagine what it was like to have been that particular offender, facing those particular obstacles with the resources of that history. Seneca's bet is that, after this imaginative exercise, one will cease to have the strict retributive attitude to the punishment of the offender. One will be inclined, in fact, to gentleness and the waiving of the strict punishment mandated in the law. The punishments that one does assign will be chosen, on the whole, not for their retributive function, but for their power to improve the life of the defendant.[43]

This merciful attitude requires, and rests upon, a new attitude toward the self. The retributive attitude has a we/them mentality, in which judges set themselves above offenders, looking at their actions as if from a lofty height and preparing to find satisfaction in their pain. The good Senecan judge, by contrast, has both identification and sympathetic understanding. Accordingly, a central element in Seneca's prescription for the judge is that he should remind himself at every turn that he himself is capable of all the failings he reproves in others. "If we want to be fair judges of all things, let us persuade ourselves of this first: that none of us is without fault. For it is from this point above all that retributive anger arises: 'I did nothing wrong,' and 'I did nothing.' No, rather you don't admit to anything" (II.28).

---

43. Some ameliorative punishments, according to Seneca, can be extremely harsh. Indeed, in a peculiar move, he defends capital punishment itself as in the interest of the punished, given that a shorter bad life is better than a longer one; he compares it to merciful euthanasia.

This part of Seneca's argument reaches its conclusion in a remarkable passage in which Seneca confronts himself with the attitude of merciful judgment that he also recommends, describing his own daily practice of self-examination in forensic language that links it to his public recommendations:

> A person will cease from retributive anger and be more moderate if he knows that every day he has to come before himself as judge. What therefore is more wonderful than this habit of unfolding the entire day? How fine is the sleep that follows this acknowledgment of oneself, how serene, how deep and free, when the mind has been either praised or admonished, and as its own hidden investigator and assessor has gained knowledge of its own character? I avail myself of this power, and plead my case daily before myself. When the light has been removed from sight, and my wife, long since aware of this habit of mine, has fallen silent, I examine my entire day and measure my deeds and words. I hide nothing from myself, I pass over nothing. For why should I fear anything from my own errors, when I can say, "See that you don't do that again, this time I pardon you." (III.36)

Seeing the complexity and fallibility of his own acts, seeing those acts as the product of a complex web of highly particular connections among original impulses, the circumstances of life, and the complicated psychological reactions life elicits from the mind, he learns to view others, too, as people whose errors emerge from a complex narrative history. Seneca's claim is that he will then moderate his retributive zeal toward the punishment of their injustices and intensify his commitment to mutual aid.

This part of Seneca's work seems very private. But there is no doubt that the primary aim of this work, and of the later *De clementia* as well, is the amelioration of public life and public judgment. The *De ira* was written at the start of the reign of the emperor Claudius. It responds to a well-known speech by Claudius on the subject of anger and irascibility, and obviously contains advice for the new regime.[44] Moreover, its explicit addressee and interlocutor is Novatus, Seneca's own brother, an aspiring orator and public man. Thus its entire argumentative structure is built around the idea of showing a public judge that the retributive attitude is unsuitable for good judging. As for the *De clementia*, its explicit addressee is none other than the new emperor Nero Caesar himself, and its explicit task is to persuade this young man to use his immense power in merciful, rather than retributive, ways. The private material provides the basis for a new sort of public and judicial life.

---

44. See Fillion-Lahille, *Le De ira de Séneque* (Paris: Klincksieck, 1984), and the summary of the evidence in Nussbaum, *The Therapy of Desire*, supra note 31, at Chapter 11.

VI.

But instead of pursuing this history further, I want now to suggest some implications of these ideas for contemporary political and legal issues. First I shall develop a general thesis concerning the connection between the merciful attitude and the literary imagination; then I shall apply it to some particular questions. The Greco-Roman tradition already made a close connection between equity and narrative. The person who reads a complex case in the manner of the reader of a narrative or the spectator at a drama is put in contact — by the structure of the forms themselves as they solicit the reader's or spectator's attention — with two features of the equitable: its attentiveness to particularity and its capacity for sympathetic understanding. This means that the spectator or reader, if he or she reads well, is already prepared for equity and, in turn, for mercy.

I could illustrate these points about the relationship between form and content in many ways. Instead I want to choose just two examples which show with particular clarity the connection between mercy and the art of the novelist, for the novel has been in recent times an especially vigorous popular literary form. The novel goes beyond tragic drama in its formal commitment to following complex life histories, looking at the minute details of motive and intention and their social formation — all that Seneca would have the good judge examine. This means that the novel, even more than the tragic drama, is an artificial construction of mercy.

My first example is from Charles Dickens's *David Copperfield*.[45] James Steerforth, we know, is a bad person, one who deserves blame for some very serious bad actions. He humiliates the kind teacher, Mr. Mell; he uses his charm to get power over those younger and weaker than himself; he uses his wealth to escape discipline and criticism. And, above all, he destroys the life of Em'ly, by convincing her to run away with him with a false promise of marriage — betraying, in the process, both David's trusting friendship and the simple kindness of the Peggotty family. These bad actions are seen and judged by Agnes Wickfield in the straightforward way characteristic of the strict moral code that is her guide in life. A reader of religious books rather than of novels and stories, Agnes has no interest in the psychology of Steerforth's acts or in seeing them from his point of view. She simply judges him and judges him harshly, calling him David's "bad angel" and urging David (even before the serious crime) to have no further association with him. (It is a subtle point in the novel that moralism here allies itself with and provides a screen for the operations of jealousy; Agnes

---

45. These issues are discussed in more detail in my essay "Steerforth's Arm," in *Love's Knowledge*.

resents the romantic hold that Steerforth has over David and uses her moral condemnation to get revenge.) David's view is more complex.

The novel—represented as written by David some years after the event, during a tranquil marriage to Agnes—does present its reader with Agnes's moral judgment of Steerforth and her reasons for that judgment. The reader is led at times—even as David shows himself being led—into the strict moral point of view and is inclined at such times to judge Steerforth harshly. But these times are moments within the novel; they do not define the overall attitude with which the novel leaves us. David tells and shows the reader that the novelist's imagination is of a certain sort—very different, in fact, from the moral imagination of Agnes. And this imagination leads to a different way of judging.

The central characteristic of the narrative imagination, as David depicts it, is that it preserves as a legacy from childhood an ability to attend closely to the particulars and to respond to them in a close and accurate manner. Like our ancient tradition, David immediately goes on to link this "power of observation" with gentleness: adults who retain it retain also "a certain freshness, and gentleness, and capacity of being pleased, which are also an inheritance they preserved from their childhood" (p. 61).[46] The nature of the connection is apparent in the manner in which the younger David sees Steerforth, and in which the mature novelist David depicts him for the reader's imagination.[47] We do become aware of Steerforth's crimes, but we see them as episodes in the life of an extremely complicated character who has enormous ability, awesome powers of attraction, great kindness and beneficence to his friends, and an extremely unfortunate family history. We do judge Steerforth's arrogance, duplicity, and self-destructiveness. But we know also, as readers of the novel, that he grew up with no father to guide him, and with the misguided and uncritical affection of a willful and doting mother who indulged his every whim. We know, too, that his position and wealth compounded this ill fortune, exempting him for too long from the necessity to discipline his character and to cooperate with others. We are led to see his crimes as deliberate in the immediate sense required by strict legal and even moral judgment, but we also know that behind these crimes is a tangled history that might have been otherwise, a history that was not fully chosen by Steerforth himself. We imagine that with a different childhood Steerforth might have made an altogether different use of his abilities—that he might have had, in short, a different character. Like Seneca's reader, we are led to see character itself

---

46. All citations from the novel are taken from the Penguin edition, ed. Trevor Blount (Harmondsworth: Penguin, 1966).

47. These are not precisely the same, since the mature novelist has achieved an integration of the erotic and the moral that eludes the character earlier on.

as something formed in society and in the family, something for which strict morality rightly holds individuals responsible, but something over which, in the end, individuals do not have full control.[48]

The result of all this is mercy. Just before Steerforth leaves to run off with Em'ly in the last conversation he has with David, we have the following exchange:

"Daisy, if anything should ever separate us, you must think of me at my best, old boy. Come! Let us make that bargain. Think of me at my best, if circumstances should ever part us!"

"You have no best to me, Steerforth," said I, "and no worst. You are always equally loved and cherished in my heart." (p. 497)

David keeps the bargain, loving Steerforth with the unconditional attention and concern of his narratorial heart. When years later, the tempest washes Steerforth's body ashore and he recognizes it, David exclaims:

No need, O Steerforth, to have said when we last spoke together, in that hour which I so little deemed to be our parting hour-no need to have said, "Think of me at my best!" I had done that ever; and could I change now, looking on this sight! (p. 866)

Just as the character David suspends punitive judgment on Steerforth's acts, so the imagination of the narrator—and of the reader—is led to turn aside, substituting for punishment an understanding of Steerforth's life story. David makes it very clear that the activity of novel writing causes him to relive this moment of mercy and that its "freshness and gentleness" can be expected to be its reader's experience as well.[49] In this sense the novel is about itself and the characteristic moral stance of its own production and reception. That stance is the stance of equity, and of mercy.

My second example is contemporary. Last year the novelist Joyce Carol Oates visited my seminar at Brown to speak about the moral and politi-

---

48. Compare the ideas on moral responsibility developed in Susan Wolf, *Freedom within Reason* (New York: Oxford University Press, 1990). Wolf holds—like the ancient tradition described here—that there is an asymmetry between praise and blame, that it is legitimate to commend people for achievements that are in large part the outgrowth of early education and social factors, but not legitimate to blame them when such forces have made them into bad characters who are unable to respond to reason. In Wolf's view, as in mine, this asymmetry will sometimes mean not holding individuals responsible for their bad acts. Unlike her, however, I make a distinction between culpability and punishment, holding that a defendant's life story may give reasons for mitigating punishment, even when requirements for culpability are met.

49. See especially p. 855, shortly preceding the discovery of Steerforth's death: "As plainly as I behold what happened, I will try to write it down. I do not recall it, but see it done; for it happens again before me."

cal dimensions of her fiction. As we discussed her recent novel *Because It is Bitter and Because It Is My Heart*, a student, silent until then, burst in with a heated denunciation of Oates's character Leslie, a well-meaning but ineffectual liberal photographer. Isn't his life a complete failure really? Isn't he contemptible for his inability to do anything significant out of his antiracist intentions? Isn't he to be blamed for not more successfully combating racism in his family and in his society? Oates was silent for a time, her eyes peering up from behind her round glasses. Then she answered slowly, in her high, clear, girlish voice, "That's not the way I see it, really." She then went on to narrate the story of Leslie's life, the efforts he had made, the formidable social and psychological obstacles in the way of his achieving more, politically, than he had — speaking of him as a friend whose life inhabited her own imagination and whom, on that account, she could not altogether dismiss or condemn. Here, I believe, was mercy and, lying very close to it, the root of the novelist's art. The novel's structure is a structure of *suggnômê*, of the penetration of the life of another into one's own imagination and heart. It is a form of imaginative and emotional receptivity, in which the reader, following the author's lead, comes to be inhabited by the tangled complexities and struggles of other concrete lives.[50] Novels do not withhold all moral judgment, and they contain villains as well as heroes. But for any character with whom the form invites our participatory identification, the motives for mercy are engendered in the structure of literary perception itself.

VII.

Now to contemporary implications. Up until now, I have been talking about a moral ideal, which has evident implications for publicly promulgated norms of human behavior and for public conduct in areas in which there is latitude for judicial discretion. I have suggested that in many ways this norm fulfills and completes a conception of justice that lies itself at the basis of the rule of law; it was to prevent incomplete, defective and biased discretionary reasoning that the rule of law was introduced and defended. But at this point and for this reason caution is in order, for the

---

50. Of course the novelist's stance is traditionally linked with compassion, as well as with mercy. Sometimes, that is, the response will be to sympathize with the plight of a character without blaming, whereas in other cases there may be both blame and a merciful punishment. The line is, and should be, difficult to draw, for the factors that make mercy appropriate also begin to cast doubt on full moral responsibility. (In other cases, of course, there is not even a prima facie offense, and therefore we will have pity without mercy).

moral ideal should not be too simply converted into a norm for a legal system. First of all, a legal system has to look out for the likelihood that the moral ideal will not always be perfectly realized, and it should protect against abuses that moral arbitrariness and bias can engender. This suggests a larger role for codified requirements in areas in which one cannot guarantee that the equity ideal will be well implemented. The equity tradition supports this. Second, a system of law must look to social consequences as well as to the just judgment on particular offenders. Thus it may need to balance an interest in the deterrent role of punishments against the equity tradition's interest in punishments that suit the agent. Both the balance between codification and discretion and the balance between equity and deterrence are enormously complex matters, with which my analysis here cannot fully grapple. What I do wish to offer here are some representative suggestions of what the equity tradition has to offer us as we think about these issues.

A. A Model of Judicial Reasoning

In other recent work,[51] I have been developing the idea that legal, and especially judicial, reasoning can be modeled on the reasoning of the concerned reader of a novel.[52] Following in some respects the lead of Adam Smith in *The Theory of Moral Sentiments*,[53] I argue that the experience of the concerned reader is an artificial construction of ideal moral and judicial spectatorship, with respect both to particularity of attention and to the sort and range of emotions that will and will not be felt. Identifying with a wide range of characters from different social circumstances and concerning oneself in each case with the entire complex history of their efforts, the reader comes to have emotions both sympathetic and participatory toward the things that they do and suffer. These emotions will be based on a highly particularized perception of the character's situation. On the other hand, since the reader is not a character in the story, except in the Henry Jamesian sense of being a "participator by a fond attention,"[54] she will lack emotions relating to her own concrete placement in the situation that she is asked to judge; her judgments will thus, I argue, be both emotionally sympathetic and, in the most appropriate sense, neutral.

---

51. The development of this idea begins in "The Discernment of Perception," in *Love's Knowledge*; it continues in *Poetic Justice* (Boston: Beacon Hill Press, 1995).

52. Or the spectator at a play. I discuss some reasons for focusing above all on the novel in *Poetic Justice*, supra note 51.

53. Discussed in "Steerforth's Arm," in *Love's Knowledge*.

54. The citation is from the preface to *The Princess Casamassima*; see James, *The Art of the Novel* (New York: Charles Scribner's Sons, 1909) p. 62.

My current inquiry into mercy takes Smith's model one step further, where judgment on the wrongdoing of others is concerned, going beyond his rather austere construction of emotional spectatorship. It construes the participatory emotion of the literary imagination as emotion that will frequently lead to mercy, even where a judgment of culpability has been made. And this merciful attitude derives directly, we can now see, from the literary mind's keen interest in all the particulars, a fact not much stressed by Smith in his account of the literary (perhaps because he focuses on classical drama, in which the concrete circumstances of daily life are not always so clearly in view). My literary judge sees defendants as inhabitants of a complex web of circumstances, circumstances which often, in their totality, justify mitigation of blame or punishment.[55]

This attitude of my ideal judge is unashamedly mentalistic. It does not hesitate to use centrally the notions of intention, choice, reflection, deliberation, and character that are part of a nonreductive intentionalist psychology. Like the novel, it treats the inner world of the defendant as a deep and complex place, and it instructs the judge to investigate that depth. This approach is opposed, in spirit if not always in outcome, to an approach to the offender articulated in some well-known writings of Justice Holmes, and further developed recently by Richard Posner.[56] According to this approach, the offender should be treated as a thing with no insides to be

---

55. John Roemer has made the following important point to me in conversation: insofar as my literary judge treats many of a person's abilities, talents, and achievements as products of circumstances beyond his or her control, this reinforces and deepens the novel's commitment to egalitarianism. (In "The Literary Imagination" I had argued that the novel is already egalitarian in asking us to identify successively with members of different social classes and to see their needs without being aware of where, in the social scheme we are to choose, we ourselves will be.) For we will then see the talents and dispositions in virtue of which people earn their greater or lesser social rewards as not fully theirs by desert, given the large role played by social advantages and other external circumstances in getting to these dispositions; we will be more inclined to treat them as social resources that are a subject to allocation as other resources. (Not, obviously, in the sense that we will take A's talents from A and give them to B, but we will regard A's talents as like a certain level of wealth, on account of which we may require A to give back more to society in other ways). On all this, see Roemer, "Equality of Talent," *Economics and Philosophy* 1 (1985): 151–86; "Equality of Resources Implies Equality of Welfare," *Quarterly Journal of Economics* (November 1986): 751–83; "A Pragmatic Theory of Responsibility for the Egalitarian Planner," 22 *Philosophy & Public Affairs*, pp. 146–66 (1992).

56. The most important sources for Holmes's view are "The Path of the Law" and *The Common Law*, now printed (the latter in extracts) in *The Essential Holmes*, ed. Richard A. Posner (Chicago: University of Chicago Press, 1992), 160–77, 237–64. For Posner's views, see *The Problems of Jurisprudence* (Cambridge, Mass: Harvard University Press, 1990), pp. 161–96.

scrutinized from the internal viewpoint, but simply as a machine whose likely behavior, as a result of a given judgment or punishment, we attempt as judges to predict.[57] The sole proper concern of punishment becomes deterrence. As law becomes more sophisticated, and our predictive ability improves, states of mind play a smaller and smaller role in judgment.

Holmes's defense of this idea takes an interesting form, from our point of view. For it begins from an extremely perceptive description and criticism of the retributive idea of judgment and punishment.[58] His own deterrence-based view is advanced as an alternative—he seems to think it the only plausible one—to retributivism, and much of the argument's force comes from the connection of the positive recommendation with the effective negative critique. The trouble begins when he conflates the retributive idea with the idea of looking to the wrongdoer's state of mind, implying that an interest in the "insides" invariably brings retributivism with it.[59] As we have seen, matters are far more complicated, both historically and philosophically. It is, I think, in order to extricate judging from the retributive view—felt by Holmes, rightly, to be based on metaphysical and religious notions of balance and proportion, and to be an outgrowth of passions that we should not encourage in society—that he feels himself bound to oppose all mentalist and intention-based notions of punishment.[60] In *The Common Law* he argues that far from considering "the condition of a man's heart or conscience" in making a judgment, we should focus on external standards that are altogether independent of motive and intention. Here he insists on the very sort of strict assessment without mitigation that the entire mercy tradition opposes:

> [The external standards] do not merely require that every man should get as near as he can to the best conduct possible for him. They require him

---

57. Posner approvingly comments on Holmes's view: "We would deal with criminals as we dealt with unreasonably dangerous machines.... [I]nstead of treating dangerous objects as people, he was proposing to treat dangerous people as objects" (*Essential Holmes*, p. 168).

58. See especially "The Common Law," in *Essential Holmes*, p. 247ff. Holmes does not mention the ancient Greek debate; he focuses on Hegel's account of retributivism.

59. See *id.* at 247: "The desire for vengeance imports an opinion that its object is actually and personally to blame. It takes an internal standard, not an objective or external one, and condemns its victim by that."

60. Holmes notes that the retributive view of the criminal law has been held by such eminent figures as Bishop Butler and Jeremy Bentham. He then quotes, without comment, Sir James Stephen's view that "The criminal law stands to the passion of revenge in much the same relation as marriage to the sexual appetite." *Id.* at 248. Presumably this means that it allows for the satisfaction of this passion in an institutionalized and civilized form, not that it causes the passion's decline.

at his own peril to come up to a certain height. They take no account of incapacities, unless the weakness is so marked as to fall into well-known exceptions, such as infancy or madness. They assume that every man is as able as every other to behave as they command. If they fall on any one class harder than on another, it is on the weakest.[61]

From our viewpoint this dichotomy between intentionalism and retributivism leaves out the real opponent of retributivism, both historical and philosophical, simply putting in its place a strict external assessment that looks suspiciously like the old Anaximandrean *dikê* in modern secular dress, despite its evident differences.

Posner follows Holmes's view in most essential respects, developing it in much more detail, referring to modern behaviorist theories of mind. Like Holmes, Posner is motivated above all by the desire to describe an alternative to retributivism, which he criticizes eloquently, with appeal to both history and literature.[62] His argument is highly complex and cannot even be accurately summarized, much less appropriately criticized, in the space available here. What is most important for our purposes is that Posner makes explicit that his behaviorist view of the criminal law requires rejecting — for legal purposes — the Kantian idea that people are to be treated as ends rather than means. It requires, in fact, treating them as objects that through their behavior generate either good or bad social consequences. This, we can easily see, is profoundly opposed to the stance of the literary judge, who may differ from some Kantians in her focus on particular circumstances, but who certainly makes the Kantian insight about human beings central to her entire project. Posner also makes it clear that the case for his account of external standards stands or falls with the case for behaviorism (perhaps eliminative materialism as well?) as an adequate and reasonably complete theory of human behavior. Since I think it is fair to say that the best current work on the philosophy of the mind and in cognitive psychology — like the best work on mind in classical antiquity — finds serious flaws in the behaviorist and reductionist views, this explicitness in Posner makes the vulnerable point in the Holmes/Posner argument especially plain. On the other hand, unlike Holmes, Posner does not seem to claim that the behaviorist view is the only available alternative to retributivist views of punishment. He shows an awareness, in fact, of the mercy tradition — strikingly enough, not in the chapter dealing with the criminal law, but in his chapter dealing with "Literary and Feminist Perspectives."[63] Posner demonstrates some sympathy with this tradition,

61. *Id.* at 253.

62. See especially Posner, *Law and Literature: A Misunderstood Relation* (Cambridge, Mass.: Harvard University Press, 1988), 25–70.

63. Posner, *Problems of Jurisprudence*, supra note 56, at 393–419, and *id.* at 105–15.

arguing that what the law should really seek is an appropriate balance between strict legal justice and a flexible and merciful discretion.[64] He is, however, pessimistic about the role that latitude for mercy is likely to play in actual cases, holding that a discretionary approach on the part of judges will frequently be harsher to defendants—especially minority defendants—than will an approach based on strict rules.[65] This is a valuable insight, and I shall return to it shortly. But first I must conclude the story where Holmes is concerned.

Holmes's *The Common Law* was written in 1881, "The Path of the Law" (where Holmes argues for a related view) in 1897.[66] It is worthy of note that toward the end of his life, in a remarkable letter, Holmes appears to endorse the mercy tradition, as a result of his reading of Roman philosophy. Writing on March 28, 1924, to his friend Harold Laski, Holmes begins by speaking of the large impression made on him by Seneca's "cosmopolitan humanity."[67] He suggests (correctly) that this notion came to Christianity from Roman philosophy, rather than vice versa. He confirms the impression by reading Plutarch in order to get the Greek perspective. After making an obligatory shocking remark—that "the literature of the past is a bore"—he vigorously praises Tacitus. Then appended to the account of his Roman reading comes the arresting insight: "Before I leave you for the day and drop the subject let me repeat if I have said it before that I think the biggest thing in antiquity is 'Father forgive them—they know not what they do.' There is the modern transcending of a moral judgment in the most dramatic of settings."

It is not terribly clear to what extent Holmes means to connect this remark about Jesus with his observations concerning the debt owed by Christianity to Roman thought. My argument has shown that he certainly could do so with justice. Nor is it clear how or whether he would apply his insight to concrete issues in the law. What is clear is that by this time

---

64. Posner, *Law and Literature*, 108ff.

65. There is another reason for Posner's skepticism about mercy: he feels that it implies a kind of interfering scrutiny of the "insides" that sits uneasily with the libertarian hands-off attitude to government intervention he has long defended. I think this is wrong; wanting to know the relevant facts in no way entails additional curtailment of individual liberty of choice.

66. In "The Path of the Law" Holmes advances his famous "bad man" theory of the law: in order to figure out the deterrent aspect of punishment correctly, the judge should think, in each case, of what a bad person, completely insensitive to legal or moral requirements except in calculating personal costs and benefits, would do in response to a particular set of legal practices. Thus he endorses the basic strictness in assessing penalties that gave rise to our asymmetry in the ancient tradition.

67. Posner, *Essential Holmes*, supra note 56 at 59–60.

in his life Holmes recognized that the transcendence of strict moralism that he recommended throughout his career need not be captured through a reliance on external behavioral standards. It seems to him to be most appropriately captured in the "dramatic setting" in which Jesus takes up toward his enemies the attitude of Senecan mercy.[68] I think that he is right.[69]

In short, in order to depart from a retributivism that is brutal in its neglect of human complexity, we do not need to embrace a deterrence-only view that treats people as means to society's ends, aggregating their good and ill without regard to what is appropriate for each. The deterrence view is all too close to the retributive view it opposes in its resolute refusal to examine the particularities of motive, intention, and story, in its treatment of people as place-holders in a larger social or cosmic calculus.[70] A merciful judge need not neglect issues of deterrence, but she is above all committed to an empathetic scrutiny of the "insides" of the individual life.

B. Mercy and the Criminal Law

I have already begun to speak about the criminal law, since the focus in mercy is on wrongdoing and the wrongdoer. The implications of the mercy tradition for issues in the criminal law are many and complex, and I can only begin here to suggest what some of them might be. I shall do this by focusing on a pair of examples: two recent Supreme Court cases involving the death penalty which raise issues of mitigation and aggravation in connection with discretionary sentencing. One is *Walton v. Arizona*;[71] the other is *California v. Brown*.[72] At stake are the roles to be played by discretion in deciding capital cases and the criteria to be used in analyzing

---

68. Senecan influence on Christianity begins with the work of writers such as Clement of Alexandria and Augustine. I mean to point to a resemblance, which is later developed in explicitly Stoic terms.

69. For the distinction between forgiveness and mercy, see my discussion of Seneca above; a good modern discussion is in Jean Hampton and Jeffrie Murphy, *Forgiveness and Mercy* (Cambridge: Cambridge University Press, 1988). The attitude of Jesus toward sinners appears to be more one of mercy than of forgiveness: for sinners will certainly be condemned and punished, not let off the hook.

70. In many cases this view is harsher than the retributivist view, since a deterrence-based view will often punish attempts at crime that do not succeed or punish harshly a relatively minor crime if there is reason to think the defendant a dangerous repeat offender.

71. 497 U.S. 639 (1990).

72. 479 U.S. 538 (1987). For discussion of both of these cases I am indebted to Ronald J. Allen, "Evidence, Inference, Rules and Judgment in Constitutional Adjudication: The Intriguing Case of *Walton v. Arizona*," 81 *Journal of Criminal Law and Criminology* 727–59 (1991). For later thoughts about the role of logic in judicial inference, see Allen,

the aggravating and mitigating features of the case. Walton was convicted by a jury of first-degree murder and sentenced to death in accordance with an Arizona statute that requires the judge first to ascertain whether at least one aggravating circumstance is present—in this case two were found[73]— and then to consider all the alleged mitigating circumstances advanced by the defendant, imposing a death sentence if he finds "no mitigating circumstances sufficiently substantial to call for mercy." The defendant is required to establish a mitigating circumstance by the preponderance of the evidence, and it was this that was the central issue in Walton's appeal. Since previous Supreme Court decisions had rejected a requirement of unanimity for mitigation,[74] Walton contended that the preponderance of the evidence test was also unconstitutional. His claim was rejected by a plurality of the court. My concern is not so much with the result as with some interesting issues that emerge from the opinions.

First, it is plain that the Arizona system, which the decision in effect upholds, establishes a lexical ordering, in which a finding of aggravation—which must be based upon criteria explicitly enumerated in the law—is used to classify an offense as a potential death-penalty offense; mitigation is then considered afterwards, in a discretionary manner. In other words, the whole range of potentially mitigating circumstances will be brought forward only when it has already been established that an offense falls into a certain class of extremely serious offenses. Discretionary concern for the entirety of the defendant's history will enter the picture only in the mitigation phase. Justice Stevens comments on this feature in his dissenting opinion, arguing that once the scope of capital punishment is so reduced, the risk of arbitrariness in sentencing is sufficiently reduced as well to permit very broad discretion and individuated decision making with the remaining class. This seems to be a correct and valuable observation. Indeed, the mercy tradition stresses that merciful judgment can be given only when there is time to learn the whole complex history of the life in question and also inclination to do so in a sympathetic manner, without biases of class or race. The tradition wholeheartedly endorses decision making by codified standards where these requirements cannot be met. (Here Posner's warnings about arbitrariness in equity seem perfectly appropriate, and they are reflected in the move away from unguided

---

"The Double Jeopardy Clause, Constitutional Interpretation and the Limits of Formal Logic," 26 *Valparaiso University Law Review* 281–310 (1991).

73. The murder was committed in an "especially heinous, cruel or depraved manner," and it was committed for pecuniary gain. Note that even here, in the nondiscretionary and codified portion of the judgment, intentional notions are prominently used.

74. *Mills v. Maryland*, 486 U.S. 367 (1988), and *McKoy v. North Carolina*, 494 U.S. 433 (1990).

discretion represented by the federal sentencing guidelines.)[75] We should not, however, say, as Stevens seems to, that the main function of such criteria is to reduce the number of cases that are eligible for the death penalty. What they do is, of course, more substantial: they eliminate from the death-eligible group many cases for which death would clearly not be an appropriate penalty, leaving the judge free to turn his or her attention to those that are more problematic, requiring a more fine-tuned deliberation.[76]

A second significant feature, and a more problematic one, is the plurality's unquestioning acceptance of the preponderance of the evidence test, which, as Allen has shown here and elsewhere, has grave defects when we are dealing with a case having multiple relevant features.[77] Suppose a defendant advances three grounds for mitigation, each of which is established to a .25 probability, and therefore to be thrown out under Arizona's rule. The probability that at least one of the factors is true, assuming they are independent, is, as Allen shows, .58.[78] If each of three factors is proved to a probability of .4, the probability that at least one is true is .78. On the other hand, if the defendant proves just one of the mitigating factors with a probability of .51 and the others with probability 0, he is successful, even though the probability that the decision is correct is in fact lower here

---

75. I have not committed myself here on the ideal scope for discretion in other areas of the law. This is an issue I feel I need to study further before making concrete claims. I focus on the capital cases because they have been the focus of an especially interesting debate about mercy, which in the penalty-setting phase has a special weight. I do think that a similar approach could be tried in another group of cases to which a finding of aggravation is pertinent, namely hate crimes. Here I think one would want to describe the grounds for aggravation very explicitly and systematically, either by setting up a special class of crimes or in the guidelines for sentencing. Once one had determined that particular offense was of this particularly severe kind, one could then consider whether the defendant's youth, family background, and so forth gave any grounds for mitigation.

76. See Allen "*Walton*," supra note 72, at 741. I agree with this point against Stevens, but disagree with an earlier one. On page 736, Allen argues that "the primary thrust of [Stevens's] argument...is for categorical rather than discretionary sentencing." This seems to me inaccurate: it is, instead, a statement about the conditions under which discretionary sentencing can be well done.

77. See also Allen, "A Reconceptualization of Civil Trials," 66 *B.U. Law Review* 410ff. (1986).

78. See Allen, "*Walton*," supra note 72, at 734–35. This is the assumption that the current test in effect makes. If they are not independent, this probablistic analysis does not follow, but there is also, then, no justification at all for treating them in isolation from one another. In either case, then, the conclusion for which I am arguing follows: the life must be considered as a whole.

than in the previous cases.[79] The law asks the judge to treat each feature one by one, in total isolation from any other. But human lives, as the literary judge would see, consist of complex webs of circumstances, which must be considered as wholes.

This same problem is present in Justice Scalia's scathing attack on the whole notion of mitigation. For Scalia thinks it absurd that we should have codified criteria for aggravation, apply these, and then look with unguided discretion to see whether a mitigating factor is present. If the criteria for aggravation are enumerated in the law, so too should be the criteria for mitigation. Only this explicitness and this symmetry can prevent total irrationality. Scalia here ignores the possibility—which Stevens recognizes—that the functions of aggravation-criteria and of mitigation are not parallel: aggravation serves to place the offense in the class to which mitigation is relevant.[80] Furthermore, in ridiculing the entire notion of discretionary mercy, Scalia adamantly refuses the forms of perception that we have associated with the literary attitude. That is, he treats mitigating factors as isolated units, unconnected either to one another or to the whole of a life. It is in this way that he can arrive at the conclusion that unbridled discretion will (absurdly) be permitted to treat traits that are polar opposites as, both of them, mitigating: for example "that the defendant had a poor and deprived childhood, or that he had a rich and spoiled childhood."[81] Scalia's assumption is that both of these cannot be mitigating and that it is a sign of the absurdity of the current state of things that they might both be so treated. But the alleged absurdity arises only because he has severed these traits from the web of circumstances in which they actually figure. In connection with other circumstances either a trait or its opposite might, in fact, be mitigating.[82] This, in Allen's argument and in mine, is the reason why categories for mitigation should not be codified in advance:

79. One might also point out that different jurors might be convinced by different factors, so long as they are treated as isolated units. One could have a situation in which all jurors agree that there is a least one mitigating factor present, but, if they disagree enough about which one it is, the defendant's attempt fails. I owe this point to Cy Wasserstrom.

80. Here the similarity to the ancient tradition is striking, especially to Seneca's insistence on separating the determination of guilt and its level from the assignment of (merciful) punishment.

81. 497 U.S. at 663.

82. See Allen, "*Walton*," supra note 72 at 739 & 742 ("Any particular fact is of very little consequence standing alone. The web of facts is what matters.") In *David Copperfield* we see a very clear example of a rich and spoiled childhood as a mitigating factor: Steerforth has no opportunity to learn moral self-restraint and is encouraged to use his talent and charm in a reckless manner.

it will be impossible for such a code to anticipate adequately the count-less ways in which factors interweave and bear upon one another in human reality.[83] Telling the whole story, with all the particulars, is the only way to get at that.[84]

In reality, of course, the mercy tradition has serious reservations about the whole idea of capital punishment. Although some of its major expo-nents, including Seneca, endorsed it, they did so on the basis of very pecu-liar arguments comparing it to euthanasia.[85] If we reject these arguments we are left, I think, with no support for capital punishment from within that tradition, and strong reasons to reject retributivist justifications. Indeed, the tradition strongly suggests that such punishments are always cruel and excessive. The question would then have to be whether the deterrence value of such punishments by itself justifies their perpetuation, despite their moral inappropriateness. Furthermore, the deterrence-based argu-ment has never yet been made out in a fully compelling way.

California v. Brown raises a different issue: that of jury instruction where emotion is concerned. The Court reviewed a state jury instruction stipulating that the jury in a capital case (in the sentencing phase) "must not be swayed by mere sentiment, conjecture, sympathy, passion, prejudice, public opin-ion or public feeling."[86] From the point of view of our account of literary judging, this instruction is a peculiar and inappropriate mixture. For the

---

83. I am not claiming that knowledge of the whole story should never give rise to aggravation of punishment. By focusing on capital cases I have left undiscussed a number of lesser cases in which such thinking might figure. One is a very interesting case recently heard by the Seventh Circuit, in which Posner defends an upward departure from the sen-tencing guidelines in a case of blackmail, on the ground that the blackmailer's victim, a married homosexual, fit the category of "unusually vulnerable victim" that justifies such aggravation. Detailed consideration of the whole story, and of American homophobia, was required in order to establish that this victim was really more vulnerable than other types of people with sexual secrets to conceal (*U.S. v. Sienky Lallemand*, 989 F.2d 936 (7th Cir., 1993)).

84. Another point against Scalia is the structure of the pardon power: a governor can pardon a criminal, but not increase a criminal's sentence or condemn someone who was acquitted. Indeed, asymmetry is built into the entirety of the criminal justice system, in the requirement to prove guilt beyond a reasonable doubt, in the safeguards surrounding the admissibility of confessions, and so forth.

85. See supra note 43.

86. 479 U.S. 538 (1987). Note that for a juror the case at issue is likely to be a rare event, and thus there is reason to think that jury deliberations will be free from at least some of the problems of callousness and shortness of time that may limit the advisability of discretion in cases involving judges. On the other hand, the limits of juror sympathy with people who are unlike themselves remains a clear difficulty. This is why I sympathize, to the extent that I do, with parts of the warning in the California juror instruction.

juror as "judicious spectator" and merciful reader would indeed disregard conjecture, prejudice, public opinion, and public feeling. On the other hand, sentiment, passion, and sympathy would be a prominent part of the appropriate (and rational) deliberative process, where those sentiments are based in the juror's "reading" of the defendant's history as presented in the evidence. It would of course be right to leave aside any sentiment having to do with one's own involvement in the outcome, but we assume that nobody with a personal interest in the outcome would end up on the jury in any case. It would also be correct to leave aside any mere gut reaction to the defendant's appearance, demeanor, or clothing, anything that could not be made a reasoned part of the "story" of the case. But the vast majority of the passional reactions of a juror hearing a case of this kind will be based on the story that is told; in this sense, the law gives extremely bad advice.[87] The Court, however approved the instruction, concluding that "[A] reasonable juror would...understand the instruction...as a directive to ignore only the sort of sympathy that would be totally divorced from the evidence adduced during the penalty phase."[88] On the one hand, this seems to me a perfectly reasonable way of articulating the boundaries of appropriate and inappropriate sympathy. On the other hand, the likelihood is so high that the sentiments of the juror would be of the appropriate, rather than the inappropriate, sort—for what else but the story told them do they have to consider?—that approving the regulation creates a misleading impression that some large and rather dangerous class of passions are being excluded.[89] The other opinions in the case confirm the general impression of confusion about and suspicion of the passions. Thus Justice O'Connor argues that "the sentence imposed at the penalty stage should reflect a reasoned *moral* response to the defendant's background, character, and crime rather than mere sympathy or emotion." She goes on to state that "the individualized assessment of the appropriateness of the death penalty is a moral inquiry into the culpability of the defendant, and not an emotional response to the mitigating evidence."[90] This contrast between morality and sympathy is a nest of confusions, as my argument by now should have shown. Justice Brennan, too, holds that "mere sym-

---

87. Compare the advice given to the prospective juror in the state of Massachusetts, in the "Juror's Creed" printed in the Trial Juror's Handbook: "I am a JUROR. I am a seeker of truth...I must lay aside all bias and prejudice. I must be led by my intelligence and not by my emotions."

88. 479 U.S. at 542–43.

89. Thus I agree in part with Allen, "*Walton*," supra note 72 at 747, although I do think it reasonable to stipulate this restriction on sentiment and believe that it is possible to think of cases where sentiments would be of the inappropriate sort.

90. 479 U.S. at 545.

pathy" must be left to one side—though he does hold (dissenting) that the instruction prohibits the juror from considering exactly what he or she should consider.[91] Justice Blackmun does somewhat better, defending the juror's ability to respond with mercy as a "particularly valuable aspect of the capital sentencing procedure." But he, too, contrasts rationality with mercy, even in the process of defending the latter: "While the sentencer's decision to accord life to a defendant at times might be a rational or moral one, it also may arise from the defendant's appeal to the sentencer's sympathy or mercy, human qualities that are undeniably emotional in nature."[92] The confusion persists: in a more recent case, the Court now speaks even more suspiciously and pejoratively of the jurors' emotions, contrasting them with the "actual evidence regarding the crime and the defendant"[93]—as if these were not the source of and basis for these emotions.[94]

In short, the insights of the mercy tradition can take us a long way in understanding what is well and not well done in recent Supreme Court writings about sentencing. It can help us to defend the asymmetry between mitigation and aggravation that prevailed in *Walton*, as well as *Walton*'s moderate defense of discretion. But it leads to severe criticism of the categories of analysis deployed in the juror-instruction cases, which employ defective conceptions of the rational.

C. Feminist Political Thought

It is now time to return to Andrea Dworkin and to feminism. Dworkin's novel has been in the background throughout this paper, providing us with a striking modern example of the strict retributivist position and

---

91. *Id.* at 548–50.

92. *Id.* at 561–63. Thus I do not agree with Allen, supra note 72, at 750, that Blackmun "gets it right." Allen, like Blackmun, is willing to give the normative term "rational" to the opposition, granting that merciful sentiment is not rational. But why not? Such merciful sentiments are based on judgments that are (if the deliberative process is well executed) both true and justified by the evidence.

93. *Saffle v. Parks*, 494 U.S. 484, 493 (1990).

94. One might think that my view entails admitting victim impact statements, for they are certainly part of the whole story, even though the victim is often no longer around to tell it. I am dubious. A criminal trial is about the defendant and what will become of him or her. The question before the court is what the defendant did, and the function of narrative is to illuminate the character and origins of that deed. What has to be decided is not what to do about the victim, but what to do about the defendant. Now of course the victim's experience may be relevant to ascertaining the nature of the offense, and to that extent it is admissible anyway. But the additional information imported by victim impact statements seems primarily to lie in giving vent to the passion for revenge, and the emotions they seek to arouse are those associated with that passion.

showing us how the retributive imagination is opposed to the literary imagination. But Dworkin's book is, after all, called a novel. One might well wonder how I can so easily say that the novel form is a construction of mercy. The problem is only apparent. For Andrea Dworkin's "novel" is not a novel but an antinovel. By deliberate design, it does not invite its reader to occupy the positions of its characters, seeing their motivations with sympathy and with concern for the entire web of circumstances out of which their actions grow. It does not invite its reader to be emotionally receptive, except to a limited degree in the case of its central figure. But this figure is such a solipsistic, self-absorbed persona that to identify with her is to enter a sealed world of a peculiar sort, a world in and from which the actions of others appear only as external movement, without discernible motive. As for the men who people the novel, the reader is enjoined to view them as the narrator views them: as machines that produce pain. We are forbidden to have an interest in their character, origins, motives or points of view. We are forbidden all sympathy and even all curiosity. We are refused perception of the particular, for, as in the male pornography that Dworkin's activism opposes, her male characters are not particulars, but generic objects.[95] In effect, we are refused novelistic readership.

Indeed, the very form of Dworkin's work causes us, as readers, to inhabit the retributive frame of mind and to refuse mercy. The inclination to mercy is present in the text only as a fool's inclination toward collaboration and slavery. When the narrator, entering her new profession as a karate-killer of homeless men, enunciates "the political principle which went as follows: It is very important for women to kill men," a voice within the text suggests the explanations that might lead to mercy.[96] As the return of the narrator quickly makes clear, this is meant to be a parody voice, a fool's voice, the voice of a collaborator with the enemy:

> He didn't mean it; or he didn't do it, not really, or not fully, or not knowing, or not intending; he didn't understand; or he couldn't help it; or he won't again; certainly he will try not to; unless, well, he just can't help it; be patient; he needs help; sympathy; over time. Yes, her ass is grass but you can't expect miracles, it takes time, she wasn't perfect either you know; he needs time, education, help, support; yeah, she's dead meat; but you can't expect some-

---

95. In "Defining Pornography," 114 *U. Pa L. Rev.* 1153 (1993), James Lindgren shows that none of the standard definitions of pornography works terribly well in separating feminist fiction from pornography, if (as MacKinnon has urged) the test is applied to passages taken out of the context of the whole work. MacKinnon's and Dworkin's definition works better than others to separate Dworkin's own fiction from pornography, but only because Lindgren has selected a rare Dworkin passage in which the woman is in control of what takes place and is not subordinated.

96. Dworkin, *Mercy*, p. 328.

one to change right away, overnight, besides she wasn't perfect, was she, he needs time, help, support, education; well yeah, he was out of control; listen, she's lucky it wasn't worse, I'm not covering it up or saying what he did was right, but she's not perfect, believe me, and he had a terrible mother; yeah, I know you had to scrape her off the ground; but you know, she wasn't perfect either, he's got a problem; he's human, he's got a problem.[97]

The only alternative to the retributive attitude, Dworkin implies, is an attitude of foolish and hideous capitulation. The novelist's characteristic style of perception is in league with evil.

This is an unsuccessful and badly written book. It is far less successful, both as writing and as thought, than the best of Dworkin's essays.[98] And yet it is in another way an important book, for it brings to the surface for scrutiny the strict retributive attitude that animates some portions of feminist moral and legal thought and allows us to see this attitude as a reasonable response to terrible wrongs. Dworkin is correct in stressing the pervasiveness of male violence against women, and correct, too, in insisting that to deny and conceal these wrongs is to condemn women of the present and future to continued bodily and psychological suffering. She is correct in protesting loudly against these wrongs and in refusing to say that they are not wrongs. The only remedy, Dworkin suggests, is to refuse all sympathy and all particular perception, moving over to a conception of justice so resolute in its denial of particularity that it resembles Anaximandrean *dikê* more than it resembles most modern retributive schemes. The narrator announces, "None of them's innocent and who cares? I fucking don't care." And it is Dworkin's position repeatedly announced in the novel as in her essays that all heterosexual males are rapists and all heterosexual intercourse is rape. In this sense, there really is no difference between him and him, and to refuse to see this is to collaborate with evil.

But Dworkin is wrong. Retributivism is not the only alternative to cowardly denial and capitulation.[99] Seneca's *De ira* is hardly a work that denies evil where it exists; indeed, it is a work almost as relentlessly obsessed with narrating tales of evil as is Dworkin's work. Like Dworkin's work, it insists

---

97. *Id.* at 329.

98. In my *Boston Review* piece on Dworkin, see supra note 1, I discuss some of the essays in *Intercourse*, which express a view of sexuality far more subtle and particularized than the views expressed here especially where women are not in the picture and Dworkin is discussing male homosexuality.

99. One might argue that Dworkin's style of retributivism, even if not morally precise, has strategic value, in publicizing the pervasiveness of harms done to women. I doubt this. For if, with Dworkin, we refuse to make distinctions we commonly make between consensual heterosexual intercourse and coercion, we are likely to get fewer convictions for rape, not more.

on the pervasiveness of evil, the enormous difficulty of eradicating it, and the necessity of bringing it to judgment. Mercy is not acquittal. In what, then, does its great difference from Dworkin's work consist? First of all, it does not exempt itself. It takes the Dworkin parody line "She wasn't perfect either" very seriously, urging that all human beings are the products of social and natural conditions that are, in certain ways, subversive of justice and love, that need slow patient resistance. This interest in self-scrutiny already gives it a certain gentleness, forces it out of the we/them mentality characteristic of retributivism. Second, it is really interested in the obstacles to goodness that Dworkin's narrator mocks and dismisses: the social obstacles, deeply internalized, that cannot be changed in an instant; the other more circumstantial and particular obstacles that stand between individuals and justice to those they love. It judges these social forces and commits itself to changing them, but, where judgment on the individual is concerned, it yields in mercy before the difficulty of life. This means that it can be in its form a powerful work of narrative art. If you really open your imagination and heart to admit the life story of someone else, it becomes far more difficult to finish that person off with a karate kick. In short, the text constructs a reader who, while judging justly, remains capable of love.

What I am really saying is that good feminist thought, in the law and in life generally, is like good judging: it does not ignore the evidence, it does not fail to say that injustice is injustice, evil evil[100] — but it is capable of *suggnômê*, and therefore of *clementia*. And if it is shrewd it will draw on the resources of the novelist's art.

I shall end by returning to Seneca's *De clementia*. Toward the end of the address to Nero Caesar, Seneca asked him a pointed question: "What... would be if lions and bears held the power, if serpents and all the most destructive animals were given power over us?" (I.26.3) These serpents, lions and bears, as Seneca well knows, inhabit our souls in the forms of our jealous angers, our competitiveness, our retributive harshness.[101] These animals are as they are because they are incapable of receiving another creature's life story into their imagination and responding to that history with gentleness. But those serpents, lions and bears in the mind still play a part today, almost two thousand years after Seneca's treatise was written, in determining the shape of our legal institutions, as the merciful atti-

---

100. Contrast Dworkin, *Mercy*, p. 334, where in epilogue entitled "Not Andrea," a liberal feminist attacks Andrea Dworkin as "a prime example, of course, of the simple-minded demagogue who promotes the proposition that bad things are bad."

101. For Seneca's use of this animal imagery elsewhere, see my "Serpents in the Soul: A Reading of Seneca's Medea," in T. Cohen et al. (ed.), *Pursuits of Reason: Essays in Honor of Stanley Cavell* (Lubbock: Texas Tech Press, 1993).

tude to punishment still comes in for ridicule, as the notion of deliberation based on sentiment still gets repudiated and misunderstood, as a simple form of retributivism has an increasing influence on our legal and political life. As judges, as jurors, as feminists, we should, I argue with Seneca, oppose the ascendancy of these more obtuse animals, and while judging the wrong to be wrong, still cultivate the perceptions, and the gentleness, of mercy.[102]

102. Cf. also *De clementia* I.17.1: "No animal has a more troublesome temperament, none needs to be handled with greater skill, than the human being; and to none should mercy more be shown."

Chapter Two

Medea and the Un-Man

Paul J. Heald

Jason: ...Thou wife in every age Abhorred, blood-red mother, who
    didst kill My sons, and make me as the dead...
Medea: I love the pain, so thou shalt laugh no more.

                           —Euripides[1]

Frate Alberigo: He answered, "I am Frate Alberigo; I am he of the evil
    garden's fruit, who here get date for fig."
Dante: "Oh," I said, "are you too now dead?"
Frate Alberigo: And he answered: "How my body is getting along in the
    world above, I have no notion. This Ptolomea is so privileged
    that often the soul falls down here before Atorpos releases it...
    I now tell you that as soon as a soul commits betrayal, as I did,
    its body is taken from it by a demon, who then controls it until
    all its time on earth is gone. The soul falls into this cistern here.

                           —Dante[2]

Ransom had the sense of watching an imitation of living motions which had
been very well studied and was technically correct, but somehow it lacked
the master touch. And he was chilled with an inarticulate, night-nursery
horror of the thing he had to deal with—the managed corpse, the bogey,
the Un-man.

                           —C.S. Lewis[3]

In 1982, William Cartwright entered the home of his ex-employer,
Hugh Riddle, to commit murder. As he made his way down the hall toward

Many thanks to Albert Alschuler, Milner Ball, Larry Biskowski, Joel Black, James
Blitch, Lief Carter, Mark Cooney, Jill Crandall, Bernard Dauenhauer, Christopher Eisgru-
ber, David Gruning, Martha Nussbaum, David Skeel, Alan Watson and James B. White
for their thoughtful comments on earlier versions of this Essay. Special thanks also go to
participants at the University of Illinois Comparative Literature Colloquium and the University of Georgia Humanities Center Faculty Colloquium. I could not have written this
Essay without the friendship and support of Professor Michael Palencia-Roth, University
of Illinois Department of Comparative Literature.

1. Euripides, *The Medea* 74–75 (Gilbert Murray trans., Oxford Univ. Press, 1912).
2. Dante Allighieri, *Inferno*, Canto 33, at 285 (Allan Gilbert trans., Duke Univ. Press,
1969).
3. C.S. Lewis, *Perelandra* 126 (1947).

the living room where Riddle watched television, he encountered Riddle's wife, Charma, whom he shot twice in the legs. After killing his ex-boss in the living room, he went back down the hall and found Mrs. Riddle trying to call the police. He stabbed her twice, slit her throat, and left her to die.[4] She survived, and on the basis of her testimony,[5] Cartwright was convicted of aggravated murder and sentenced to die in the Oklahoma electric chair.[6]

Oklahoma, like most states with the death penalty, requires the sentencing authority to weigh a specific list of statutory aggravating circumstances against mitigating evidence that the convicted murderer offers.[7] In Cartwright's case, the jury found two aggravating circumstances, one of which was that the murder was "especially heinous, atrocious, or cruel."[8] On appeal, Cartwright challenged Oklahoma's heinousness factor as unconstitutionally overbroad.[9] He argued that the statutory language which was read to the jurors did not adequately confine their discretion.[10] How was the jury to guess what the legislature meant by an "especially heinous murder" as opposed to a "just-plain-vanilla heinous murder"? The language invited, according to Cartwright, the sort of arbitrary, capricious, and standardless sentencing scheme struck down in *Godfrey v. Georgia*.[11] *Godfrey* had held that when a life is at stake, the sentencer cannot be given an open opportunity to condemn for whatever reason it pleases.[12]

In vacating Cartwright's sentence, the Supreme Court affirmed *Godfrey*'s requirement that the state must channel jury discretion with more than vague statutory language.[13] It refused, however, to strike down the statute on its face. Instead, it suggested that the heinousness factor could be constitutionally applied in light of a limiting judicial construction or statutory amendment that would flesh out what was meant by "especially heinous,

---

4. *Maynard v. Cartwright*, 486 U.S. 356, 358 (1988).

5. See *Cartwright v. State*, 695 P.2d 548, 551 (Okla. Crim. Ap.) (discussing the testimony at trial of Charma Riddle), *cert. denied*, 473 U.S. 91 (1985).

6. *Maynard*, 486 U.S. at 358–59.

7. Okla. Stat. tit. 21 § 701.11 (1991).

8. *Id.* § 701.12(4). Many jurisdictions include "heinousness" or something like it as an aggravating circumstance. See, e.g. Fla. Stat Ann. § 921.141(5)(h) (West Supp. 1995) ("especially heinous, atrocious, or cruel"); Ariz. Rev. Stat. Ann. § 13-702(c)(5) (1994) ("especially heinous, cruel or depraved"); Ga. Code Ann. § 17-10-30(7) (Michie 1990) ("outrageously or wantonly vile, horrible, or inhuman").

9. *Maynard*, 486 U.S. at 359.

10. *Id.* at 361–62.

11. 446 U.S. 420 (1980).

12. *Id.* at 428–29.

13. *Maynard*, 486 U.S. at 362–64.

atrocious or cruel."[14] The sentencer, whether judge or jury, must be told more precisely what sort of murders fit the bill.

The heart of the opinion mandates that states do a better job of sorting out the kinds of murderers who deserve to be executed from those who do not. The Court refused to perform the task itself—it was unwilling to hold, for example, that the jury could find heinousness as an aggravating factor only if torture or serious physical abuse were present.[15] Instead the Court invited the states to tell stories to their sentencers about what kind of people should die. The content of these stories would be basically up to judges or legislatures, but the sentencer's discretion must be guided by the story told.[16]

The Court had earlier, in a number of decisions beginning with *Lockett v. Ohio*,[17] authorized defendants to tell their own stories: stories about their childhoods, their religious conversions, their experiences in prison, their addictions—anything that might remotely be considered mitigating in the eyes of the sentencer.[18] The state typically must plead and prove the existence of at least one enumerated statutory aggravating factor,[19] but the defendant may offer character evidence that falls outside the mitigating factors specifically listed in the capital sentencing statute.[20] The defendant usually seeks to make himself a more sympathetic individual in the eyes of the sentencer. In requiring the admission of such evidence, the Court has already invited the sentencers to listen to one sort of deathtime story.

The state's tale is usually different. Under *Cartwright*, it must categorize defendants rather than individualize them and pose the question whether the defendant is the type of person who should be executed. When this ethical dilemma arises, literature can become relevant. Fiction comprises a huge repository of stories about who should live and who should die, what is good and what is evil, what is heinous and what is merely pathetic. Because we constitute ourselves as a community through both art and law, artists and lawmakers spend considerable time pondering the fates of those who transgress societal norms. To give content to the term "heinous," a judge might just as plausibly look to fiction as to a dictionary or to history, legislative or otherwise.

In fact, given the narrowness of our actual experiences, perhaps resort to fiction should be mandated. In considering the relevance of fiction to living, Nussbaum ponders:

---

14. *Id.* at 364–65.
15. *Id.* at 365.
16. *Id.* at 364–65.
17. 438 U.S. 586 (1978).
18. *Id.* at 604–05 (plurality opinion).
19. E.g., Fla. Stat. Ann. § 921.141(2)–(3) (West 1985).
20. *Lockett*, 438 U.S. at 604–07 (plurality opinion).

But why not life itself? Why can't we investigate whatever we want to investigate by living and reflecting on [life]? Why, if it is the Aristotelian ethical conception we wish to scrutinize, can't we do that without literary texts, without texts at all...

One obvious answer was suggested already by Aristotle: we have never lived enough. Our experience is, without fiction, too confined and too parochial.[21]

In her commentary on Kant's theory of political judgment, Hannah Arendt addresses a similar point:

The "enlargement of the mind" plays a crucial role in the *Critique of Judgment*. It is accomplished by "comparing our judgment with the possible rather than the actual judgment of others, and by putting ourselves in the place of any other man." The faculty which makes this possible is called imagination...[By] force of imagination it makes the others present and thus moves potentially in a space which is public, open to all sides; in other words, it adopts the position of Kant's world citizen. To think with the enlarged mentality—that means you train your imagination to go visiting.[22]

In the hope of enlarging our understanding through a mix of fiction and historical examples, I would like to tell the following *Maynard* stories for the state.

When Dante nears the end of his journey through Hell and finally reaches the lake of ice that surrounds the trunk of Satan himself, Dante encounters a special group of murderers whose acts were so evil that they merited punishment in the lowest circle of the great pit. They are the killers of kin and guests—frozen in eternal torment. In pausing to speak with Friar Alberigo, whose servants murdered his dinner guests upon his signal to serve dessert (hence the reference to figs at the beginning of his speech[23]), Dante expresses surprise that the Friar has died. In fact the Friar's body is not really dead at all, although his soul resides in Hell. His body, now possessed by a demon, is alive and well and committing who knows what sort of horrors on the populace of Italy.[24] His irredeemably corrupt soul has perished, leaving behind a husk of unspeakable evil.

We encounter the husk itself in C.S. Lewis's *Perelandra*, not the shell of Friar Alberigo, but the body vacated by the fictional physicist, Dr. West-

---

21. Martha C. Nussbaum, *Love's Knowledge* 47 (New York: Oxford Univ. Press, 1992).

22. Hannah Arendt, *The Life of the Mind* 257 (Mary McCarthy ed., 1978) (quoting Immanuel Kant, *Critique of Judgment* (1790)).

23. See Dante, supra note 2, canto 33, at 285 ("I am he of the evil garden's fruit, who here get date for fig."); see also supra text accompanying note 2.

24. See Dante, supra note 2, canto 33, at 285 ("How my body is getting along in the world above, I have no notion."); see also supra text accompanying note 2.

on. Bloated by his fabulous scientific success, Weston has committed the ultimate sin of making himself into God.[25] He admits he is capable even of genocide to advance what he describes as the spirit of the universe.[26] Just before his soul vacates his body, Weston raves to Lewis's hero, Dr. Ransom:

> There is no possible distinction in concrete thought between me and the universe. In so far as I am the conductor of the central forward pressure of the universe, I am it. Do you see, you timid, scruple-mongering fool? I am the Universe. I, Weston, am your God and your Devil. I call that Force into me completely.[27]

At the moment of invocation, Weston's personality is gone in a violent contorting shudder, but his body remains, the Un-man, an empty yet terrifying creature of purposeful violence against which Ransom wages a passionate struggle for the rest of the novel.

Unfortunately for us, the Un-man is not only an imaginary creature, a character from fiction. We find him purposefully searching the streets and countryside for vulnerable women to rape, torture, and murder. He visits the corner convenience store and calmly shoots the teenage clerk in the back of the head when he turns to empty the till. He has led nations and political movements. When he is caught, he often describes his acts in the third person. Psychologists who interview him frequently note the "inappropriate affect" exhibited by the Un-man when discussing the crime—the trademark monotone, the emotionless recitation of acts of deliberate annihilation.[28] Joe Aloi, a private investigator who helped the infamous serial killer Theodore Robert Bundy in one of his murder defenses, described the "altered state" Bundy would seem to enter when he discussed one of his serial killings. According to Aloi, Bundy would emit a strong odor, freezing those around him in fear.[29] In the eyes of many, when Bundy was executed in 1989, the state of Florida switched off a managed corpse—the person inside had disappeared long before.

Dante and Lewis may help the state describe one sort of murderer that might merit capital punishment. They provide an illustration of what "heinousness" could mean for the purposes of *Maynard*, an insight that

---

25. Lewis, supra note 3, at 97.

26. *Id.* at 96–97.

27. *Id.* at 97.

28. See, e.g., Myra MacPherson, "The Roots of Evil," *Vanity Fair* (May 1989) at pp. 140, 196 ("[Ted] Bundy, like other serial killers, dehumanized his victims, seeing them as only symbolic objects to 'hunt'."). See generally Stephen G. Michaud & Hugh Aynesworth, Ted Bundy, *Conversations with a Killer* (1989).

29. MacPherson, supra note 55, at 190.

focuses on a rare type who embraces and nurtures the darkest side of human nature—one who develops a taste for killing.

Before suggesting further attributes of the Un-man and discussing the practical dangers and theoretical problems of appealing to Dante and Lewis for help, let me tell another story—the myth of Medea, wife of Jason and murderess of their children.[30] Whatever her faults, Medea is not an Un-person—in fact, few murderers are. This does not necessarily mean her punishment should be lenient. *Maynard* does not say who should live and who should die, but the telling of the Medea myth, in conjunction with the myth of the Un-man, clarifies and refines the state's options in defining heinousness.

After Jason and Medea flee from Iôclos, where Jason has failed to regain his deposed father's throne after completing his quest for the Golden Fleece, they come to Corinth where King Creon offers Jason the hand of his daughter. Jason, who owes his life and virtually all his accomplishments to the help of Medea, but whose wealth is depleted and who is tired after years of wandering, accepts Creon's offer. He claims to Medea that he does not love his attractive young betrothed, but that he is strategically doing what is best for Medea and their children. In her anger over his betrayal, she kills Creon's daughter and her own children.

Medea's anguish goes far beyond mere jealousy. She has given up everything in her obsessive devotion to Jason. When he arrived in her barbarian home of Colchis on his quest, she fell in love with him and enabled him to defeat her family. Without her help, he could not have taken the Golden Fleece and recovered the soul of his kinsman Phrixus, as demanded by Pelias, his father's usurper. Because she needed to kill her own brother to prevent him from ambushing Jason, she fled Colchis with Jason and the Argonauts. She proved an invaluable addition to his crew as his ship wandered its way home to Iôclos. Unfortunately, once Jason arrived back home to his civilized Greek city-state, Medea's violent determination to advance Jason's interest backfired and resulted in their exile to Corinth after her killing of King Pelias.

Despite the obsessive nature of Medea's love, she remains, at least in part, a sympathetic character, especially in the face of Jason's eagerness to abandon her. Jason provides one of fiction's first examples of male midlife crisis. The quest of his youth has been completed. What can he look forward to, other than bedding an aging wife, watching his sons grow, and continuing the struggle to survive? How can he resist a beautiful young princess and a chance to see his children on the throne of Corinth? One can hardly fault Jason for being tempted. Medea's attendant confronts her nurse's surprise at Jason's behavior by declaring "[W]hat man on earth is different?"[31] But Jason is tempted by more than a young body. He is tempted by

---

30. Euripides, supra note 1.
31. *Id.* at 7.

the illusion that he can both have his new life and discharge the enormous debt he owes Medea.

Jason will not admit that he is a traitor. As Medea exclaims, " 'Tis but of all man's inward sicknesses/The vilest, that he knoweth not of shame...."[32] He clings stubbornly to the illusion that Medea and the children will be better off after the marriage. He never admits that he is attracted to Creon's daughter. He tries to turn his treachery into a favor:

> Yet, even so, I will not hold my hand
> From succoring mine own people. Here am I
> To help thee, woman, pondering heedfully
> Thy new state. For I would not have thee flung
> Provisionless away—aye and the young
> Children as well; nor lacking aught that will
> Of mine can bring thee. Many a lesser ill
> Hangs on the heels of exile...[A]ye, and though
> Thou hate me, dream not that my heart can know
> Or fashion aught of angry will to thee.[33]

Like many modern American men, Jason believes that if he pays his child support and remains civil to his abandoned family, he may blithely start a new life. No responsibility need be taken for the severing of old ties.

Jason's failure to acknowledge the legitimacy of Medea's pain provokes her ultimate act of violence—the stabbing deaths of their two children. Having tried all manner of words, Medea murders to make Jason feel her pain. To the surprise of no one who has seen this story played out on a less epic scale, Jason's blindness remains even in the face of the horrific result of his faithlessness. He takes no responsibility for the tragedy. Looking back, Jason (but not the audience) finds Medea accursed and wicked from the beginning: She has not killed because of his abandonment, but because she was evil from the day they met. His response to the murder is not insight into Medea's tortured soul. He does not see her as the victim she wants to be. Rather, he rejects her entire being as poisonous. Medea has not only murdered her children but also finished the process by which Jason blinded himself both to reality and to his own responsibility for Medea's crimes.

In fact, Medea's love for Jason was probably never very healthy. Healthy love does not lead a woman to kill her brother, at least one king, the daughter of another, and her own two children. But the issue here is not whether Medea is culpable—she is. The question is whether the play sheds any light on how a state should describe a heinous murder. Should the murder of Medea's children be described as "especially heinous" for the purposes of

---

32. *Id.* at 27
33. *Id.* at 26–27.

Maynard v. Cartwright? This point is especially relevant in that Medea is not any more a purely mythic character than the Un-man.[34]

According to Jungian critics, Medea is so common, so much a part of every person, that she can easily stand for the archetype of the wronged feminine in both women and men.[35] For Jung, the feminine represents the part of a personality that seeks connection with others, that casts its lot with mate, friends, and family, that seeks meaning in relationship rather than material accomplishment.[36] When a relationship is severed, and particularly when the wrong goes unacknowledged, Medea raises her head. "If only my spouse knew what pain he was causing me, I'm sure he would stop." Obviously, most Jason-like wrongings of the feminine do not result in murder, but sometimes they do. Spouses, ex-spouses and ex-lovers sometimes pay a lethal last visit to their families.[37] Fired workers (those who have a greater emotional investment in their jobs than I do) return to work one last time to kill their employers or co-workers.[38]

The problem with executing Medea is that we know her too well. Although the obsessiveness of her love pushes her much further out of control than any reader of this Essay is likely to get, we empathize with her. Do we dare execute an archetype of our own pain? Might we not diminish ourselves in the process? The Court's decision in *Maynard* does not provide us with an answer to that question; however, it does imply that a state should at least ask it. Irrespective of the answer chosen by the state, reading Euripides helps us describe and identify a type of murderer that differs significantly from the Un-man.

Having discussed Medea in relatively familiar terms, we encounter difficulties improving our description of the Un-man. Neither Dante nor Lewis lets us into the Un-man's mind—if they think he even has one.[39] Per-

---

34. See Martha C. Nussbaum, "Serpents in the Soul: A Reading of Seneca's Medea" in *Pursuits of Reason: Essays in Honor of Stanley Cavell* 307, 330 (Ted Cohen et al. eds., 1993) (noting the real life connection between violence and erotic love).

35. Cf. John A. Sanford & George Lough, *What Men are Like* 140, 136–41 (1988) (surveying the archetypal powers of major Greek goddesses in order to emphasize "the scope and importance of the feminine archetype in a man's psychology"). My presentation of the facts of the Medea myth is heavily influenced by Sanford.

36. *Id.* at 149, 131–50 (noting that the feminine side of a man—the anima—"gives a man heart, enabling him to be courageous in the face of life's burdens and afflictions").

37. See, e.g., Bill Harmon, "Retired Cop Charged in Slaying: Police say the Former Officer Stabbed His Estranged Wife Four or Five Times," *Tampa Trib.* Jan.17, 1995 at 1.

38. See, e.g., Doron P. Levin, "Slayings at Michigan Post Office Spur a review of All Employees," *N.Y. Times*, Nov. 16, 1991, at 6.

39. For an interesting attempt, see Anne Rice, *The Tale of the Body Thief* 1–23 (New York: Knopf, 1992) (describing the thoughts and impulses of a killer—the Un-man—as sensed by the book's narrator, a vampire).

haps a fuller description of the interior life of the Un-man would prick our sympathies as much as the Medea story. Our view of the Un-man is clouded by his own unwillingness or inability to describe his motivation.[40] Ted Bundy, the prototypical Un-man for the purposes of this Essay, sheds a little light. He responded to the following question about his need to "possess" his victims:

> [Interviewer]: Would the feeling of physical possession be met, or satisfied...if the victim was unconscious or dead?
> Bundy: ...I think we see a point reached—slowly, perhaps—where the control, the possession aspect, came to include, uh, uh, within its demands, the necessity...for the purposes of gratification... the killing of the victim...Perhaps it came to be seen that the ultimate possession was, in fact, the taking of the life. And then the purely...physical possession of the remains.[41]

Bundy savored the God-like power of exerting ultimate control over another human being. Perhaps the Un-man is the murderer who enjoys killing for its own sake. Although our understanding of the Un-man is still incomplete, Dante and Lewis are clearly attempting to describe a different kind of murderer than is Euripides.

*　*　*

Before discussing whether the state, having separated Medea and the Un-man, should treat them differently, we should note potential difficulties with using literature to answer the question. For example, the state should not abstract from Dante and Lewis and tell its sentencers that especially evil and inhuman murderers merit the death penalty. To do so would authorize the same sort of ambiguous and standardless charge that does not guide discretion and that has frequently led to an overabundance of ethnic minorities on death row (those of different races are too easily perceived to be inhuman[42]). Aristotelian ethics would suggest that the safeguard and usefulness of the stories lies in their particularity.[43] The specific imagery of Dante and Lewis, the "night-nursery horror...of the managed corpse"[44]

---

40. Unlike Medea, who explains to Jason, "I love the pain, so thou shalt laugh no more." Euripides, supra note 1, at 75.

41. Hugh Aynesworth & Stephen G. Michaud, "A Killer's Words," *Vanity Fair*, May 1989, at 146, 147 (transcript of interview).

42. Martha C. Nussbaum, "Equity and Mercy," 22 *Philosophy and Public Affairs* 83, 113–14 (1993).

43. See Nussbaum, supra note 34, at 338 (arguing of Medea that "it is only in [this particular story] that the limits of Aristotelianism can be clearly seen").

44. Lewis, supra note 3, at 126.

in all its vividness, identifies a very special type of killer. The point cannot be made too emphatically that what is most true in literature is most potent in the particular expression of the work itself. Even talking about Dante and Lewis as we have is one step removed from the power of the original works.[45] Law and literature works best when we stay with particular literary works, talk about narrow legal questions, and avoid the real dangers of making literature merely part of the competitive rhetoric of law.

For this reason, literature and myth may be most appropriately integrated by an appellate judge reviewing a trial court's finding of heinousness. An appellate judge, removed from the impassioned argumentation of the courtroom, may be better able to apply dispassionately the lessons taught by literature. And through the institution of the written opinion, the logos of decision, conversation about confining the sentencer's discretion can be carried on by judges within the case law. This institutionalized narrative may incorporate the stories of Medea and the Un-man less dangerously than the relatively unconstrained speechmaking of lawyers before juries.

Of course, these stories may be integrated into the legal process before other audiences. The story of Medea and the Un-man might be told to a judge before she drafts her instructions to a jury, to a district attorney considering whether to seek the death penalty,[46] to a legislature considering an amendment to its capital sentencing scheme, to a class of law students struggling with their own ethical sensibilities, or to literature students threatened with marginalization by a culture that finds little pragmatic use for literary criticism. We should not presume that the only useful legal audience for art is the jury.

But what art? What stories? Another danger lies in the misconception that a particular canon of works would provide the "correct" solution to legal problems.[47] Dante, Lewis, and Euripides do not provide the last word in the heinousness debate. Other works are probably equally or more relevant. The assertion made in this Essay is that reading increases wisdom—not that the truth is confined to a particular list of books, poems, or plays. Dante, Lewis, and Euripides challenge us, increase our options, raise our consciousness, and trouble us. They make us wiser. But they are not the only authors capable of enriching our understanding.

---

45. See Richard Weisberg, *Poethics* 5 (New York: Columbia Univ. Press, 1992) ("We can rearticulate...words to state their meaning, but we know that not only their beauty is thereby impoverished; the *meaning itself* is lessened through each restatement." (emphasis in original)).

46. See Heinzelman, Chapter Three (describing a Texas district attorney's decision to reduce the charge of the killer of a child).

47. See Richard Delgado & Jean Stefancic, "Norms and Narratives: Can Judges Avoid Serious Moral Error?," 69 *Tex. L. Rev.* 1929, 1955–56 (1991) (suggesting that the legal-literary canon is composed of a body of works representing a narrow range of interests).

The life of the law, however, may not always need enrichment. Perhaps the integration of law and literature will only muddy the water and make decision making more complex. Dante, Lewis, and Euripides do not provide crystal-clear answers. Literature may have a disruptive and destabilizing influence. Bringing increased complexity to the law, however, is not necessarily problematic. Rendering the answer to a particular question less black and white is beneficial if we have been oversimplifying. For instance, before reading *Medea*, one could much more easily define multiple child murder as per se heinous. Destabilization of existing decision-making models may be a good thing. We proceed ethically even if the wisdom sought in literature makes decision making more, rather than less, agonizing. More information should be desirable; although any information, derived from literature or otherwise, potentially can be abused.

Finally, we need to be wary of the information we purport to glean from a work. *Medea* was written long ago in a very different cultural context. The danger of taking a work out of context is manifest. We must try to distinguish what Euripides is saying about Greek culture in particular from what he is saying about human nature in general. This is often a difficult, if not impossible, task. And yet, it is the routine work of the law. By keeping historical and cultural contexts in mind, competent judges and academics learn much from decades or even centuries-old precedent. *The Thorns Case*[48] still teaches students the fundamentals of tort law. The point here is not that all legal commentators perfectly distill the truth from culturally distant texts, but rather that our current system flourishes in spite of contextual limitations in the case law and faces no greater problem in considering literature. In other words, the argument against the legitimacy of using texts as distant as those of Euripides proves too much.

*   *   *

A question has been left hanging concerning the precise use the state should make of the stories told by Dante, Lewis, and Euripides. With the aforementioned caveats in mind, let us consider whether Medea should be treated differently than the Un-man in light of post-*Maynard* developments in the law. The response to *Maynard* by state courts has been mixed, evidencing two sorts of approaches. For example, the Arizona Supreme Court has defined "especially heinous, cruel or depraved" to identify a "perpetrator [who] inflicts mental anguish or physical abuse before a vic-

---

48. Y.B. 6 Edw. 4, fol. 7, pl. 18 (1466), reprinted in Richard A. Epstein, *Cases and Materials on Torts* 62 (Boston: Little, Brown, & Co., 5th ed. 1990). Students in Epstein's first-year torts class report that he has sometimes spent more than a week on this ancient two-page case.

tim's death" or who "relishes the murder, evidencing debasement or perversion" or "shows an indifference to the suffering of the victim and evidences a sense of pleasure" in the crime.[49] This narrowing language was approved by the U.S. Supreme court in *Walton v. Arizona*.[50] Although far from a model of clarity, this language suggests an emphasis on the mental state of the murderer that complements the foregoing discussion of Lewis. The Un-man characteristically relishes the murder or exhibits the type of "indifference toward the suffering of the victim"[51] that the *Walton* court focuses on.

Florida, on the other hand, focuses somewhat more on the category of crime, holding rather consistently, for example, that the sentencer can infer heinousness as a matter of law from the strangling of a conscious—but not semiconscious—victim.[52] The Court approved of this crime-specific approach in *Sochor v. Florida*.[53] A reconsideration of Dante, Lewis, and Euripides helps frame the question whether line drawing should be based on the type of crime or mental state of the defendant.

In his organization of Hell in *Inferno*, Dante tends to categorize sinners by type of sin. Panderers are together in one level; adulterers have their own place; gluttons, usurers, and others all suffer torment commensurate with their sort of sin. Medea, perhaps, is down with Friar Alberigo, frozen in the ice for killing her own kin.[54] We do not know whether Dante would have considered her an Un-person—he gives no indication whether all killers of guests and kin descend to Hell before their bodies perish. At first glance, his cosmology might support Florida's categorization of murderers by type of crime—for example, its treating of stranglers of conscious victims the same as far as the determination of heinousness is concerned.[55]

Lewis, on the other hand, seems initially to be more concerned with the mental states of individuals he depicts. He describes the original and greatest sin (and in a sense the only sin) as surely one of mental state—making

---

49. *State v. Walton*, 769 P.2d 1017, 1032–33 (Ariz. 1989), *aff'd* 497 U.S. 639 1990).

50. 497 U.S. 639, 654–55 (1990).

51. *Walton* 769 P.2d at 1033.

52. See *Sochor v. State*, 580 So. 2d 595, 603 (Fla. 1991), *rev'd on other grounds*, 504 U.S. 527 (1992); see also *Cannady v. State*, 620 So. 2d 175, 169 (Fla. 1993) (holding that a quick shot to the heart was not heinous because the victim had no forewarning).

53. 504 U.S. 527 (1992).

54. Dante does not explicitly place Medea in Hell in *Inferno*, although she is referenced in the Canto that consigns Jason to the level where seducers are punished. Dante, supra note 2, Canto 18, at 147.

55. We will see later, however, that this use of *Inferno* is unconvincing and provides an example of how literature can be misused—a misuse that, nonetheless, can be persuasively rebutted. See infra text accompanying notes 94–95.

oneself God. The serpent told Adam that eating from the tree of knowledge would make him like God. Being like God makes anything possible, and those who exercise the most God-like power may lose their humanity altogether. Although Lewis's imagery is primarily biblical, Ted Bundy echoed these themes in interviews when he described his mental state as he killed and mutilated young women.[56] Just as Lewis's Professor Weston eventually identified himself with the universal life force, Bundy sought to possess life itself through killing. A focus on how Bundy killed, often hitting the victim on the back of the head with a tire iron before she knew what was happening, as opposed to his mental state while he killed, fails to name fully the evil that ended in Florida's electric chair in 1989.

A reading of Dante and Lewis illustrates the significance of the choice between a bright-line rule treating identically all those who commit certain types of crimes—multiple victims, strangulation of the conscious, and others—and an ad hoc inquiry focused on the mental state of the murderer. In which direction should we channel sentencing discretion? Using Medea as an example, should the sentencer find the act of infanticide per se heinous (if we are going to have per se rules, certainly multiple child murder is likely to be one of them), or should the sentencer be directed to look first into her soul? Although literature has proven useful in framing this question (and that alone justifies its use), it may prove equally useful in suggesting an answer.

Let us pose the question in light of two real cases. The State of Florida executed two men in the spring of 1989 for killing young girls: Theodore Robert Bundy and Aubrey Dennis Adams. Working on their final habeas corpus appeals while clerking for a judge of the United States Court of Appeals for the Eleventh Circuit altered my own ethical sensibilities.[57] The state of Florida's heinousness findings in the two cases demonstrate the ethical problems presented by focusing primarily on circumstantial evidence.

The trial court made the following findings of fact relevant to heinousness in the prosecution of Ted Bundy for the murder of Kimberly Leach:

> [T]he victim was a twelve year old female junior high school student attending the Lake City Junior High School. The Defendant kidnapped her from the said Junior High School sometime between 9 and 10 a.m. on February 9, 1978, and her deteriorated body was found in a hog pen approximately 45 miles from the scene of abduction on April 7, 1978. The victim died of homicidal violence to the neck region of the body. At the time the body was found it was unclothed except for a pull-over shirt around the neck. There were semen stains in the crotch of her panties

---

56. See supra note 41 and accompanying text.

57. None of the discussion herein violates judicial confidentiality. My views are my own and not those of the judge for whom I worked. Moreover, the issues raised in the final appeals did not directly address the heinousness issue.

found near the body. Blood was found on the bluejeans also found near her body, and there were tears and rips in some of her clothes. The Court finds this kidnapping was indeed heinous, atrocious and cruel in that it was extremely wicked, shockingly evil, vile and with utter indifference to human life.[58]

In *Bundy v. State*,[59] the Florida Supreme Court *reversed* the trial judge's finding of heinousness.

Another trial court made the following findings of fact relevant to heinousness in the prosecution of Dennis Adams for the murder of Trisa Thornely:

[T]he capital felony was especially heinous, atrocious or cruel.... [T]he autopsy...showed a bruise on one arm, inflicted prior to death,...swelling in the hands induced by tight binding with tape prior to death...[T]he autopsy showed that the body was a nude body of an eight year old girl whose hands were tightly taped behind her back prior to death, which showed that Trisa Gail Thornely had time to anticipate her murder and that the autopsy and photographs showed seven coils of rope with circumference of nine and three fourths inches around the neck...and that the child's body was placed in a plastic garbage bag and thrown in a wooded area some three miles from her home.[60]

In *State v. Adams*,[61] the Supreme Court of Florida *affirmed* the trial court's finding of heinousness.

Apart from the additional physical evidence of sexual abuse present in the *Bundy* case, the similarity between the circumstances relied on by the judges in the two cases is striking. Wholly apart from the question of whether the ultimate sentences themselves were merited, one could strongly argue that given the state's focus on similar circumstances, the consideration of the heinousness factor in both cases should have been the same. If anything, stronger evidence of sexual abuse would seem to make Bundy's crime more heinous, although his victim was four years older. The result in these cases casts doubt on the strongest argument that can be made in favor of focusing on circumstances rather than mental state—that predictability is enhanced.

An ad hoc inquiry into mental state, rather than circumstance, is not necessarily more predictable, but predictability is only one goal of sentencing. Another critical goal is the labeling of the behavior meriting pun-

58. *State v. Bundy*, No. 70-149-CF, slip op. at 3–4 (Fla. Cir. Ct. 1980), quoted in *Bundy v. State*, 471 So. 2d 9, 21 (Fla. 1985), *cert. denied*, 479 U.S. 894 (1986).

59. 471 So. 2d 9 (Fla. 1985), *cert. denied*, 479 U.S. 894 (1986).

60. *State v. Adams*, No. 78-474-CF, slip op. at 4 (Fla. Cir. Ct. 1979), quoted in *State v. Adams*, 412 So. 2d 850, 856 (Fla.), *cert. denied*, 459 U.S. 882 (1982).

61. 412 So. 2d 850 (Fla.), *cert. denied*, 459 U.S. 882 (1982).

ishment by the state. An execution is a communicative act whereby the state names, correctly or incorrectly, what is most evil in people. A reading of Lewis would suggest that what makes a crime especially heinous is the mental state of the murderer, not the circumstances surrounding the act of killing.[62]

For example, Ted Bundy killed purposefully—to possess as fully as possible the body and life force of his victim. He is the classic Un-man: devoid of empathy, completely self-centered, and above all social norms. His enjoyment of killing for its own sake is what renders his crime heinous. On the other hand, Dennis Adams was a hardworking prison guard with no criminal record or history of violence.[63] He was spurred to a homicidal catatonia by his wife's chronic infidelity—she spent the night before the murder sleeping with one of Adams's coworkers across the street from their house.[64] He confessed to the crime.[65] Although his behavior was inexcusable and his execution may be defensible, he was a much different type of killer than Bundy. He looks more like a version of Medea than the prototypical Un-man. Whether or not the State of Florida should treat Medea and the Un-man differently, its current focus on circumstance rather than mental state appears to lead to arbitrary results.

The state, however, relying on *Inferno*, could argue that a rigid focus on circumstance might reduce arbitrariness, asserting that our notions of punishment are equally well informed by the type of crime. For example, each circle in Dante's Hell is reserved for specific types of crimes. Wouldn't clear rules for heinousness based on the circumstances of the murder be consistent with Dante's cosmology? Florida's equating of choking a conscious victim to death with special heinousness seems to take such an approach. A set of bright-line rules might be desirable. Maybe the correct response to the comparison of Bundy and Adams should be to intensify the focus on circumstance: murdering children is per se heinous, or concealing remains is per se heinous. This suggestion, if consistently applied (a big if), might lead to greater predictability, but it does injustice to Dante. Not all murderers go to Hell. Dante's purgatory contains murderers who confessed their sin and asked for forgiveness.[66] Mental state is hardly irrelevant to

---

62. The facts surrounding the crime will, of course, often provide strong clues as to mental state—the fact a victim was tortured reveals a lot about the mental state of the defendant.

63. *Adams*, 412 So. 2d at 854.

64. *Id.* at 857.

65. See *id.* at 851 (stating that the defendant's involvement in the crime was shown through circumstantial evidence and the defendant's oral and written statement to police officers).

66. Dante Alighieri, *Purgatorio* (Laurence Binyon trans., Macmillan & Cough., 1938).

Dante. Mental state sends one to Hell—circumstance merely helps determine the type of punishment. In fact, severity of punishment is closely related to mental state. Francesca and Paolo, suicidal lovers who fell victim to their own erotic passions, are less far down in Hell than those who killed in betrayal.[67]

Inferno then cannot convincingly be read as supporting the notion that special heinousness as an aggravating factor should be determined merely from looking at the circumstances surrounding the crime.[68] In the final analysis, Dante and Lewis both make mental state critical. If mental state is the key, then a focus on circumstance does a poor job of separating the Un-man from Medea.

Of course, the question remains whether Medea should be treated identically to the Un-man. I believe the answer should be no. When the fax machine chattered the death of Ted Bundy, I felt ambivalent. The execution of Dennis Adams continues to trouble me. The trial court found three aggravating factors in his case and three mitigating factors.[69] Had the Florida Supreme Court invalidated the finding of heinousness in his case, as it did in Bundy's, the balance would have tipped in his favor. The vast majority of people cannot imagine committing a crime such as Adams's, yet most have felt the rage and disorientation of rejection by a loved one.

In a powerful essay, Nussbaum explores the lessons of Seneca's *Medea* and concludes:

> The message to the Aristotelian is, then, that there is no combining deep personal love with moral purity. If you set yourself up to be a person who cherishes all the virtues, whose every act is done justly and appropriately, towards the right person in the right way at the right time, you had better omit erotic love, as the Stoics do. If you admit it, you will almost surely be led outside the boundaries of the virtues; for this one constituent part likes to threaten and question all the others. And then the very perfectionism of the Aristotelian, who so wants all of life to fit harmoniously together, will produce rage upon rage—angry violence towards one's own violence, a sword aimed at one's own aggression.[70]

---

67. Francesca and Paolo were found in the second circle of Hell, see Dante, supra note 2, Canto 5, at 37, whereas those who killed in betrayal were found in the ninth circle of Hell, see *id*. canto 32 at 271–77. For a discussion by Nussbaum of the differences between Medea's erotic nature and Francesca's "erotic flame that is 'quickly kindled in the gentle heart,'" see Nussbaum, supra note 34, at 335–36.

68. The attempt, however, is useful to illustrate a misuse of literature and also to demonstrate the possibility of convincingly diffusing the attempt.

69. *Adams*, 412 So. 2d at 854.

70. Nussbaum, supra note 34, at 336.

If Medea's violence is a natural, although unacceptable, outgrowth of erotic love, then it is hard to label the violence heinous. Acknowledging the destructive capacity of love should not lead us to condemn it because "if we leave love out, as the play also teaches us, we leave out a force of unsurpassed wonder and power."[71] As a community, we will sometimes pay the price for choosing to accept the gift of *eros*. Because we choose love, we find Medea's crimes tragic, but not heinous. The Un-man, on the other hand, is not the outgrowth of any part of our nature we choose as a community to embrace. His nihilistic spirit may lurk within us, but we have no excuse to feed and nurture it.

Only a focus on mental state and the interior life of the particular defendant can fully reveal the distinctions that lie at the heart of *Maynard v. Cartwright*. Although the inquiry at issue is conducted within the brutal confines of capital sentencing procedure, the purpose of the inquiry is inherently merciful. In examining the contrast between *epiekeia* (roughly translated as "mercy") and *dikê* (roughly translated as "retribution"), Nussbaum concludes that notions of retribution are most appropriately focused on a category of crime unconcerned with the individual criminal,[72] while equity and mercy are exercised when the "notions of intuition, choice, reflection, deliberation, and character that are part of a nonreductive intentionalist psychology" are applied to the particular individual at issue.[73]

Her understanding of mercy leads Nussbaum's "ideal judge [to be] unashamedly mentalistic" and to treat "the inner works of the defendant as a deep and complex place."[74] This inner world is considered "[l]ike a novel"[75] and is based on a highly particularized perception of the character's (defendant's) situation.[76] Most importantly, she concludes that "the motives for mercy are engendered in the structure of literary perception itself."[77] In other words, mercy will naturally be exercised when we seek to understand the individual's mental state. She properly rejects Holmes's "conflat[ion of] the retributive idea with the idea of looking to the wrongdoer's state of mind, implying that an interest in the insides invariably brings retributivism with it."[78] Perhaps equity and mercy are the strongest reasons to reject Florida's crime-specific approach to heinousness.

---

71. *Id.*

72. See Nussbaum, supra note 42, at 111–13 (agreeing that retributive notions should be based on external standards).

73. *Id.* at 111.

74. *Id.*

75. *Id.* at 110.

76. *Id.*

77. *Id.* at 109.

78. *Id.* at 112.

To conclude, I think that the strongest thesis—strongest in the sense of most specific—that can be supported by a reading of Euripides, Dante, and Lewis is that Medea's crimes are not heinous for the purposes of *Maynard*, but that the Un-man's are. An intermediate thesis suggests more generally that a focus on mental state rather than circumstance would reduce arbitrariness in determining heinousness and improve and refine the labeling function of punishment.[79] A yet broader suggestion might be made that Euripides, Dante, and Lewis improve the quality of the heinousness debate, raising the ethical level of the discussion irrespective of what standard the state eventually decides to implement. On the most general level, the consideration of particular works of literature can be seen to help identify the ethical parameters of specific legal issues.

---

79. In holding that the term "pitiless" was not unconstitutionally ambiguous, the Supreme Court remarked that

> some within the broad class of first-degree murders *do* exhibit feeling. Some, for example, kill with anger, jealously, revenge or a variety of other emotions...Idaho has identified the subclass of defendants who kill without feeling or sympathy as more deserving of death. By doing so, it has narrowed in a meaningful way the category of defendants upon whom capital punishment may be imposed.

Creech v. Arave, 507 U.S. 463, 475–76 (1993) (emphasis in original).

Chapter Three

"Going Somewhere": Maternal Infanticide and the Ethics of Judgment

Susan Sage Heinzelman

This essay explores several interconnected issues: the representation of crisis, and, in the case of infanticide, representation *in* crisis; and the ethics and aesthetics of judgment. I do not intend to discuss the substantive legal nature of maternal infanticide, except as it concerns my interest in the symbolic systems by which we represent this event and thereby accommodate it within our culture. My interest in infanticide as a problem of ethical and aesthetic representation should not be interpreted as indifference to the act of child murder. I believe it is necessary, however, to recognize that the politically charged nature of representations of violent women, whether those representations are sympathetic or hostile, makes the question of how we come to judgment, upon what narrative of guilt and innocence we choose to rely, especially important.

For feminists, infanticide, like abortion and fetal abuse, raises a set of questions about women's social and reproductive responsibilities that are especially difficult to adjudicate. As Marie Ashe and Naomi Cahn succinctly argue: "A war of interpretation...surrounds the bad mother figure and centers on the issue of agency. This struggle involves competing understandings of such women, one which defines them as fully responsible moral agents and another which defines them as victims of individual men and of patriarchal society."[1] These "hard cases," where women act violently against the vulnerable, are the ones that test the resilience and integrity of feminism in its claim to be ethical politics.

Maternal infanticide has always been represented as an unnatural crime that is beyond comprehension; like witchcraft, with which it is often connected, it is the *crimen exemplum*, the sure sign of Satan in the world, the

---

1. Marie Ashe & Naomi Cahn, "Child Abuse: A Problem in Feminist Theory," 2 *Texas J. of Women & the Law* 75, 84 (1993).

work of hidden and unknowable forces.[2] The murder of a child by its father, however reprehensible, is nevertheless represented as within the "imaginable," sometimes as even within the "rights" of the father, a right connected to the responsibilities of paternity and the expectations of violence associated with the patriarchy. By its very nature a quintessentially domestic crime and an attack upon the reproduction of the patriarchy, maternal infanticide is frequently employed to summon up images of a radical social malaise — and not just in the ancient Greek or Judeo-Christian tradition — witness Newt Gingrich's claim that Susan Smith's drowning of her two children was evidence of the moral corruption of the nation under the Democrats.

Smith was indicted just a few days before the November 1994, Congressional elections. Newt Gingrich's comments that her behavior was emblematic of what was happening to America under the moral leadership of Clinton and the Democrats made her the "Willie Horton" of those elections — ironically so, given the way she had herself played the "race card," stereotyping male African-Americans as likely to commit this most heinous of crimes (and thus as more "naturally" unnatural than women). Outraged by Smith's savagery, Gingrich called for a purging of the Susan Smiths, the murdering mothers, and the Democrats, from the body politic: "I think that the mother killing the two children in South Carolina vividly reminds every American how sick the society is getting and how much we need to change things," he said. "The only way you get change is to vote Republican."[3]

In a slick rhetorical move, Gingrich calls up the ancient horror of infanticide to fuel his emotional appeal and simultaneously denies the historicity of that appeal by insisting that such horrors have happened only under the rule of the Democrats. Thus, the former history professor situates Susan Smith's murder of her two children within a violently antagonistic political discourse that casts the Democrats as players in a national tragedy much like those ancient figures from the house of Atreus, who served up infants to their fathers, or that consummate bad mother, Medea. In Gingrich's staging of this national morality play, infanticide comes to represent

---

2. The complexity of the word, the image, the symbol of the "witch" and its function in myth, history and reality are traced in Sylvia Bovenschen, "The Contemporary Witch, the Historical Witch, and the Witch Myth: The Witch, Subject of the Appropriation of Nature and Object of the Domination of Nature," 15 *New German Critique* 83–119 (1978).

3. Quoted in Frank Rich, "The Mother Next Door," *The New York Times* (Section 4, November 13, 1994): 15. Ron Rosenbaum put it this way: "It wasn't Susan Smith who pushed the Mazda into the lake; it was George McGovern." See "Staring into the Heart of Darkness," *The New York Times Magazine* (June 4, 1995): 36–72.

all that has gone wrong with society.[4] Smith's crime is exemplary of all crimes against the state and its individual citizens. And only, it seems, can the catharsis of voting expunge this sickness from the state.

In his comments, Gingrich relies on an assumption entirely consistent with our culture's sense of social responsibility and political action: that the moral and the political are linked in a powerful, mutual relationship. In fact, the relationship between the moral and the political, or between individual conscience and communal action, is analogous in Western culture to the relationship between the audience of a Greek tragedy and its actors, who together figuratively embody the sickness of the state that needs purgation. The audience, both as individuals and as a community, must feel in their bodies the dis-ease that weakens the state, cathartically purify (and thus cure) themselves through pity and fear, and thereby restore the state to health. *This relationship between representation and response enables both compassion and judgment.* Despite his instinctive reliance on this dialectical assumption, however, Gingrich's comments are couched in a rhetoric so antagonistic that the *polis* (audience) is divided against itself, forced to dis-member the communal body, and thus render judgments that are both partial and reductive.

To play out the possibilities both of his explicit and his implied model of social and moral relationships, I want to look at the narrative representation of infanticide in light of the two possibilities for judgment invoked by Gingrich's comments — what I will call the antagonistic and the dialectical. By dialectical, I mean a mutually affective relationship between the individual and the community(ies), between the self and the other(s). In this model of engagement, narrative can transform by negotiating social, moral and jurisprudential compromises in seemingly unresolvable conflicts. In arguing for this narrative efficacy, I am placing narration, here understood as a managed account of individual actions in their cultural contexts that allows apparently irreconcilable discursive structures a space for compromise, against prosecution, here understood as an adversarial strategy by which guilty parties are punished and innocent parties exonerated.

My essay has four parts : the first is a discussion of infanticide in the context of Kenneth Burke's theory of catharsis. Burke is a critic who has explicitly connected the political and the aesthetic in his theorizing about Aristotelian catharsis, shifting attention away from the merely psychoan-

---

4. One of the ultimate ironies of Gingrich's appeal was revealed in the trial when Susan's step-father, a prominent Republican politician and member of the Christian Coalition, confessed to molesting her as a child and to maintaining an adulterous relationship with her as an adult.

alytical value of the cathartic experience. Burke points out that, aside from a single reference to catharsis in Aristotle's definition of tragedy, the *Poetics* contains no account of the concept. In his *Politics*, however, Aristotle discusses musical catharsis and intimates that the subject will be treated at greater length in the *Poetics*. Burke argues that:

> [t]hose paragraphs in the *Politics* at least give reason to infer that the treatment in the *Poetics* was not essentially different, and that the kind of 'purge' produced by tragedy may have been specifically considered from the 'civic' point of view (as a species of political purge), in contrast with the stress on intimate, family relationships in Freud's views on the cathartic effects of psychoanalysis.[5]

Burke therefore invites us to attend to the social nature of representation and the cathartic experience, suggesting that representation carries with it the weight of ethical, as well as aesthetic, constraints and promises.

The second part of the essay will re-tell the contemporary story of a Texas mother charged with the murder of her newborn infant, focusing specifically on how an adversarial system produces two competing, antagonistic versions of a univocal narrative of motherhood. The third part of the paper will offer an alternative to this confrontation by examining the concept of what I call narrative jurisprudence as a model for ethical judgment. I will also turn to another mode of judging—the literary critical model employed in the interpretation of poetry. My turn to aesthetics is not intended to lessen the crisis of infanticide, but rather to invoke a feminist ethic of representation and judgment in the context of literature. The fourth part will narrate another Texas version of infanticide—that of a mother in Houston who drowned two of her children. This story illustrates narrative jurisprudence: a model of listening and judging that accommodates the complexity of an other's experience and draws from the audience an ethical response that is fittingly complex.

I. Burke and Catharsis

Gingrich's rhetoric was hyperbolic, but he accurately pinpointed the tendency of the American media to represent wrongdoers through essentialized narratives of motive and action, narratives that require a public, and highly publicized, resolution in the image of the offender brought to judgment. This performative quality of legal representation (seen *in extremis* in the Simpson trial) is one of the many ways in which law and literature share a common culture; indeed, both legal and literary performances are

---

5. Kenneth Burke, "On Catharsis, or Resolution," 3 *Kenyon Review* 337, 337 (1959).

representative practices of social institutions. Within those performances, "[n]arratives are not just stories told *within* social contexts; rather *narratives are social practices*, part of the constitution of their own context."[6] My choice of Aristotle's critical term "catharsis" as read through Burke is intended to stress both this social aspect of narrative and the commonality between legal and literary narratives.

Catharsis, or purgation, is the term Aristotle uses to define the experience of those who witness the dramatic representation of a tragic event. Cleansing itself of—and through—pity and fear, the citizenry restores the state to health. In this Greek model of (limited) participatory democracy, catharsis, the key to civic health, is enabled both by compassion and by judgment, leading to reconciliation between the offended and the offender. This reconciliation is crucial; it affords society the chance to re-affirm its communal values at the same time as it integrates the offender back into its midst.

According to the philosopher Kenneth Burke, the term "catharsis" enforces a connection between the aesthetic and the political, in both their individual and communal forms.[7] The audience who witnesses a tragedy enacted on the stage recognizes the individual and social nature of the dramatic representation, and, in witnessing, the audience realizes both its individual agency and its social responsibility. Thus catharsis refers both to the specific emotional and political response of the individual spectator, who acknowledges her own complicity in the tragedy by suffering with the transgressor in the drama, and to the larger relationship between the spectator and her community, a relationship that enables the transgressor to be reintegrated into that community. Of course, the difficulty of reintegration is enormously complicated when the community is heterogeneous, distinguished by marks of race, gender, ethnicity, religion, class, and culture. The Simpson case, once again, illustrates the difficulty of coming to a consensual judgment when the community is radically divided within itself.

I want to theorize an ethics of feminist judgment by applying this concept of dramatic catharsis to the performance of legal drama in order to analyze the relationship between the offender and those who judge her. I

---

6. Patricia Ewick & Susan Silbey, "Subversive Stories and Hegemonic Tales," 29 *Law and Soc'y Rev.* 197, 211 (1995).

7. I am indebted to Brian Bremen's discussion of Burke's rhetoric of disease and cure in his *William Carlos Williams and the Diagnostics of Culture* (New York: Oxford Univ. Press, 1993). My account of Burke's definition of catharsis is drawn from Kenneth Burke, *A Grammar of Motives* (Berkeley: Univ. of Calif. Press, 1969); "Catharsis—Second View," 5 *Centennial Review of Arts and Sciences* 107–32 (1971); and "On Catharsis, or Resolution," 3 *Kenyon Review* 337–69 (1959).

am offering this model of catharsis as an alternative to the adversarial model of legal discourse, employing the term "catharsis" in its Burkean sense to mediate between the demands of the adversarial system, on the one hand, and claims of compassion, on the other. Catharsis is clarification, another term for truth-telling. If we apply this cathartic model to legal drama, we see that the jury (and by extension the public) are invited to witness the political and social consequences of justice enacted, as well as to reflect upon the personal consequences of crime and punishment. These witnesses to the trial respond both as individuals and as members of a shared community to the ritualized representation of the law's drama, a ritual enacted in the form of the narratives of prosecution and defense. The individual offender is represented in those narratives both as an autonomous agent, with full responsibility for her actions, and as a member of a society that has directly and indirectly coerced her to behave in certain ways. The recognition of the tension between autonomy and coercion constitutes one of the hallmarks of justice.

The witnesses to the trial attend to the particular conditions represented to them as not merely a contemporaneous, unique enactment of a crime, but also the inevitable recalling and historicizing of all such moments of disruption, an act of history that can reach back symbolically to previously performed narratives. Thus, just as catharsis in its theatrical embodiment is not simply an individual's singular, emotional release provoked by the dramatic rendition of tragic events, so too, in a legal drama, catharsis is more than simply the satisfaction of an emotional need for revenge. It is the ethical and social response of a member of a community who has been provoked by the public re-enactment of an offense committed by a member of that same community; the response works to recall the common stories shared by the community and thereby to re-integrate the offender into that community.[8]

To summarize, in my reading, catharsis is a multiple response generated by a realization of: 1) how the present is related to the past—this event is not one isolated aberration from the normal continuum of events, but a

---

8. For an extended meditation on the way in which the narrative of crime and punishment can reintegrate the offender into the community, see Sacvan Bercovitch, *The Office of The Scarlet Letter* (Baltimore: Johns Hopkins Press, 1991), especially where he speaks of Hester's return to the community that has exiled her. He argues that the "bond [Hester] forges anew with the community reconstitutes Hester herself, as a marginal dissenter, into an exemplum of historical continuity." *Id.* at 3. This reference to Hester Prynne and her homogenous community only reinforces, however, the problems faced when the offender is perceived as outside, rather than merely marginal to, the community that is rendering judgment. I am grateful to Nan Goodman for bringing Bercovitch's argument to my attention.

rehearsal of previous, similar crises, and 2) how the individual citizen (witness and offender) is related to her larger community. The insistence upon relatedness lessens the possibility that the individual narrative will be seen as isolated from its social context. As Ewick and Silbey point out in their essay on subversive and hegemonic narratives in legal representation, the "law's insistent demand for personal narratives achieves a kind of radical individuation that disempowers the teller by effacing the connections among persons and the social organization of their experiences."[9]

When I employ the term "catharsis" as a way of describing an ethical reading of someone's story, I am insisting, as Ewick and Silbey do in their account of subversive stories, on the "emplot[ment]" of "connections... between biography and history."[10] In this complex recognition of the network of symbolic identities in which we participate, simplistic categories are rendered useless as a basis for judgment, especially so in crimes that seem unrepresentable, unspeakable, like infanticide. In my interpretation of Burke's description of catharsis, then, only an understanding of the full political, ethical and aesthetic context of a social crisis has value as a basis for judgment.

How can this principle of catharsis be employed in legal decision making, especially concerning the proper punishment for infanticide? It is not possible to stand apart, to separate oneself from the suffering or the cruelty of others once one recognizes that one's sense of self is produced by complex social narratives. And, I would suggest, one specifically acknowledges that complex production of the self by identifying simultaneously with those who offend the state and with those who are the victims of that offense. The histories of self and society, and the identification of disruptions in those histories, are essentially narrative acts. Indeed, the bridge between the offended and the offender occurs most particularly and most acutely in the act of narration: "Storytelling... is never innocent. If you listen with attention to a story well told, you are implicated by and in it."[11] There is, to quote Kenneth Burke, a feeling of "going somewhere" in narrative, a movement away from the paralysis of accusation and "othering." He argues, "There should be a 'curative' value in the sheer *irreversibility* of narrative," because once you have heard another's story, you cannot return to the judgments produced by ignorance of that narrative.[12]

---

9. See supra note 6, at 217.

10. *Id.* at 218.

11. Peter Brooks, "The Law as Narrative and Rhetoric," in *Law's Stories: Narrative and Rhetoric in the Law* 16, Peter Brooks and Paul Gewirtz, eds. (New Haven: Yale Univ. Press, 1996).

12. See Burke, supra note 4, at 366.

"Going somewhere" metaphorically describes the active aesthetic and emotional perception of narrative and the product of that perception, which is ethical reasoning. Identification through narrative with the offender and the victim is at the heart of the cathartic experience, and it produces both vicarious malevolence and vicarious suffering, neither one of which should be discounted in coming to judgment. Ethical judgment is sharply distinguished from the moral indignation of those who do not wish to be moved and who thus only scapegoat the offender. The figure of the "scapegoat is a concentration of power,"[13] the locus of a culture's anxiety or confident truths. "Criminals either actual or imaginary may...serve as scapegoats in a society that 'purifies itself' by 'moral indignation' in condemning them, though the ritualistic elements operating here are not usually recognized by the indignant." [14] Scapegoating sidesteps history: it transforms the individual and local into the universal and the abstract by ignoring history.[15] The universal narrative then covers up the particularity of the crisis, flattening its complexity into monothematic representation. In legal drama, the frequent avoidance of "history" — apart from the specific "legal" history of the particular case — stems from the law's pretense to objectivity.

Relying on an essentialist narrative as a way of managing crisis can cover up the individual's responsibility to address the particular cultural crisis.[16] I employ the term "cover" here in its legal sense, as in "femme coverte"

---

13. Kenneth Burke, *A Grammar of Motives* 407 (Berkeley: Univ. of Calif. Press, 1969).

14. *Id.* at 406. A Freudian reading of this social pathology is suggested in Joseph H. Smith, "Ambivalence, Instincts, and Mourning," 1 *Common Knowledge* 97 (1992). I am grateful to Marianna Adler for bringing this analogy to my attention:

> The meanness of prejudice shows itself when the love of one's own kind has as corollary the fear and hatred of others. It is a prolongation of primitive splitting in which the mother is not yet one person but two—the good mother and the bad mother...The persistence of such grossly infantile "good us/bad them" splitting is based on the fantasy that one's self and one's kind has overcome splitting. It is a fantasy of having achieved impossible unity, of being in charge, centered, whole, and transparent to one's self...The inner dangers that one has turned away from...are projected onto "them." The fantasy, then, is that the destruction of "them" would allow for the millennium.

Id. at 101–02.

15. *Id.* at 407.

16. Compare Burke's use of the term "covered":

> ...insofar as the idea of catharsis is objectified in terms of offscourings (*katharmata*), there is a sense in which the cleaning has led to the un-clean. Or, otherwise put: the unclean is either displaced, or 'covered.' And this principle of removal introduces in effect the principle of substitution, or vicarage, since the cleansing of

(the husband "covers" the legal acts and responsibilities of his wife, who assumes thereby a covert identity). I am suggesting that when one relies on essentialist narratives as a way of explaining crises and rendering judgment, one acts "under cover of" an ahistorical and generic identity, denying one's own complicity and inferring a similar ahistoricism and generality for the offender. I am arguing for a different gesture: we should assume, and assume responsibility for, a specific social and individual identity, both for ourselves and for the offender.

This responsibility is acutely demanded when we are confronted with crimes like infanticide. In those cases, infanticide is frequently represented as the prototype of uncivilized behavior, consistent with an ancient narrative about women, their irrationality, and violence. The mother is demonized not only for the horror provoked by her individual actions, but as the representative of the principle of evil, the personification of all that must be cut out from the body politic. In this reductive narrative, the one summoned up by Gingrich, the murdering mother embodies all that threatens civilization and apparently nothing short of a re-birth into a new polity, with new parentage, can relieve that threat.[17] But this moral and political call to action only offers the appearance of resolution. Catharsis does not operate through a metonymic calculus: one does not simply work through the individual and social tragedy by substituting another troupe (trope) of actors/agents to replace those who are not "doing it right." In judging the mother who has acted against her child, we must do more than put in opposition two essentialist narratives of motherhood, the good mother against the bad. Such adversarial discourse excludes alternative stories of a less than perfect world in which one's class, race, religious beliefs, or health (to name but a few contingencies) can make mothering unbearable.[18]

What if there were some way to narrate a story or stories in a legal context that had the power to bring us face-to-face with what Martha Nussbaum calls "complex particularity." Perceiving an event as a story can reveal moral complications that a merely accusatory statement hides. One necessarily engages in an ethical reading of the other's narrative when one confronts the complications of the other's life.[19] Indeed, following Levinas,

---

one place incidentally involves the polluting of another. See "Catharsis—Second View," supra note 7, at 125.

17. Kenneth Burke points out that the act of scapegoating—that is, "the alienating of iniquities from the self to the scapegoat—amounts to a rebirth of the self." See *Grammar*, supra note 7 at 407.

18. Compare Marie Ashe, "The "Bad Mother' in Law and Literature: A Problem of Representation," 4 *Yale Journal of Law and Feminism* 1017–37 (1991).

19. This act of confrontation, the standing face to face with another, explains how a jury in the court with Susan Smith, a witness to her responses and to her story, can so

Adam Newton argues that even before the act of narrating those complications, in merely recognizing that such complexity exists, one acknowledges the ethical imperative. Ethics "refers to the radicality and uniqueness of the moral situation itself, a binding claim exercised upon the self by a concrete and singular other whose moral appeal precedes both decision and understanding."[20]

Attending to or narrating someone else's story functions as a kind of mediation between the other and the self, situating the listener or narrator within her own historical and political realities. This historical situating is distinguished from ahistorical assumptions about the other that come from the oft-repeated narrative, or stereotyping, whose legitimacy resides in repeatability, not in relationship to specific historical circumstances. Ethical narration emphasizes contingency and particularity, calling up the past as a way of reinvesting the present with meaning, rather than invoking the past to "cover" the crises of the present.[21] In such a narrative model, the woman who commits infanticide is not pre-judged to have committed a crime so awful as to be unrepresentable except by essentialist narratives of maternity. Rather, the complex particularities of the offender's life are judged to be of importance. The narrative of her crime actively places these historical contingencies before the audience: "Stories that are capable of countering the hegemonic are those which bridge, without denying, the particularities of experience and subjectivities and those which bear witness to what is unimagined and unexpressed... Subversive stories are narratives that employ the connection between the particular and the gener-

---

quickly arrive at a decision so decidedly different from that shared by the general public. "The outcome of [the Smith trial] flatly contradicts current public opinion....Now more than ever, Americans support the death penalty by striking majorities. And a nation... voted 62 percent to 28 percent in a NEWSWEEK survey that she should have been put to death...Citizens support the death penalty in general, but frequently refuse to apply it when, as in the Smith case, they are confronted with a face, a name, and human frailties that, however lurid, bear at least some resemblance to their own." Tom Morganthau, "Condemned to Life," *Newsweek*, August 7, 1995: 19.

20. Adam Newton, *Narrative Ethics* 12 (Cambridge, Mass.: Harvard Univ. Press, 1995).

21. To argue that contingency and particularity are part of an ethical narrative is not to deny that some appeal to collective beliefs and values might also be made. The fact that those values are collective (and may even appear to be "universal") does not, however, make them ahistorical. "Whatever truth we may have is to be gotten not in spite of but through our historical inherence." Maurice Merleau-Ponty, *Signs* 109 (Richard C. McCleary trans., 1964). For a general discussion of the tension between contingency and abstract values, see the essays by Martha Nussbaum, Pierre Schlag, and Steven L. Winter in *Yale Journal of Law & the Humanities* (vol. 6) (1994).

al by *locating the individual within social organization.*"[22] In other words, the offender has not severed her relationship to her community by her offense; she has re-defined it, and the ethical response facilitated by narrative is to conceptualize the nature of that re-definition.[23]

II. The Case of Susan Bienek, Smithville, Texas

In the case of Susan Bienek, convicted of murder in the death of her newborn son, both the prosecution and the defense crafted their strategies around maternal narratives, arguing respectively that she was a "bad" mother, in fact the worst kind of mother, or that she was a "good" mother, such a good mother that she erred only in protecting her family from the burden of the newborn's death. The structure of the trial was adversarial; the rhetoric of the trial was oppositional; and the symbolic narrative of the trial was maternal. Given that the jury could only chose between two essentialist narratives and that no alternative was offered that made sense of what she did, it is hardly surprising that it convicted her.

Susan Bienek was 34 years old when charged on January 6, 1993, with the murder of her infant son, Daniel, around midnight on December 30, 1992. She was accused of abandoning him in a garbage bag early in the morning of December 31. The body was found in a county dump six days later and traced to Susan Bienek through the mail and assorted household items in the garbage bag. Susan came to trial with a court-appointed lawyer on October 4, 1993, in the 21st Judicial District Court of Bastrop County, Judge Harold R. Towslee presiding. On October 9, after 6 hours deliberation, the jury of seven men and five woman returned a verdict of guilty of murder, rejecting lesser verdicts of involuntary manslaughter or crimi-

---

22. Ewick & Silbey, supra note 6, at 220.

23. Part of that re-conceptualization of the relationship between the offender and her community is undertaken by those who critique the traditional representation of the liberal subject—the autonomous, rights-bearing, self-identified subject. In place of the liberal subject, we are asked to imagine a multiple subjectivity, generated and constrained by ethnicity, race, class, and gender. This multi-faceted subject can tell stories of power and subordination, of success and failure, of action and victimage because the real world in which this subject is constituted is fluid and equivocal. See Linda Alcoff, "Cultural Feminism versus Post-Structuralism: The Identity Crisis in Feminist Theory," 13 *Signs* 405, 433 (1988) (arguing for identity relative to "a constantly shifting context, to a situation that includes a network of elements involving others, the objective economic conditions, cultural and political institutions and ideologies and so on"). Compare Martha Minow, "Identities," 3 *Yale Journal of Law & the Humanities* 97, 98 (1991) ("...the cultural, gender, racial, and ethnic identities of a person are not simply intrinsic to that person, but depend upon that person's self-understanding in conjunction with communal understandings").

nally negligent homicide. On October 12, after 8 1/2 more hours of deliberation, they recommended nine years imprisonment, rejecting a plea from her family for a probated sentence. Judge Towslee commented that her sentence was "not as bad as it sounds. She was quite fortunate under the circumstances."

Susan Bienek had been married for seventeen years and was the mother of four children, ranging in age from fourteen to five. She had left school after 12th grade and had worked since 1987 for the IRS in Austin, a distance of 45 miles from Smithville, where she lived in a four-room, 500-square-foot house. Susan frequently worked a 60-hour week and was the sole support of the family. She took home approximately $1600 a month after taxes. Her husband, Kelly, had not worked for some years due to back problems. She got up at four each morning, left home just before five and arrived at work at six. After the long drive home from work, she was still primarily responsible for the care of her family. She is an ideological conservative and has always attended the local Lutheran church in Smithville. She had never been involved with the police in any way before Daniel's death.

Susan Bienek described what happened on December 30 in a deposition she gave a week later:

> I started feeling cramps on the 30th of December about 11:30 to 12:30. I was in bed. My husband was in the living room. I think he was lying on the couch. I went into the bathroom. I was bleeding pretty heavy. I was standing in the bathroom and the baby came out. Once the baby came out, I broke the cord. I pulled it apart with my hands. The reason I did that was to make it breathe. I didn't use scissors or a knife. The baby wasn't breathing, it just laid there. I held the baby for awhile, then I went in the kitchen and got a sheet that was on a chair. I didn't call 911 because I didn't think of it. I wrapped the baby in the sheet...Once I wrapped the baby in the sheet, I went outside through the back door. I sat on the back steps, I still had the baby in my arms. After awhile I got up and put the baby in the bassinette...I went back in the house to the bathroom. I was bleeding all this time...I started to feel dizzy so I went to bed and laid down. I had thrown the sanitary napkins in the trash can that's in the bathroom. I started feeling dizzy because I lost so much blood. I woke up a little later, it was still dark outside. I was still cramping...I laid in bed for awhile... It was getting on towards morning. I got up and dressed. I went outside through the back door. I brought the plastic trash bag and the bag containing the sanitary napkins out to the shed. I held the baby for a little bit. I put the baby in the trash bag...I carried the bag outside and put it in the passenger side seat of the truck. I went back inside the house. Rachel [my daughter] was up. I got my purse and keys and told her I'd be back in a little bit. I drove off and rode around. I thought about my family and the baby all this time...I stopped at a roadside park on Highway 21. I

put the bag with the baby and the sanitary napkins in a cardboard box that was by the trash can. This was Thursday morning…I went back home… everybody was up. I laid on the couch for awhile and fell asleep. I did what I did because the baby was dead and I can't afford funeral expenses. I didn't take it to a doctor because it was dead and they'd say I did it. The baby was dead. He wouldn't move, he wouldn't breathe. He just laid there. [Very blue, he was very blue. I picked his arm up. It fell down. I tried to make him cry. He looked like a rag doll I hit his bottom to try and make him cry, but he did not cry. He didn't breathe. I thought he was dead.]

The prosecution characterized Susan Bienek's behavior as covert because she had told no one she was pregnant and had, in fact, specifically denied it when asked by one of her co-workers. In fact, she had not told her husband because she was not sure until she was six months gone and soon thereafter the baby had stopped moving, leading her to believe that she was mistaken. She explained on cross-examination that she had not known for sure she was pregnant with any of her children because she gained so little weight and continued to have her periods throughout the pregnancy. In response, the prosecution emphasized repeatedly her secret and duplicitous behavior, her capacity to hide her body and its procreative power from public view.

In addition to her secrecy, the prosecution also highlighted her self-control before the baby's birth and after his death, emphasizing the rationality of her behavior and thereby undermining any attempt by the defense to argue that she was mentally disturbed rather than evil. Susan's only defense, as argued by her lawyer, was that she had believed the child to be stillborn; her crime was disposing the body in a garbage bag. She was a good mother who had made a terrible but not felonious mistake. In contrast, the prosecution's narrative asserted that Susan was, despite the evidence of fourteen years of good mothering, a bad mother, a force of evil in the community.

The conflict between these two versions of the maternal story occurred most prominently in the presentation of the forensic evidence and in the lawyers' closing statements. The forensic evidence produced by the prosecution suggested that the child had indeed been alive and, even if distressed at birth, could have been saved by medical intervention. The Assistant District Attorney asked Susan why she hadn't performed CPR, called for help from her husband, dialed 911, or phoned her father who was a volunteer fireman. To all of these questions, she replied: "I don't know. I was weak. I was bleeding" or "He wasn't breathing. He was blue." Arguing that no normal mother would abandon her newborn infant without seeking some assistance, the prosecutor insisted that Susan's failure to call for help confirmed her secretive behavior and evidenced cold-hearted cruelty toward her son. On the other hand, a county pathologist argued for the defense that sufficient evidence suggested that air found in the child's lungs and stomach could have been caused by decomposition and not by respiration. Under this narrative, Susan had acted in a state of shock and distress when she took the body of her child and placed him in a sheet and then in a garbage bag. The epitome of the good mother, Susan was momentarily deranged by the death of her son.

What both advocates lacked, however, was a convincing explanation for her secrecy. Despite the Chief Investigating Officer's attempt to supply Susan with one by suggesting various reasons why she abandoned the baby in the garbage bag, for example, that she did not want to bother with a funeral—the absence of a compelling and coherent motive that would conform to the "mother narrative" of either lawyer was disconcerting. Both lawyers agreed that Susan's behavior that night was unnatural, what they disagreed about was the significance of that unnaturalness. In one version, Susan is the scapegoat for all that is evil and disruptive in society; in the other, she is the scapegoat for all the potential frailty and instability of women, especially reproducing women. These are both mythic narratives, generalized representations of family disorder which cloak Susan's specific identity and story.

The role of the scapegoat is evoked in both the prosecuting and defense lawyers' closing remarks. The case of Susan Bienek is, the prosecutor argues, not simply the case of an individual mother who has harmed her child. Her conduct is a threat to the community, a harbinger of moral decline: "This is not about Susan Bienek; this case is about a whole community, an outraged community. And I'll tell you another thing...this verdict...goes out and it sets standards for a lot of people for a long time to come...We've got a kid that will never see a ball game, that will never see scouting, and this community will never know that this kid would have had an affect [sic] on all of them...Believe it or not, the whole concept of justice and the importance of human life falls in your hands. You've got to stand tall."[24] The prosecutor moves the jury's attention from the specifics of this case to the pervasive presence of crime and anti-communal behavior. He marks this case of infanticide as representative of all evil that threatens the community but offers that community, through the jury, the chance to cleanse itself of the transgressor: "[S]omeone," he said, "some force, brought this woman to justice."[25] The prosecutor asks the jury to compare the death of the newborn to the savagery of a mother who gouges out the eyes of her child. Summoning up vaguely Oedipal images of abandonment and blindness, the prosecutor invokes mythic fears of unnatur-

24. Trial Transcript at 980, 988, 992.
25. *Id.* at 972.

al mothering. "It runs against our human side that this crime could have been committed by a mother…The baby died from exposure, from the cold, freezing to death.…The trust was broken in this case…by a mother. The trust placed by God in a mother to a child. That is serious. That's a violation of a duty so sacred that it should tear at the very strings of your heart."[26] Her crime must be punished, argued the prosecutor, "punished severely. Not even five years, not even ten years."[27]

Susan's lawyer relied on an equally essentializing narrative about motherhood in his closing statement, arguing that "Mommas don't kill babies. Especially this mother don't kill babies; this mother of these four children who love her. If she did kill babies, these four children wouldn't be here."[28] Rejecting the myth of the devouring mother, the defense offers instead the ultimate symbol of the nurturing mother: "Daniel Bienek… has been wrapped in the arms of God since before his birth."[29] In this drama of maternal suffering, Susan Bienek is the medium through which the infant is united with his ultimate Parent. No longer the cruel and cold-hearted murdering mother, she is represented as the anguished mother, consoled only by the knowledge that her son is with God. Her error is transformed into a fortunate fall. She has in some way, it appears, worked God's will.

In both narratives, the power of the mythic mother narrative to compel assent to a certain kind of judgment overwhelms any opportunity for an alternative narrative, one that might come closer to Susan Bienek's individual story. I have spoken with a former neighbor of Susan's and with the school teacher who taught three of her four children and with other residents who knew her and her husband's families well. I was also told that Susan's husband, Kelly, had been thrown out of the house by his parents when he was in his teens because he was frequently in trouble with the police. I was told repeatedly that "the real story would never be heard in court" or "There's a lot more going on here than will ever be known." There were, apparently, calls to the police over domestic disturbances at the Bienek's house. From their hints, I inferred that Susan was intimidated and bullied by her husband. Concealing her pregnancy from him may have been the result of her fear of his response. None of this evidence came out at the trial. Her husband did not testify in her defense at the trial, although both parents and other close friends did testify on her behalf. Kelly Bienek disappeared from Smithville after the trial. Two years after the trial, in December 1995, the court of appeals affirmed her sentence. Susan Bienek

---

26. *Id.* at 991.
27. *Id.* at 115.
28. *Id.* at 943.
29. *Id.* at 971.

is now serving time in a prison in Gatesville, Texas. Her earliest release date is 2005.

III. Dialectical Narrative and Ethical Judgment

The Bienek case illustrates the need to conceptualize a dialectical and mediatory alternative to antagonistic narratives that derive their authority and plausibility from univocal representations of human agency and morality. The case demands a form and style of narrative that represents crisis so that catharsis, and therefore ethical judgment, is possible.

The community, in the form of the specific legal or popular audience, should not judge the offender against a model of causal and historical relationships that flattens her particular experience. Rather, they should come to an ethical judgment by examining "a multiplicity of possible connections" that keep "all contextual and ethical elements in play."[30] This mediatory narrative should remind the jury that they, too, are subject to the passing of time and the contingency of events: their "historical sense...[should be] an ethical force, acting to break down static conceptions of right and wrong."[31]

Let me repeat what I have already said: *The offender has not severed her relationship to her community by her offense; she has re-defined it, and the ethical response facilitated by dialectical narrative is to conceptualize the nature of that re-definition.* Stereotypical narratives of motherhood rehearsing the apparently ageless quality of a mother's relationship to her community threaten to cover up particularities like class, gender and race. The mother's crime can become the essence of what she is, regardless of the specifics of her individual life. The complex narrative that might mediate between the demands of the community for retribution and the right of the defender to justice should not be reduced to a fixed, single action, emptied of local meaning and isolated from the complexities that produced it.

As a way of imagining narrative mediation, one might contemplate how we more easily accept and judge compassionately that which is represented as "not real" as opposed to that which is represented as "real." When reading fiction, we can suspend our judgment until we have understood the complexities of the protagonist's life: witness our sympathetic response to Sethe's murder of her infant daughter in Toni Morrison's *Beloved*. Recognizing the possibilities present in our ethical response to fiction is rele-

---

30. Virginia Anderson, "Antithetical Ethics" 19 (unpublished paper on file with author). We are reminded again of how the jury in the Susan Smith trial responded to the particular details of her life and circumstances and not simply to the incontestable narrative of horror generated by her actions.

31. *Id.*

vant because the literary text is not a discrete, aesthetic object, separate from the social, but rather "its value [is] as activity and its meaning [is] as a gesture and a response to a determinate situation. Thus conceived, literary and cultural criticism takes its place among the social sciences [and offers] a unique means of access to the understanding of social relations."[32] I'm suggesting here that the combination of literature, literary critical thinking and legal hermeneutics provides yet another richly nuanced way of "understanding...social relations."

Considering a specific critical response to a literary text illustrates this ethical act of interpretation and imagination. I am not suggesting that the consequences of literary interpretation are analogous to those of legal interpretation. (And this essay is not the place to enter into the debate about the social construction of taxonomical distinctions that allow me to designate the poem as "literary" and trial testimony as "legal.") Something, however, in the act of interpretation, ethically undertaken, compels the interpreter to arrive at a just reading of the text, and thus in criminal cases, to arrive at an appropriate judgment. What follows is a poem by Seamus Heaney about infanticide.[33]

Limbo

Fishermen at Ballyshannon
Netted an infant last night

Along with the salmon.
An illegitimate spawning,

A small one thrown back
To the waters. But I'm sure
As she stood in the shallows
Ducking him tenderly

Till the frozen knobs of her wrists
Were as dead as the gravel,
He was a minnow with hooks
Tearing her open.

She waded in under
The sign of her cross.
He was hauled in with the fish.
Now limbo will be

---

32. Fredric R. Jameson, "The Symbolic Inference; or Kenneth Burke and Ideological Analysis," in Hayden White & Margaret Brose, eds., *Representing Burke* 68, 70–71 (Baltimore: Johns Hopkins Press, 1982).

33. Seamus Heaney, *Wintering Out* (London: Faber & Faber, 1972).

A cold glitter of souls
Through some far briny zone
Even Christ's palms, unhealed,
Smart and cannot fish there.

Seamus Heaney's poem is about a child drowned by its mother in the cold waters of the Irish Sea and abandoned. What judgment might we render if faced with the facts unmediated by this poem? The poem does not excuse us from judgment. It asks us to comply with its own reasoning, articulated through the imagery of Christian sacrifice and Catholic theology, or to take a stand against its ethical position. In either case, we find the simple response —either the mother is a "demonic and unrepentant murderer"[34] of her unwanted child or the mother is a passive victim of a harsh patriarchal world — unavailable. The poem insists upon the complexity of the narrative through which this incident must be viewed. Critic Elizabeth Butler Cullingford alerts us to the techniques through which complexity is achieved. The poet assumes the first-person pronoun, "But I'm sure," and thus "interprets the mother's motives through a non-appropriative act of personal trust."[35] She notes, "He guarantees that her act was not lightly undertaken. He does not speak in her voice, but he speaks on her behalf, with empathy"[36] (like a defense lawyer?). In other words, the poet assumes the voice of the mother, compelling the reader to assume the mother's position, at least for the duration of the poem.

The mother who ducks her child "tenderly" in the water is both the specific woman trapped, like the spawning salmon, in the nets of men and the representative Irish woman who lives in a culture that controls her "spawning" body (the Irish Republic constitutionally forbids contraception and abortion) and that condemns her to a "limbo" of desperation and despair, to live "with hooks/Tearing her open."[37] She is not just, howev-

---

34. See Elizabeth B. Cullingford, "Seamus and Sinead: From 'Limbo' to 'Saturday Night Live' via 'Hush-a-Bye Baby'," 1 *Colby Quarterly* 43, 49 (1994), quoting Anne O'Connor, "Women in Irish Folklore: The Testimony Regarding Illegitimacy, Abortion and Infanticide," in Margaret MacCurtain & Mary O'Dowd, eds., *Women in Early Modern Ireland* 304, 309 (Dublin: Wolfhound, 1991).

35. *Id.* at 52.

36. *Id.*

37. Cullingford quotes from a letter written by filmmaker Margo Harkin whose film "Hush-a-Bye Baby" uses Heaney's poem "as an objective correlative for the national trauma" caused by the Irish Republic's policy on abortion: "he collapsed into that poem the anguish and loss and the love that may have clashed so violently in that destroying act and which we absolutely know is part of the desperate condition of so many women imprisoned in a religious culture so completely intolerant of a woman's right to choose." Cullingford, supra note 34, at 53.

er, the passive victim of her culture—she affirmatively "ducks" her child. She "wade[s] in under/The sign of her cross," becoming in that moment both the sacrificer and the sacrificed, identified with Christ. [38]

What happens to us when we enter into the experience of this poem? We are moved by its narrative beyond the first horror at the thought of a mother drowning her child to see that mother as neither evil nor innocent. The murdering mother is not isolated from her community, scapegoated to carry the burden of violence and sin; rather, she is re-inserted into her community, immersed, as it were, in the waters of a shared cultural narrative. Her terrible deed recapitulates the actions of others who have been driven to kill their children and thus situates her in human history. Throwing back the "small one," she is associated with the community of fishermen who have netted her baby, and as the "spawning" salmon, she is netted herself by the men who fish and by that most charitable fisher of men, Jesus Christ. Set against this potentially redemptive reading, however, is the image of the "cold glitter" of limbo, where according to Roman Catholic dogma the baby's unbaptized soul must linger forever. Even Christ "cannot fish there." And so the mother, who may be redeemed by the promise of Christ's forgiveness, is nevertheless sentenced to remember her crime forever. She, too, must dwell in limbo. According to Cullingford, "the 'child murderess' endures a female Calvary that is compounded by her religious beliefs: the cross weighs heavily upon her because infanticide outrages both her feelings as a mother and her conscience, her sense of sin."[39] The judgment suggested by the poem on the mother is ambivalent and fraught with irresolution and is for these very reasons more ethical than simple condemnation or exoneration would be. The legal system, of course, sometimes requires a verdict of innocence or guilt, or at least a formal plea by the accused. Most cases, however, are handled outside the formal constraints of the courtroom. Considerable leeway resides in prosecutorial discretion and the omnipresent plea bargaining process. Even if the case gets to court, one frequently sees the presence of the kind of ambivalence I am addressing here—probated sentences or probation instead of jail, reduced charges or pleas.

---

38. Compare Burke, *A Grammar of Motives* 406 (Berkeley: Univ. of California Press, 1969) ("...the scapegoat is 'charismatic,' a vicar. As such, it is profoundly consubstantial with those who, looking upon it as a chosen vessel, would ritualistically cleanse themselves by loading the burden of their own iniquities upon it....In representing their iniquities, it performs the role of vicarious atonement...").

39. Cullingford, supra note 34, at 53. She also states, "[The Church] has created a Limbo for women in the same way it so conveniently created one for unbaptized babies. No one can go in there, no one can talk about this experience, it is the loneliest place; it must be endured. It is a prison sentence without appeal." *Id.*

Placed within the complex political, ethical,and aesthetic context of the mother's own life, infanticide is authentically unrepresentable *except in the terms of the culture out of which the mother has acted*. Fiction like Heaney's demands that we respond as temporary members of *that same culture*, that we put aside our habitual responses and enter "so intensely 'inside' [the] symbol system [of the poem's world] that a new quality or order of motives emerges from within it."[40] This "new...order of motives" does not recast the mother as innocent victim, simply reversing an oppositional ideology that would demonize the mother. The point is not to avoid judgment (or punishment), but to render a judgment consonant in its complexity with the crime.

As a concluding example of the capacity for narrative to facilitate ethical judgment, let's consider the case of Juana Léija, charged with two counts of capital murder for the drowning deaths of her children.

IV. The Case of Juana Léija, Houston, Texas

Eleven-year-old Eloisa Léija, the daughter of Juana Léija, was deposed on April 18, 1986, the day her mother tried to kill her seven children:

> This morning before school my mother told me that today we were going to go to the water and make us [sic] jump in and she told me not to be scared like the other time she did this. She told me not to say anything about it cause my sisters and brothers would get scared. In March of this year, it was on a Saturday when my mother got all of my brothers and sisters together and took us down to the little river near Crockett Street. She said she was going to put us all in the river and then she was going to go in too. She was mad at my father because he drinks too much and says that he is going to kill her. He hits her a lot and all of us kids too. Mother has called the police on him but they don't do nothing to him.
>
> We went to the river and then she couldn't do it so we all went back home. My Grandmother found out that my mother was going to do that to us and she got mad at my father and said she was going to call the police on her own son because he shouldn't do that and my mother had good reason the way he does her. One time he pointed a rifle at her and told her he was going to kill her. He always drinks and gets mean when he drinks....
>
> My mother and father have been fighting ever since I was a little baby. He has a lot of friends he goes with to drink and gets drunk a lot....
>
> My mother is good to us all and takes care of us but she cries a lot and doesn't want my father to be mean to us.[41]

---

40. Burke, "Catharsis—Second View," supra note 7, at 127.
41. Statement of Eloisa Léija, April 18, 1986, Harris County District Attorney.

Juana Flores was 16-years old when she first met 20-year-old Jose Luis Léija in Matamoros, Mexico. She wanted to "work, to study, and more than anything, [she] wanted to be a teacher."[42] In an interview shortly after her arrest, Juana Léija said that she "never even wanted to be his girlfriend... But from the beginning, Jose Luis kept insisting that he wanted to get married, and I kept telling him I wanted to work and study. Someday, marriage. Someday, children. But I just wasn't ready yet, I told him."[43] One day, Jose Luis picked her up from school, offering to take her home. But when she got into the car, "he immediately started going in a different direction from home, and I couldn't stop him. I kept telling him to take me home, but he kept driving no matter what I said until we got to this place where it was very dark and secluded and ugly. And then he raped me."[44] Despite her insistence that he leave her alone, Jose Luis persisted in calling on her at home and demanding again and again that she marry him. She refused until he threatened to "go from block to block throughout her neighborhood shouting to the world that he had taken his pleasure with her and that any man who wanted could do the same."[45] "I couldn't bear to hurt my parents," she said, "especially my father who always said he didn't care very much if I made good grades... but only asked that, when I finally left his home, I'd leave it dressed in white."[46] Seventeen-year-old Juana dropped out of school and married Jose Luis in 1973. Soon after they entered the U.S. illegally, heading for Houston.

Juana had seven children between 1975 and 1987. In 1983, Jose Luis lost his job and all but stopped looking for another. "Every day, it was the same," said Juana. "He would leave the house, he would stay gone all day, and he would come home in the evening very drunk and very angry. And every night, there were beatings."[47] Eleven-year-old Eloisa said that her father was "always mean to Esther," the oldest child who was retarded, "and [hit] her with his fist all the time because she doesn't understand him. He hits on [5-year-old] Juana a lot too. He puts bruises on all of us."[48] Toward the end, Jose Luis no longer cared if the neighbors and police knew that he was beating his family. Neither did Juana. "[T]he more he did it," she said, "the less and less I cared."[49] In August 1985, eight months before she tried to remove herself and her children from this nightmare,

---

42. *Houston Chronicle*, June 19, 1987, Section 1, 1.

43. *Id.* at 1, 21.

44. *Id.*

45. *Id.*

46. *Id.*

47. *Id.*

48. Statement of Eloisa Léija to Harris County District Attorney (April 18, 1986).

49. *Houston Chronicle*, June 19, 1987, section 1, 21.

Juana was found in a delusional state at a hospital with her hands cupped. The doctors said that she "seemed to believe that her children were tiny and contained within her hands."[50]

After years of brutal abuse Juana Léija took her children to the edge of Buffalo Bayou, in Houston, and threw them in the water, intending afterward to drown herself. In her testimony she said, "I saw no way out for us. I saw that the best thing was to end my life and their lives and that would end all our suffering."[51] "I wanted to end my life and the lives of my children because I knew that sooner or later my husband was going to kill me and I didn't want my children to stay with him or someone else that was going to mistreat them. I knew that my children would suffer if they stayed behind."[52] All but two of the children were rescued: five-year-old Juana and six-year-old Judas died. Juana Léija was charged with two counts of capital murder. Her lawyer faced the extraordinarily difficult task of defending a mother, an illegal Mexican immigrant, against charges of infanticide—every class, race, and gender prejudice would be overwhelmingly against her.[53]

The psychiatrist engaged by Juana Léija's lawyer, who believed that the evidence would support an insanity defense, pointed out that the most difficult issue would be "to convince the jury that it is not wrong for a mother to want to take the lives of her children and herself if she believes (knows) that is the only safe way for them. That is a psychotic and unreasonable thought process but is, I believe, the way that Mrs. Léija was functioning at the time."[54] However, the case never went to a jury. Juana's priest was able to secure the assistance of local Hispanic leaders and they, in turn, managed to convince Dick De Guerin, one of the best criminal lawyers in Texas, to take her case.[55] Eventually, Juana Léija was permitted to plead no contest to murder and attempted capital murder charges. She received

---

50. *Id.* at 2

51. *Id.* at 21.

52. Statement of Juana Léija, April 19, 1986, Harris County District Attorney.

53. Cynics might say that these things might work for her—after all, who cares if a crazy illegal immigrant drowns her children. It's just two fewer kids for the system to take care of. On the other hand, there is the need to insist that "real" Americans don't behave as Léija—that the madness and horror of her action is to be attributed to her otherness, her illegality. For a study of the way in which evidence itself can be "partisan," functioning to transform the social attributes of the defendant into a successful or unsuccessful legal claim, see Mark Cooney, "Evidence as Partisanship," 28 *Law and Society Review* 833 (1994).

54. Letter from psychiatrist to Dick De Guerin, February 24, 1987.

55. As Cooney, supra note 53, at 852, points out, "the poor and socially isolated are not always disadvantaged. Sometimes they act (to borrow a term from chaos theory) [citation omitted] as 'strange attractors' obtaining support from high-status individual[s] or organizations."

a ten-year probated sentence, described by the Houston Chronicle as a "gentle form of probation," and used when there is no judgment of guilt or innocence. Léija was required to remain under the care of Harris County mental health officials.

In convincing the authorities to render a probated sentence, Juana Léija's lawyer situated her horrifying actions within a narrative that addressed the pain of her life, the desperation she was driven to, and the active agency of her solution. Moreover, De Guerin, a white male, had to speak for a client who was marginalized in terms of her gender, her ethnicity and her class. Narrative mediation was accomplished in the case by De Guerin with the help of a psychiatrist and Mexican folklorist José Limón who situated Léija's particular tragedy within a larger cultural narrative through the figure of La Llorona. The central components of the legend of La Llorona are that she appears "weeping and . . . as a ghost in the form of a woman. Closely associated elements include white clothing, walking at night, appearance near water . . . continous searching, betrayal [and] the loss or murder of the child who is the object of the search."[56] The loss of the child, argues José Limón, does not necessarily signify the oppressive conditions of motherhood or a threat to rebellious mothers, but rather suggests "the humanly understandable, if extreme and morally incorrect, reaction of a woman to sexual and familial betrayal by a man in a Mexican cultural context where such betrayal was a common and recurrent experience for women."[57]

De Guerin's narrative accommodated both the specific details of Juana Léija's life as an immigrant woman married to an abusive husband and the way in which her individual history recapitulated the relationship of a marginalized Latino culture to a dominant Anglo order. Juana's experience was not articulated merely as an example of a mythic or prototypical narrative of motherhood. It was articulated in the details of her lived experience within its cultural context. Both the individual and collective representation of disempowerment and its consequences can be simultaneously witnessed, and even the murdering mother, La Llorona, has a story to tell that demands an audience.

By providing Juana Léija with a voice that represents not only her victimization but also her active agency, her lawyer invoked both the individual and cultural history to which she was subject, empowering her to

---

56. Lomax B. Hawes, "La Llorona in Juvenile Hall," in 27 *Western Folklore* 155–70 (1968).

57. José Limón, "*La Llorona*, the Third Legend of Greater Mexico: Cultural Symbols, Women and the Political Unconscious," in Ignacio M. Garcia (ed.) *Renato Rosaldo Lecture Series Monograph*, 59–93 (Tucson: Univ. of Az. Mex. Amer. Studies & Research Ctr., 1986).

resist the prolongation of that subjection. This is not a voice that is imposed upon her from the outside, "Yo soy La Llorona," she said in one of her interviews with José Limón. Under pressure from symbolic narratives, the legal narrative in her case accepted the complexity of an individual woman's life and generated, I believe, the appropriate ethical and legal judgment. Juana Léija's narrative did not remain unavailable to us "en el otro" (on the other side) covered by our myths of maternity. [58]

The other side for me, a white, middle-class, academic feminist and mother of two children, is the place where the unthinkable happens—the place where La Llorona walks; the place where a mother murders her children. The bridge that allows me to cross over to that other side—the only pathway to alterity—is narrative. "The gift-giving, consummating potential (as Bakhtin puts it) that one bears another is most meaningfully bestowed narratively—across time, and through a call of/for stories."[59] This "crossing over," or "going beyond," as Burke characterizes it, is neglected as a strategy in the representation of difference, especially in law courts where the pretense of objectivity and autonomy may frustrate our longing for justice. The experiences of those whom the legal process has often cloaked cannot expect to be recognized unless their stories are told in voices that represent them as more than simply powerless. It is not sufficient to assert that one is telling one's own version of what happened, a version of the "truth," unless that truth can be recognized as such by those who listen. This means that we have to go beyond simply recognizing that "the same empirical events can give rise to very different amounts and types of evidence."[60] We must also recognize that some stories will not even appear to have a prime facie claim to be heard, their weak "evidentiary strength"[61] rendering them implausible.

The richly contextualized story of Juana Léija's life challenges the categories of what is legally relevant, putting pressure on the boundaries of legal narrative to yield to other narrative conventions. A powerful and central cultural symbol was invoked to make representable what was otherwise unrepresentable, in both the aesthetic and the legal sense. The narrative of La Llorona mediates between the individual, historical facts of Juana Léija's life and the collective symbolic narrative out of which her individual manifestation has emerged. The consequence of this mediation—of this "crossing over"—is a new relationship between the particular story of a woman's life, the culture from which she draws her symbolic

---

58. For a contemporary, Chicana fictional version of La Llorona, see Sandra Cisneros, *Women Hollering Creek* (New York: Random House, 1991).

59. See Newton at 48.

60. Cooney, supra note 53, at 834.

61. *Id.*

life, the culture from which she feels alienated, and the legal context that draws all these disparate elements together. The voice of La Llorona does not simply echo ballads and folk stories. What happens when the judge hands down a probated sentence is that La Llorona, the betrayed and ghostly matricide, is heard in the court, demanding an ethical inquiry heretofore unavailable.

The discourse of ethical feminism has direct application to the hardest of legal cases, even when theorized in terms of a traditional, Aristotelian aesthetic. Such a political reconceptualization not only "reinvents" classical literary theory for feminism, but provides us with an alternative to adversarial jurisprudence. The central concern of catharsis is the reconciliation between the offender and the community that has defined the terms of the offense. One might be willing to go even further and argue that certain "crimes," like abortion, are produced by the community and that the community shares responsibility with the individual offender for the social crises that follow. As a political, ethical, emotional and aesthetic response, catharsis also affirms the power of difference *qua* difference, insisting that a conscious recognition of that difference accompany the reintegration of the offender into the community. The adversarial system, on the other hand, can only figure difference as opposition and requires its erasure in order to ensure the appearance of consistency and objective treatment under the law.

Infanticide raises questions about culture's deepest anxieties, and its presence opens up otherwise hidden seams of ethical and social crises. Feminism's responsibility, as a political and ethical discourse, is to respond to the presence of female violence in our culture and to reconfigure the relationship between the community and the offender who, despite her crime, remains part of our world.

Chapter Four

Rational Emotions

Martha C. Nussbaum

> "Bitzer" said Mr. Gradgrind, broken down, and miserably submissive to him, "have you a heart?"
> "The circulation, sir," returned Bitzer, smiling at the oddity of the question, "couldn't be carried on without one. No man, sir, acquainted with the facts established by Harvey relating to the circulation of the blood, can doubt that I have a heart."
> "Is it accessible," cried Mr. Gradgrind, "to any compassionate influence?"
> "It is accessible to Reason, sir," returned the excellent young man. "And to nothing else."
>
> Charles Dickens, *Hard Times*

I. Reason and Nothing Else

Literature is in league with the emotions. Readers of novels, spectators of dramas, find themselves led by these works to fear, to grief, to pity, to anger, to joy and delight, even to passionate love. Emotions are not just likely responses to the content of many literary works; they are built into their very structure, as ways in which literary forms solicit attention. Plato, describing the "ancient quarrel" between the poets and the philosophers, saw this clearly: epic and tragic poets lure their audience by presenting heroes who are not self-sufficient and who therefore suffer deeply when calamity befalls. Forming bonds of both sympathy and identification, they cause the reader or spectator to experience pity and fear for the hero's plight, fear, too, for themselves, insofar as their own possibilities are seen as similar to those of the hero. Plato saw correctly that it was no trivial matter to remove those (to him) objectionable emotional elements from tragedy, for they inform the genre itself, its sense of what has importance, what a suitable plot is, what needs recognition as a salient part of human life. To take the emotive elements away, you must rewrite the plot, reshape the characters, and restructure the nature of the interest that holds the spectator to the unfolding story (or, if sufficiently altered, non-story).

One can make a similar point about the realist novel. As Dickens says, such novels are stories of "human hopes and fears." The interest and pleasure they offer is inseparable from the readers' compassionate concern for "men and women like themselves" and the conflicts and reversals that beset them. But then a lover of literature who wishes to question Plato's banishment of literary artists from the public realm must, in pleading her case, make some defense of the emotions and their contribution to public rationality.

Today, too, they badly need defending. The contrast Bitzer draws between emotion and reason has become a commonplace of our public discourse, although its conceptual value is marred both by a failure to define what emotions are and by equivocation between a descriptive and a normative use of "reason" and "rational." Bitzer takes for granted that reason is defined in terms of the Gradgrind economic conception, according to which reason does indeed exclude emotive elements such as sympathy and gratitude. Then this highly controversial conception is used without further defense as if it were a norm so that whatever it excludes can be from then on treated as dispensable or even contemptible. "It is accessible to Reason, sir, and to nothing else," he proudly boasts of his heart.

Bitzer's contemporary heirs are quick to make the same move. Thus in his 1981 book *The Economics of Justice*, Richard Posner, leading thinker of the law-and-economics movement, begins by announcing that he will assume "that people are rational maximizers of satisfactions." Without defending this conception of the rational, he then justifies his proposed extension of economic analysis to all areas of human life by appealing to the conception as if it were an established norm, and as if this norm excludes all emotion-based decision making:

> Is it plausible to suppose that people are rational only or mainly when they are transacting in markets, and not when they are engaged in other activities of life, such as marriage and litigation and crime and discrimination and concealment of personal information?...But many readers will, I am sure, intuitively regard these choices...as lying within the area where decisions are emotional rather than rational.[1]

In other words, we can respect people's choices as rational in the normative sense only if we can show that they conform to the utilitarian conception and do not reflect the influence of emotional factors. (Posner offers us no account of the emotions or of their relationship to belief.) According to this conception, works like Dickens's novel, which suggests that emotions of certain sorts are frequently essential elements in a good decision, would be misleading and pernicious works—"bad books" indeed, as Mr. Gradgrind zealously stated.

Nor is this denigration of emotion confined to theoretical utilitarian works on public rationality. In one or another form, it plays an important

---

1. Richard Posner, *The Economics of Justice* (Cambridge: Harvard University Press, 1981), 1–2.

part in public practice. Consider, for example, a jury instruction issued by the state of California. At the penalty phase, the jury is cautioned that it "must not be swayed by mere sentiment, conjecture, sympathy, passion, prejudice, public opinion or public feeling."[2] As Justice Brennan demonstrated with a wealth of examples, such instructions are generally understood by both prosecutors and jurors to entail that the juror completely disregard emotional factors in reaching a decision. In a representative case, the jury was informed that its assessment of aggravating and mitigating factors "is not a question, I believe, that should be guided by emotion, sympathy, pity, anger, hate, or anything like that because it is not rational if you make a decision on that kind of basis." The prosecutor continues: "It would be very hard to completely filter out all our emotions, make the decision on a rational basis"—but that, he adds, is what a good juror will do.[3] This filtering process would exclude, as Brennan persuasively argues, factors of sympathetic assessment of the defendant's background and character that are actually indispensable to a rational judgment about sentencing, and a central part of what such judgments have traditionally been understood to involve. Clarifying the unexamined contrast between emotion and reason thus makes a practical difference in the law.[4]

II. Objecting to Emotions

In order to answer the charge that emotions are in a normative sense irrational and thus inappropriate as guides in public deliberation, I must, first of all, make the charge more precise. A number of very different arguments have been made against the emotions, all of which can be expressed using the convenient umbrella term "irrational." In some cases, these argu-

---

2. The instruction is assessed in *California v. Brown*, 479 U.S. 538 (1986).

3. *Id*. at 554–55 (Brennan, J., dissenting). The majority held that the instruction was constitutional because it would be understood by any reasonable juror to mandate the exclusion only of "untethered" or "inappropriate" sympathy; Brennan argues effectively that this has not been the case. All the justices agreed that certain types of emotion are in fact legitimate as guides to a rational decision about sentencing.

4. On the emotion-reason distinction in the law, see Paul Gewirtz, "Aeschylus' Law," 101 *Harvard Law Review* 1043–55 (1988); Lynne Henderson, "Legality and Empathy," 85 *Michigan Law Review* 1574–1652 (1987); Toni Massaro, "Empathy, Legal Storytelling, and the Rule of Law: New Words, Old Wounds," 85 *Michigan Law Review* 2099–2127 (1989); and Martha Minow and Elizabeth V. Spelman, "Passion for Justice," 10 *Cardozo Law Review* 37–76 (1988) (commenting on Justice Brennan's paper in the same issue). Only Minow and Spelman question the sharp dichotomy between reason and emotion, and none of the articles investigates the role of belief and judgment in the emotions themselves.

ments are not only distinct, but also built on incompatible views of what emotions are. So any defense must begin by disentangling them. I shall focus on only four of the much larger family of objections that can be found. But these are, I believe, the most germane to the debate about the public role of literature.

First, then, there is the objection that the emotions are blind forces that have nothing (or nothing much) to do with reasoning. Like gusts of wind or the swelling currents of the sea, they push the agent around, surd unthinking energies. They do not themselves embody reflection or judgment, and they are not very responsive to the judgments of reason. (This picture of emotion is sometimes expressed by describing emotions as "animal," as elements of a not fully human nature in us. It has also been likened with the idea that emotions are somehow "female" and reason "male"—presumably because the female is taken to be closer to the animal and instinctual, more immersed in the body.) It is easy to see how this view of emotions would lead to their dismissal from the life of the deliberating citizen and the good judge. Forces of the sort described do seem to be a threat to good judgment, and their dominance in an individual would indeed seem to call into question the fitness of that individual for the functions of citizenship.

A very different argument is made in the chief anti-emotion works of the Western philosophical tradition. Variants of it can be found in Plato, Epicurus, the Greek and Roman Stoics, and Spinoza. These philosophers all hold a view of emotions incompatible with the view that underlies the first objection. They hold, namely, that emotions are very closely related to (or in some cases identical with) judgments. So lack of judgment is not at all their problem. The problem, however, is that the judgments are false. They are false because they ascribe a very high value to external persons and events that are not fully controlled by the person's virtue or rational will. They are acknowledgments, then, of the person's own incompleteness and vulnerability. Fear involves the thought that there are important bad things that could happen in the future and that one is not fully capable of preventing them. Grief involves the thought that someone or something extremely important has been taken from one; anger the thought that another has seriously damaged something to which one attaches great worth; pity the thought that others are suffering in a non-trivial way, through no fault of their own or beyond their fault; hope involves the thought that one's future good is not fully under one's control.

In all of these cases, the emotions picture human life as something needy and incomplete, something held hostage to fortune. Ties to children, parents, loved ones, fellow citizens, country, one's own body and health—these are the material on which emotions work; and these ties, given the power of chance to disrupt them, make human life a vulnerable business, in which complete control is neither possible nor, given the value of these attachments for the person who has them, even desirable. But according to the anti-emotion philosophers, that picture of the world is in fact false. As Socrates said, "The good person cannot be harmed." Virtue and thought are the only things of real worth, and one's virtue and thought cannot be damaged by fortune. Another way of expressing this is to say that the good person is completely self-sufficient.

This argument is sometimes connected with a relative of the first argument, through the idea of stability.[5] A good judge, these philosophers insist, is someone stable, someone who cannot be swayed by the currents of fortune or fashion. But people in the grip of emotions, because they place important elements of their good outside themselves, will change with the gust of fortune and are just as little to be relied upon as the world itself is. Now hopeful, now in tears, now serene, now plunged into violent grief, they lack the stability and solidity of the wise person, who takes a constant and calm delight in the unswerving course of his own virtue. Thus this second picture can lead to some of the same conclusions as the first. But it is important to notice how different, in the two cases, the reasons for the conclusions are. On the first view, emotions are neither taught nor embodied in beliefs; on the second, they are taught along with evaluative beliefs. On the first, they can be neither educated nor entirely removed; on the second, both are possible. On the first, emotions are unstable because of their unthinking internal structure; on the second, because they are thoughts that attach importance to unstable external things.

This second objection is what led Plato to urge that most existing literature be banned from the ideal city; it led the Stoics to urge their pupils to pay attention to literature only from a viewpoint of secure critical detachment—like Odysseus, they said, lashed to the mast so that he could hear, but not be swayed by, the sirens' song. It led Spinoza to select a form of communication with his reader as far from the literary as possible: the geometrical method, in which, as he says, "I shall regard human actions and desires exactly as if I were dealing with lines, planes, and bodies." As all of these writers saw, most great literature treats the events that befall finite and vulnerable people as deeply significant, involving the audience in their good or ill fortune. It shows a hero like Achilles grieving for the death of Patroclus, rolling in the dirt and crying out, rather than recognizing that such things have no true importance. Thus it elicits bad desires in the very act of reading or watching, and it gives the audience bad paradigms to take into their lives. Once again, we should insist that this is not a point about literary content simply, but a point about form: for the tragic genre,

---

5. I state the Stoic view in its full form, and it is a rather extreme view; as we shall see below, one may accept their claim in a modified form, as true of some instances of emoting, without getting rid of emotions completely.

as we have said, is committed to grief, pity, and fear. Thus its very shape, its characteristic choices of character and plot structure, are subversive of philosophical attempts to teach rational self-sufficiency.

As will become clear in what follows, I very much prefer the second objector's view to the first, in the sense that I think it is based on a far more profound and better-argued view of the relationship between emotion and belief or judgment. But it should already be plain that one might accept this analysis of the emotions and yet refuse to accept the Stoic conclusion that the emotions are (in the normative sense) irrational and totally to be avoided when we seek to deliberate rationally. For, as one can see, that conclusion is based on a substantive and highly controversial ethical view, according to which ties to loved ones, country, and other undependable items outside the self are without true worth. But one might dispute this. And then one would wish to retain any evaluative judgments contained in emotions that one has judged to be true and to draw on those judgments in practical reasoning.[6]

A third objection, while compatible with some respect for the emotions in private life, assails their role in public deliberation. (It is compatible with the second objector's analysis of emotions as closely linked to judgments about the worth of external objects and probably not compatible with the first objector's claim that they are altogether without thought.) Emotions, this objector charges, focus on the person's actual ties or attachments, especially to concrete objects or people close to the self. They consider the object not abstractly, as one among many, but as special—and special, in part at least, on account of its prominence in the agent's own life. Emotions always stay close to home and contain, so to speak, a first-person reference. Thus love ascribes great worth to a person who is in an intimate relationship with the agent, and its intensity usually depends on the existence of a connection of some sort between agent and object. Grief, again, is grief for a loss that is felt as cutting at the roots of one's life. Fear is usually either completely self-centered or felt on behalf of friends, family, loved ones. Anger is aroused by slights or damages to something that is important to oneself. In all these cases, emotions bind the moral imagination to particulars that lie close to the self. They do not look at human worth or even human suffering in an even-handed way. They do not get worked up about distant lives, unseen sufferings. This, from the point of view of both utilitarian and Kantian moral theory, would be a good reason to reject them from a public norm of rationality, even though they might still have some value in the home. Even pity, which initially looks more universal, may not be so, for on Aristotle's analysis at least, it too contains a first-person reference, in the thought that one's own possibili-

---

6. On the different positions in the tradition regarding the relationship between belief and emotion, see below.

ties are similar to those of the sufferer. On this view then, novels, by arousing and strengthening emotions, would be encouraging a self-centered and unequal form of attention to the sufferings of other human beings. We should prefer the impartiality of the calculative intellect and of the prose in which it is embodied, for here each person counts for one, and none for more than one.

Closely related, the fourth objection is that emotions are too much concerned with particulars and not sufficiently with larger social units, such as classes. This is a point that has seemed to many Marxists, and to other political thinkers as well, to make the novel an altogether unsuitable instrument for political reflection—or in some versions, an instrument so committed to bourgeois individualism that it is unsuited for critical political reflection. Irving Howe made this point against Henry James, alleging that his insistence on a fine-tuned perception of particulars, his close scrutiny of subtle emotions, betrayed an incapacity for understanding the political, which is "a collective mode of action."[7] In Doris Lessing's *The Golden Notebook*, the heroine, a Marxist novelist, faces a related objection from her Marxist friends: that her attachment to the novel and its emotional structures betrays a residual attachment to the bourgeois world and is inconsistent with her politics. On some versions of this objection, novels may be useful enough in the private domain, so long as they do not overstep their bounds; on the Marxist version, which does not grant the existence of an ethical domain separate from the political, they are altogether worthless.

Each of these four objections is a profound one. To answer them all definitively would require me to elaborate and defend a full theory of the emotions. This obviously cannot be done here.[8] Instead, I shall map out plausible answers to the four objections and then ask how public emotions might best be filtered or winnowed in order to make sure that we are relying on the truly trustworthy ones.

III. Answering the Objections

A. Emotions as Blind Animal Forces

The first objector insists that emotions are irrational in the normative sense, that is, bad guides to choice, because they do not partake of reason

---

7. Irving Howe, *Politics and the Novel* (New York: Horizon Press, 1957). The chapter on James is reprinted in *Henry James: A Collection of Critical Essays*, ed. Leon Edel (Englewood Cliffs, N.J.: Prentice-Hall, 1963), 156–71.

8. For an attempt to do this, see my *Upheavals of Thought: A Theory of the Emotions* (Cambridge: Cambridge University Press, 1997).

in even the broadest descriptive sense. Emotions are just blind impulses that neither contain a perception of their object nor rest upon beliefs. This position is in one sense, I feel, hardly worth spending time on, since it has never been strongly supported by major philosophers who have done a great deal of their most serious work on the emotions—including those who for other reasons dislike the emotions intensely. By now it has been widely discredited even where it once was popular, in cognitive psychology, for example, and in anthropology.[9] But it still has a hold on much informal thinking and talking about emotions, which retains the legacy of earlier behaviorist and empiricist theories. Therefore it seems important to say something about what has led to the widespread conclusion that it is not a tenable view.

Western philosophers as diverse as Plato, Aristotle, the Greek and Roman Stoics, Spinoza, and Adam Smith have agreed that it is very important to distinguish emotions such as grief, love, fear, pity, anger, and hope from bodily impulses and drives such as hunger and thirst.[10] This distinction is made in two ways. First, emotions contain within themselves a directedness toward an object, and within the emotion the object is viewed under an intentional description. That is to say, it figures in the emotion as it appears to, is perceived by, the person who experiences the emotion. My anger is not simply an impulse, a boiling of the blood: it is directed at someone, namely, a person who is seen as having wronged me. The way I see the person is itself intrinsic to the nature of my emotion. Gratitude contains an opposed view of another person's relation to my good; distinguishing anger from gratitude requires giving an account of these opposed perceptions. Love is not, in the relevant sense, blind: it perceives its object as endowed with a special wonder and importance. Once again, this way of perceiving the object is essential to the character of the emotion. Hatred differs from love in nothing so much as the opposed character of its perceptions. Emotions, in short, whatever else they are, are at least in part ways of perceiving.

---

9. In psychology, see, for example, Richard Lazarus, *Emotion and Adaptation* (Oxford: Oxford University Press, 1991), and A. Ortony, G. Clore, and G. Collins, *The Cognitive Structure of Emotion* (Cambridge: Cambridge University Press, 1991); in anthropology, Jean Briggs, *Never in Anger* (Cambridge: Harvard University Press, 1981), and Catherine Lutz, *Unnatural Emotions* (Chicago: University of Chicago Press, 1988). The lack of support among philosophers would not be significant in and of itself, since philosophers have been known to agree about wrong conclusions over a long period of time; I mean, however, to focus on the fact that no good arguments have been produced to support the point.

10. The Stoics trace their position to Plato (whether rightly or wrongly), and Spinoza and Smith base theirs on that of the Stoics.

Second, emotions are also intimately connected with certain beliefs about their object. The philosophical tradition I have mentioned is not unanimous about the precise relation between emotion and belief. Some hold that the relevant beliefs are necessary conditions for the emotion, some that they are both necessary and sufficient, some that they are constituent parts of what the emotion is, some that the emotion is just a certain sort of belief or judgment. Let us begin, therefore, with the weakest view, on which all agree: the view that emotions are so responsive to beliefs of certain sorts that they cannot come into being without them. What leads these philosophers to accept that view? Consider, again, the emotion of anger. Being angry seems to require the belief that I, or something or someone important to me, have been wronged or harmed by another person's intentional action. If any significant aspect of that complex belief should cease to seem true to me—if I change my view about who has done the harm, or about whether it was intentional, or about whether what happened was in fact a harm, my anger can be expected to abate or to change its course accordingly. Much the same is true of other major emotions. Fear requires the belief that important damages may happen to me or someone important to me in the future, and that I am not fully in control of warding them off. Pity requires the belief that another person is suffering in some significant way, through no fault of her own or beyond her fault and so forth. Some of the beliefs in question, especially those concerned with value or importance, may be very deeply rooted in one's psychology; getting rid of them cannot be expected to be the job of a one-shot argument. But without these beliefs, no emotion can take root.

Most of the thinkers in the tradition go further, holding that the beliefs in question are also constituent parts of the emotion, part of what identifies it and sets it apart from other emotions. It seems highly implausible that we can individuate and define complex emotions such as anger, fear, and pity simply by reference to the way they feel. To tell whether a certain pain is fear or grief, we have to inspect the beliefs that are bound up in the experience. To tell whether a certain happy feeling should be called love or gratitude—again, we must inspect not just the feeling, but also the beliefs that go with it. For this reason, definitions of emotion in the philosophical tradition standardly include beliefs as well as feelings.

It appears to many thinkers, furthermore, that the beliefs we have mentioned are—usually, at any rate—sufficient for the emotion. That is, if I really succeed in making you believe that B has been insulting you behind your back, and you believe that insults of that type are important damages, that will suffice to make you angry with B. I do not need, as well, to light a fire under your heart. Whatever fire there is, is fire about the insult and is sufficiently produced by awareness of the insult. Much of the ancient science of rhetoric rests on this observation, and modern political speech is no stranger to it either. When George Bush wanted to make the American public fear the prospect of a Dukakis presidency, he did not need to inject ice water into their veins. All he needed to do was to make them believe that a Dukakis presidency would mean significant dangers for them that they would be powerless to ward off—namely, Willie Hortons running free in the streets of every city, ready to prey on innocent women and children. This position is compatible with the view that emotions have other noncognitive components (such as feelings or bodily states) in addition to beliefs, but it insists that the relevant beliefs are sufficient causes of these further components.

The greatest Stoic thinker, Chrysippus, went one step further, holding that emotions are simply identical with a certain type of belief or judgment. No specific feeling or bodily state is absolutely necessary for a given type of emotion. His position is, I believe, a powerful one, and far less counterintuitive than we might at first think.[11] But since it is an intricate matter to defend it, and since the weaker cognitive views of emotion are all we need to rebut the first objector, I shall forego that task here.

Notice that the family of cognitive views I have laid out still makes ample room for saying of some (or even perhaps of all) emotions that they are, in the normative sense, irrational, for emotions must now be assessed by inspecting the relevant beliefs or judgments. These may be either true or false, either appropriate or inappropriate to their object, and they may be either rational or irrational. (These are two independent dimensions of assessment: a belief might be false but rational, if I formed it on the basis of good evidence, but it happens to be wrong; it may also, and more often, be true but irrational, if I formed it hastily and uncritically, but it happens to be the case). But in no case will emotions be irrational in the sense of being totally cut off from cognition and judgment.

It is important to notice that it is this way of assessing emotions—one that grants their cognitive content and then asks how appropriate they are to their object and situation—that has been the dominant tradition in the criminal law, where the common-law formulation of the notion of reasonable provocation, to take just one example, appraises the appropriateness of a defendant's anger to the situation by asking what the response of a reasonable person in that situation would be. Some events are judged to be events that provoke a reasonable person to extreme anger—for example, an attack on one's child. This anger and its consequences will be differently treated by the law from the anger of someone who is just an ill-tempered and uncontrolled character. Even though the "reasonably provoked"

---

11. I defend it in Chapter 10 of *The Therapy of Desire: Theory and Practice in Hellenistic Ethics* (Princeton: Princeton University Press, 1994), and also in *Upheavals of Thought*, see supra note 8.

person who commits an act of violence as a result will still be convicted of a crime (unless the violent act is shown to have been in self-defense), the existence of reasonable provocation will be likely to reduce the level of the offense—from murder, for example, to voluntary manslaughter. In these and other ways, the common-law tradition treats emotions not as blind forces that can overwhelm volition by sheer strength, but as elements of a person's character; it is assumed that people are responsible for modifying their emotions to make them parts of a reasonable person's character.[12]

In short, there is no more reason to think emotions unsuited for deliberation just because they can go wrong, than there is reason to dismiss all beliefs from deliberation just because they can go wrong. There might of course be an argument that this class of cognitive attitudes is for some reason especially likely to go wrong—whether because of its content or the manner of its formation. But such an argument would have to be produced and assessed. To the assessment of the most famous such argument I now turn.

B. Emotions as Acknowledgments of Neediness

I now turn to the second objector, the ancient Stoic. In answering the first objector, I have endorsed the Stoic account of what emotions are, finding in them both object-directed intentionality and a close relation to beliefs of a certain sort, beliefs that ascribe high importance to things and persons outside the self's secure control. To make these judgments of worth is to acknowledge one's own neediness and lack of self-sufficiency. We can now locate the cognitive dimension of the emotions more precisely: they enable the agent to perceive a certain sort of worth or value. For those to whom such things really do have worth, emotions will be necessary for a complete ethical vision. Louisa Gradgrind says that, lacking emotion, she has been "stone blind." Her blindness has been a value-blindness, an inability to see the worth and importance of things outside herself, to see what she needs and what she doesn't, to see where her life needs to be completed by ties to others.

But are such acknowledgments of neediness and incompleteness good? The Stoic objector states that beliefs that people have deep needs from the world are always false: the only resources one really needs come from within oneself and one's own virtue. These false beliefs are, moreover, socially damaging, sapping confidence and robbing action of its stability. One can get rid of them, and life will be more satisfactory as a result. This

---

12. See Kahan and Nussbaum, "Two Conceptions of Emotion in Criminal Law," 96 *Colum. L. Rev.* 269 (1996).

means, for the Stoics, radically rewriting the vision of the world that their young pupils would have absorbed from their literary education. Instead of dramatic stories, they say, we should have paradigms of self-sufficiency and detachment, since a good person's life contains no dramatic suspense or tension. "Behold how tragedy comes about," writes the Stoic Epictetus, "When chance events befall fools." Socrates' calm demeanor in prison shows the way a wise person will greet misfortune. This example becomes Stoicism's antitragic ideal of the hero. About Socrates no conventional literary work can be written, for Socrates does not treat the events around him as worthy of much regard. The only "plot" in which he takes an interest is the unfolding of the argument; but this, Stoics hold, is always within his power.

This is a profound vision of the ethical life—profound, first of all, because it is based on a powerful conception of what emotions are, one that I believe to be more or less correct; profound, as well, because it raises deep questions about what a good human life should be, what sorts of vulnerabilities are compatible with the constancy that the ethical and political life require. And the view is profound, finally, because, like all the most searching philosophical thought, it shows its own argumentative structure to the reader and thus shows, as well, how and where one might take issue with it. In particular, it shows both friends and opponents of the emotions that the radical anti-emotion conclusion rests on normative claims about self-sufficiency and detachment that are highly controversial. Let me at least begin to question those premises.

Consider the emotion of compassion (pity).[13] As Aristotle long ago argued, this emotion requires the belief that another person is suffering in a serious way through no fault of her own, or beyond her fault. Those who feel compassion must also, in most cases at least, believe that their own possibilities (or as Aristotle adds, those of someone they love) are, broadly speaking, similar to those of the sufferer. This acknowledgment that one might oneself suffer similar things is traditionally and plausibly linked with beneficence, and the refusal of pity (as in Dickens's Bitzer) with a hard and ungenerous disposition.

The foundation of compassion (as of its near relative, fear) is the belief that many common forms of bad luck—losses of children and other loved ones, the hardships of war, the loss of political rights, bodily illness and deficiency, the prospect of one's own death—are in fact of major importance. In order to remove compassion and its relatives from human life, the Stoics must remove that fundamental belief. But then we must ask what rea-

---

13. I use both words because "pity," in recent times, has acquired connotations of condescension that it did not have earlier, and still does not have when used as a translation of Greek *eleos*, latin *misericordia*, or Rousseau's *pitié*.

sons they give us to care profoundly about the bad things that happen to others, what reasons to get involved, to take risks, for the sake of social justice and beneficence.

It has always been difficult for philosophies based on an idea of the self-sufficiency of virtue to explain why beneficence matters. No major thinker of this sort is willing to say that it does not matter, and yet for Socrates, for the Greek and Roman Stoics, for Spinoza, for Kant, it is difficult to motivate it consistently, given the alleged moral irrelevance of external goods, the self-sufficiency of virtuous will. Repudiating pity, as the Stoics do, leaves few motives for the acts usually prompted by pity; and if they are performed out of very different motives, say on account of pious obedience to Zeus's will, it is not clear that their moral character is the same. In effect, the person deprived of the evaluations contained in pity seems to be deprived of ethical information without which such situations cannot be adequately, rationally appraised.

The moral vision of Dickens's novel, by contrast, as of most mainstream realist novels and tragic dramas—begins from the profound importance of the vulnerabilities of human life and its need for "external goods." It begins, therefore, from fear, gratitude, and pity or compassion. Indeed, we can say of the mainstream realist novel what Aristotle said of tragic drama—that the very form constructs compassion in readers, positioning them as people who care intensely about the sufferings and bad luck of others and who identify with them in ways that show possibilities for themselves. Like tragic spectators, novel-readers have both empathy with the plight of the characters, experiencing what happens to them as if from their point of view, and also pity, which goes beyond empathy in that it involves a spectatorial judgment that the characters' misfortunes are indeed serious and have indeed arisen not through their fault. Such judgments are not always available within the empathetic viewpoint, so the novel-reader, like a tragic spectator, must alternate between identification and a more external sort of sympathy. What the ancient pity tradition claims for epic and tragedy might now be claimed for the novel: that this complex cast of mind is essential in order to take the full measure of the adversity and suffering of others, and that this appraisal is necessary for full social rationality. Rousseau shrewdly observes that the absence of a belief in one's own potential vulnerability can easily lead to social obtuseness and unresponsiveness:

> Why are kings without pity for their subjects? It is because they count on never being human beings. Why are the rich so harsh to the poor? It is because they do not have fear of becoming poor. Why does a noble have such contempt for a peasant? It is because he never will be a peasant.... It is the weakness of the human being that makes it sociable, it is our common sufferings that carry our hearts to humanity; we would owe

it nothing if we were not humans. Every attachment is a sin of insufficiency.... Thus from our weakness itself, our fragile happiness is born. (*Emile* bk.4)

Utilitarianism takes its start from the fact of common suffering and is, at its best, motivated by a wish to relieve pain. So it is a very serious internal criticism of utilitarianism if it can be shown that the ways of reasoning it designates as "rational," by excluding emotion, deprive us of information we need if we are to have a fully rational response to the suffering of others.

Hard Times pursues these criticisms, showing that it is only when Mr. Gradgrind becomes aware of his own need and feels "a wretched sense of helplessness" that he is able to address productively the needs of those around him. By contrast, Bitzer, for whom all human relationships are market transactions and gratitude an irrational, "untenable" response, fails to be a good Utilitarian agent in the sense of the original motivations of that view, since he fails utterly to comprehend and respond to another person's pain.[14]

In short, if we reject the Stoic tradition in the matter of self-sufficiency, we must, to be consistent, reject its normative arguments for the dismissal of emotion. There might be other arguments for the dismissal, but these will need to come forward for adjudication. Meanwhile, it would appear that many emotional responses embody correct perceptions of value, worthy of guiding deliberation: for example, the correct evaluation of the importance of children and other loved ones in a person's life. And one can go further. If one agrees with most of the philosophical tradition in holding that certain sorts of beliefs about the importance of worldly events and persons are not only necessary, but also sufficient, for emotion—and this seems to be a very plausible position[15]—then one will have to grant that if emotion is not there, those beliefs are not (or not fully) there. And that means

---

14. Consider Gradgrind's appeals to Bitzer to have gratitude for his education and sympathy for Gradgrind's predicament:

"I really wonder, sir," rejoined the old pupil in an argumentative manner, "to find you taking a position so untenable. My schooling was paid for, it was a bargain; and when I came away, the bargain ended."

It was a fundamental principle of the Gradgrind philosophy, that everything was to be paid for. Nobody was ever on any account to give anybody anything, or render anybody help without purchase. Gratitude was to be abolished, and the virtues springing from it were not to be. Every inch of the essence of mankind, from birth to death, was to be a bargain across a counter. And if we didn't get to Heaven that way, it was not a politico-economical place, and we had no business there.

15. It is plausible only if we carefully bear in mind that the relevant beliefs include evaluations of the importance of the object for the person experiencing the emotion. Two people may judge that "Socrates is dead." If only one also judges, "Socrates is one of the most important people in the world to me," then only that one will experience grief; but for

that a part of social rationality is not fully there. Those who accept the judgments about the value of the "goods of fortune" that the Aristotle/Rousseau tradition puts forward against the Stoics must, if consistent, admit emotions are essential elements in good reasoning about these matters. Thus judges or jurors, who deny themselves the influence of emotion deny themselves ways of seeing the world that seem essential to seeing it completely. It cannot be (normatively) rational to think this way—even when we are doing economics!

C. Emotions and Impartiality

The calculating intellect claims to be impartial and capable of strict numerical justice, while emotions, it alleges, are prejudiced, unduly partial to the close at hand. Each human being should count as one, and none as more than one, the utilitarian plausibly insists. But in the emotions attachments to family and close friends seem all-encompassing, blotting out the fair claims of the distant many. So, too, the reader of novels, taught to cherish particular characters rather than to think of the whole world, receives a moral formation subversive of justice.

This we may doubt. As I have argued elsewhere, the abstract vision of the calculating intellect proves relatively shortsighted and undiscriminating, unless aided by the vivid and empathetic imagining of what it is really like to live a certain sort of life. I can now add that emotions are an integral part of this more comprehensive vision. Louisa complains that her father's failure to educate the emotions has made her "unjust," and we see, in truth, that the absence of a quick intelligence of others' misery has in fact made her very slow to grasp the situation of the Coketown workers. By contrast, Sissy's robust emotional responses to the needs of others are essential ingredients in her ability (in her economics lesson) to come up with sensible answers about distant hypothetical cases. Let us now consider two further examples from that lesson.

Sissy is told by her utilitarian teacher that in "an immense town" of a million inhabitants only twenty-five are starved to death in the streets. The teacher, M'Choakumchild, asks her what she thinks about this—plainly expecting an answer expressing satisfaction that the numbers are so low. Sissy's response, however, is that "it must be just as hard upon those who were starved, whether the others were a million, or a million million." Again, told that in a given period of time a hundred thousand people took sea voyages and only five hundred drowned, Sissy remarks that this low

---

that one, the belief-set will be sufficient for grief. See my *Upheavals of Thought*, supra note 8.

percentage is "nothing to the relations and friends of the people who were killed." In both of these cases, the numerical analysis comforts and distances: what a fine low percentage, says M'Choakumchild, and no action, clearly, need be taken about that. Intellect without emotions is, we might say, value-blind: it lacks the sense of meaning and worth of a person's death and what the judgments internal to emotions would have supplied. Sissy's emotional response invests the dead with the worth of humanity. Feeling what starvation is for the starving, loss for the grief-stricken, she says, quite rightly, that the low numbers don't buy off those deaths, that complacency simply on account of the low number is not the right response. Because she is always aware that there is no replacing a dead human being, she thinks that the people in charge of sea voyages had better try harder. Dealing with numbers it is easy to say, "This figure is all right"—for none of these numbers has any nonarbitrary meaning. (And really, notice that 500 deaths out of 100,000 is incredibly high for ocean crossings, whether by sea or air.) Dealing with imagined and felt human lives, one will (other things equal) accept no figures of starvation as simply all right, no statistics of passenger safety as simply acceptable (though of course one might judge that other factors make further progress on these matters for the present unwise or impossible). The emotions do not tell us how to solve these problems; they do keep our attention focused on them as problems we ought to solve. Judge which approach would lead to a better public response to a famine at a distance, to the situation of the homeless, to product testing and safety standards.

This does not mean that one would not use economic models of the familiar type. Frequently in such cases they can provide valuable information. But one's use of them would be steered by a sense of human value. Nor need emotion-based reasoning hold that human life is "sacred" or "of infinite value," vague notions that probably do not capture many people's intuitions when these are closely examined and that have generated much confusion in arguments about animal rights, the termination of life, the treatment of severely handicapped humans.[16] We may concede that in some of these cases the emotion-based vision of a single death might distort judgment if steered by such a vague notion of infinite value and that the "cold" techniques of economics might give more accurate guidance. (For example, we certainly should be ready to accept a relatively low risk of death or disease to attain considerable social gains.) But in this case, I claim, what we are saying is not that the calculation per se is more reli-

16. For valuable critiques along these lines, see James Rachels, *Created from Animals* (New York: Oxford University Press 1990), Jonathan Glover, *Causing Death and Saving Lives* (Harmondsworth: Pelican, 1976); and Richard Posner, *Sex and Reason* (Cambridge: Harvard University Press, 1992).

able than emotion per se: we are saying instead that a certain degree of detachment from the immediate—which calculation may help to foster in some people—can sometimes enable us to sort out our beliefs and intuitions better and thus to get a more refined sense of what our emotions actually are and which among them are the most reliable. If we had only numbers to play with and lacked the sense of value embodied in emotions of fear and compassion, we would not have any nonarbitrary way of answering such questions. (To the issue of detachment I shall shortly return.)

We may add to this general argument a genetic thesis. Intimate bonds of love and gratitude between a child and its parents, formed in infancy and nourished in childhood, seem to be indispensable starting points for an adult's ability to do good in the wider social world. These initial attachments need further education, to be sure, but they must be there if anything good is to come of education. This point is at least as old, in the Western tradition, as Aristotle's criticism of Plato in Book 2 of the *Politics*. Aristotle insists that removing the family, rather than ensuring impartial and equal concern for all citizens, will ensure that nobody cares strongly about anything. The point is vividly developed in *Hard Times*, in Dickens's chilling account of the education of the young Gradgrind children, who are taught to calculate but never encouraged to love. And the story of Louisa's tragic collapse shows us something further: that a reliance on emotion in the developmental process can actually (by providing good guidance about important attachments) diminish the more damaging kinds of need and vulnerability in later life, creating a personality that has a more stable center than a personality raised in Louisa's way, a personality that has balanced emotional commitments and therefore balanced practical judgments. Repression of childhood emotion, by contrast, may simply bring emotion back in a more destructive and genuinely irrational form.[17]

D. Emotions and Classes

As for the related objection, that the emotions are too concerned with the individual, too little with larger social units such as classes, we must grant that in fact the whole commitment of the novel as genre, and not least of its emotional elements, is indeed to the individual, seen as both qualitatively distinct and separate. In this sense, the vision of community embodied in the novel is, as Lionel Trilling long ago argued, a liberal vision, in which individuals are seen as valuable in their own right, and as hav-

---

17. Indeed, we might say that Louisa is attracted to Harthouse precisely because her attachment-world has previously been so empty and uncultivated: she knows how to embrace only the emptiness she feels.

ing distinctive stories of their own to tell.[18] While the genre emphasizes
the mutual interdependence of persons, showing the world as one in which
we are all implicated in one another's good and ill, it also insists on respect-
ing the separate life of each person and on seeing the person as a separate
center of experience.

It is in that sense no accident that mass movements frequently fare badly
in the novel, to the extent that they neglect the separate agency of their
members, their privacy, and their qualitative differences. The British bureau-
cracy in *Little Dorrit*, the trade union movement in *Hard Times*, the divorce
laws that cause Stephen Blackpool's misery, the entire legal system in *Bleak
House*, the revolutionary movement in Henry James's *The Princess
Casamassima*—all are seen as guilty of obtuseness toward the individual.
To the extent that they are guilty, the novel in its very form is bound to be
their enemy and subverter. This means that from the point of view of such
movements the novel is a dangerously reactionary form—as the Com-
munist friends of Doris Lessing's novelist heroine in *The Golden Notebook* are eager to observe, as Lukács was quick to emphasize when he
condemned as "petit bourgeois" the liberal-cosmopolitan political vision
of Rabindranath Tagore's novel *The Home and the World*.[19]

This political attitude has its dangers, and sometimes the novelist's suspicion of any form of collective action leads to error—as when, in *Hard
Times*, Dickens seems to suggest that it would be better to divert and enter-
tain the workers rather than to change, through trade union action, the
conditions of their labor; as when he portrays trade unions as in their very
nature repressive toward individual workers. But such a failure in no way
indicts the whole approach. More often, I think, the vision of individual
life quality afforded by novels proves compatible with, and actually moti-
vates, serious institutional and political criticism—as when, in Sissy Jupe's
lesson, the reader's emotions themselves indicate the meaning of the hunger
and misery of millions, directing the calculative intellect to interpret the
numbers in an urgently activist spirit; as when, in Tagore's mordant portrayal of Indian nationalism, we find the movement's leaders neglecting,
in their abstract zeal, the real economic misery of the poor traders who
cannot earn a living unless they sell the cheaper foreign wares, while we,

---

18. Lionel Trilling, *The Liberal Imagination: Essays on Literature and Society* (New
York: Charles Scribner's Sons, 1950).

19. Lukács calls *The Home and the World* (which is intensely critical of the early Indi-
an nationalist movement) "a petit bourgeois yarn of the shoddiest kind" (quoted in Anita
Desai's introduction to the 1985 Penguin edition of the novel, p. 7). For the case of *The
Princess Casamassima*, see Trilling, *The Liberal Imagination*, and my discussion in "Per-
ception and Revolution" in *Love's Knowledge: Essays on Philosophy and Literature*
(New York: Oxford University Press, 1990).

with the author's surrogate Nikhil, understand better what it really is to make each human life count for one.[20]

It seems appropriate, in fact, for any form of collective action to bear in mind, as an ideal, the full accountability to the needs and particular circumstances of the individual that the novel recommends, in its form as well as its content. This does not entail a romanticism that scorns modeling and measurement, as I have insisted repeatedly. Such "literary" insights underlie much of what is best in recent economic approaches to the measurement of the quality of life. A story of human life quality, without stories of individual human actors, would, I argued, be too indeterminate to show how resources actually work in promoting various types of human functioning. Similarly, a story of class action, without the stories of individuals, would not show us the point and meaning of class actions, which is always the amelioration of individual lives. Raymond Williams puts this point very well, defending traditional realist narrative against socialist criticism:

> Moreover we should not, as socialists, make the extraordinary error of believing that most people only become interesting when they begin to engage with political and industrial actions of a previously recognized kind. That error deserved Sartre's jibe that for many Marxists people are born only when they first enter capitalist employment. For if we are serious about even political life we have to enter that world in which people live as they can as themselves, and then necessarily live within a whole complex of work and love and illness and natural beauty. If we are serious socialists, we shall then often find within and cutting across this real substance—always, in its details, so surprising and often vivid—the profound social and historical conditions and movements which enable us to speak, with some fullness of voice, of a human history.[21]

In a realist novel such as *Hard Times* we enter, I claim, that full world of human effort, that "real substance" of life within which, alone, politics

---

20. As the impoverished trader Panchu says to Nikhil:
"I am afraid, sir…while you big folk are doing the fighting, the police and the law vultures will merrily gather round, and the crowd will enjoy the fun, but when it comes to getting killed, it will be the turn of only poor me." We see the commitments of the genre, as well, in Nikhil's refusal to dismiss the English governess: "I cannot…look upon Miss Gilby through a mist of abstractions, just because she is English. Cannot you get over the barrier of her name after such a long acquaintance? Cannot you realize that she loves you?"
This is a self-referential moment: for it is evident that the vision of the novel as a whole is this sort of particularized vision.

21. Raymond Williams, *The Politics of Modernism: Against the New Conformists* (London and New York: Verso, 1989), 116.

can speak with a full and fully human voice.[22] This human understanding, based in part on emotional responses, is the indispensable underpinning of a well-guided abstract or formal approach.

IV. The Judicious Spectator

So far I have argued only that emotions can sometimes be rational and that the emotions of sympathy, fear, and so on, constructed by a literary work such as *Hard Times* are good candidates for being rational emotions. I have not yet said very much about which emotions we are to trust or how literary readership helps us to discriminate the trustworthy from the untrustworthy. But if we have no reliable filtering device, we might still wonder whether we should trust emotions at all. I shall now argue that such a device can be found in Adam Smith's conception of the judicious spectator and that literary readership (as Smith himself suggests) offers an artificial construction of the position of such a spectator. It thus supplies a filtering device for emotion of just the sort that Smith thought necessary for emotions to play the valuable role they ought to play in public life.

We must begin by noting that Adam Smith, in many respects the founder of modern economics, did not believe that ideal rationality was devoid of emotion. In fact, he devoted a major part of his career to developing a theory of emotional rationality, since he believed that the guidance of certain emotions was an essential ingredient in public rationality. In *The Theory of Moral Sentiments*, he describes a figure whom he calls the "judicious spectator," whose judgments and responses are intended to provide a paradigm of public rationality (whether for the leader or for the citizen). The spectator's artificially constructed situation is designed to model the rational moral point of view, by ensuring that he will have those, and only those, thoughts, sentiments, and fantasies that are part of a rational outlook on the world.[23]

The judicious spectator is, first of all, a spectator. That is, he is not personally involved in the events he witnesses, although he cares about the participants as a concerned friend. He will not, therefore, have such emotions and thoughts as relate to his own personal safety and happiness; in that sense he is without bias and surveys the scene before him with a certain sort of detachment. He may of course use any information about what

---

22. Williams would certainly agree. See his valuable account of the novel in Chapter 5 of *Culture and Society, 1780–1950* (London: Penguin, 1958).

23. This device, in which circumstantial and informational restrictions are used to model the moral point of view, was in many respects the origin of John Rawls's device of the Original Position in *A Theory of Justice* (Cambridge: Harvard University Press, 1971).

is going on that he derives from his own personal history—but this information must be filtered for bias in favor of his own goals and projects. On the other hand, he is not for that reason lacking in feeling. Among his most important moral faculties is the power of imagining vividly what it is like to be each of the persons whose situation he imagines.

> [T]he spectator must...endeavor, as much as he can to put himself in the situation of the other, and to bring home to himself every little circumstance of distress which can possibly occur to the sufferer. He must adopt the whole case of his companion with all its minutest incidents; and strive to render as perfect as possible, that imaginary change of situation upon which his sympathy is founded. (1.1.4.6)

But sympathetic identification with the parties before him is not sufficient for spectatorial rationality. Smith understands that often the misfortunes that befall the parties damage their ability to assess their own situation correctly. At the most extreme we may imagine a case in which an accident has caused the person before us to lose the use of reason altogether. If the person's life is painless, empathy might well show us the pleasure of a contented child. But, Smith observes, the judicious spectator will nonetheless view the calamity as "of all the calamities to which the condition of mortality exposes mankind... by far the most dreadful." What this shows us is that both empathetic participation and external assessment are crucial in determining the degree of compassion it is rational to have for the person: "The compassion of the spectator must arise altogether from the consideration of what he himself would feel if he was reduced to the same unhappy situation, and, what is perhaps impossible, was at the same time able to regard it with his present reason and judgment."

Since Smith, a follower of ancient Greek cognitive conceptions of emotion, holds that emotions such as pity, fear, anger, and joy are based on belief and reasoning, he does not hesitate to describe the point of view of the spectator as one rich in emotion. Not only compassion and sympathy, but also fear, grief, anger, hope, and certain types of love are felt by the spectator as a result of his vivid imagining.[24] It would seem bizarre to omit these emotions: Smith's position (like mine) holds that they are entailed by certain thoughts that it is appropriate to have about what is happening to the person before us and its importance, indeed that they are part of the equipment with which we register what is happening. The spectator's responses are not just willed attitudes of concern, but really emotions; and

---

24. Smith would include the love we have for friends and fellow citizens, as well as the love of humanity; he excludes only erotic love, which he takes to be based on morally irrelevant particularities and to be inexplicable by any kind of public reason-giving process.

Smith plainly believes that the cultivation of appropriate emotions is important for the life of the citizen. Appropriate emotions are useful in showing us what we might do, and also morally valuable in their own right, as recognitions of the character of the situation before us. Furthermore, they motivate appropriate action.

On the other hand, not all emotions are good guides. To be a good guide, the emotion must, first of all, be informed by a true view of what is going on—the facts of the case, of their significance for the actors in the situation, and of any dimensions of their true significance or importance that may elude or be distorted in the actor's own consciousness. Second, the emotion must be the emotion of a spectator, not a participant. This means not only that we must perform a reflective assessment of the situation to figure out whether the participants have understood it correctly and reacted reasonably; it means, as well, that we must omit that portion of the emotion that derives from our personal interest in our own well-being. The device of the judicious spectator is aimed above all at filtering out that portion of anger, fear, and so on, that focuses on the self. If my friend suffers an injustice, I become angry on his behalf; but, according to Smith, that anger lacks the special vindictive intensity of much anger at wrongs done to oneself. Again, if my friend is grieving for the loss of a loved one, I will share his grief, but not, it appears, its blinding and disabling excess. For Smith, thinking of this distinction helps us to think of what we should be as citizens: passionate for the well-being of others, but not inserting ourselves into the picture that we responsively contemplate.

What we now should notice is that throughout this discussion Smith uses literary readership (and spectatorship at dramas) to illustrate the stance, and the emotions, of the judicious spectator. Smith attaches considerable importance to literature as a source of moral guidance. Its importance derives from the fact that readership is, in effect, an artificial construction of judicious spectatorship, leading us in a pleasing natural way into the attitude that befits the good citizen and judge. As we read we are immersed and intensely concerned participants, yet we lack concrete knowledge of where we are in the scene before us. We care about both Louisa and Stephen Blackpool, to some extent we identify with both, and yet we lack that special and often confused intensity of emotion that would derive from thinking that it is really our own life that is at issue in one or the other case. This also means that we are not prejudicially located: we can feel for both Louisa and Stephen in a more balanced way than can either of them, precisely because we are at the same time both of them and neither. Once again, there are many different readers with different personal histories, and judicious readers are permitted to make use of information about what is going on that derives from their histories. (That is why ideally the process of reading must be completed by a conversation among readers.) But this information, being exercised toward lives that are not ours, will lack the personal bias of the interested participant.

The view of human hopes and fears that the judicious reader forms in the process of reading the novel is not foolproof. As I have said, emotions are good guides only if they are based on a true view of the facts of the case and a true view of the importance of various types of suffering and joy for human actors of many types. (Like other judgments, they must be tested for coherence with our other experiences and with our moral and political theories.) It is obvious that literary works can distort the world for their readers in these two ways. They can present historical and scientific fact falsely, as Dickens to a great extent falsely depicts the labor union movement, and as many novelists present a distorted picture of the capacities of women or of religious and racial minorities. They can also misrepresent the importance of various types of suffering or harm, leading us to think them either graver or lighter than they really are. Thus Dickens suggests that workers will flourish if only they are diverted and given some leisure time; he does not rate high enough the harm involved in class hierarchy itself. Dickens also fails to take note of harms caused to women by inequalities of autonomy that are endemic to marriage as it was lived in his time. Aspects of the imagination of the reader that lead toward social equality rather than its opposite tend to detect and undermine hierarchies of race and class and gender. But one must concede that this tendency is not universally practiced, and to this extent novels (like any other text) will offer a guidance that is, if promising, still fallible and incomplete.

This shows us that we need to exercise critical judgment in our selection of novels and to continue the process of critical judgment as we read, in dialogue with other readers. Wayne Booth has aptly called this process "coduction," since it is by its nature a nondeductive, comparative type of practical reasoning that is carried on in cooperation with others. In the process of co-duction, our intuitions about a literary work will be refined by the criticisms of ethical theory and of friendly advice, and this may greatly alter the emotional experience that we are able to have as readers—if, for example, we find ourselves convinced that the novel's invitations to anger and disgust and love are based on a view of the world we can no longer share.

In short, my view does not urge a naive uncritical reliance on the literary work.[25] I have insisted that the conclusions we are apt to draw on the basis of our literary experience need the continued critical scrutiny of moral and political thought, of our own moral and political intuitions, and of

---

25. On the need for reflective criticism, see also the title essay in *Love's Knowledge*, supra note 19.

the judgments of others. I have, however, argued, with Smith that the formal structures implicit in the experience of literary readership give us a kind of guidance that is indispensable to any further inquiry—including a critical inquiry about the literary work itself. If we do not begin with "fancy" and wonder about the human shapes before us, with sympathy for their sufferings and joy at their well-being, if we do not appreciate the importance of viewing each person as separate with a single life to live, then our critique of pernicious emotions will have little basis. Readership, as I have argued, gives us this basis—and it also gives us the stance of judicious spectatorship essential to the critique. The reader of *Hard Times* is well placed to begin a critique of the novel's picture of the happiness of workers, well placed by the structures of attention and sympathy inherent in the act of reading itself.

The reader cultivates concern with human agency and autonomy and, at the same time, a capacity to imagine what the life of a worker such as Stephen Blackpool is like. This combination is likely to engender in Dickens's readers a dissatisfaction with Dickens's own somewhat glib and condescending solution. Thus one does not need to think the politics of a novel correct in all ways to find the experience itself politically valuable.

I now return to the California jury. The judicious spectator/reader learns an emotional repertory that is rich and intense but free from the special bias that derives from knowing one's own personal stake in the outcome. A reader's emotions will also be constrained by the "record"—by the fact that they are restricted to the information presented in the text. In this way, we can now see, the judicious spectator is an extremely good model for the juror. The juror, of course, is not simply the judicious spectator. Jurors will be constrained in specifically legal ways in what they may consider, not only by the restrictions on bias already built into Smith's model. All the same, keeping Smith's requirements in mind would help us to sort out some of the complex issues involved in the discussion of relevant and irrelevant juror sympathy.

All the opinions in *California v. Brown* agreed that a jury at the penalty phase should ignore only "the sort of sympathy that was not rooted in the aggravating and mitigating evidence introduced during the penalty phase."[26] "Extraneous emotion" was indeed to be disregarded, but emotion appropriately grounded in the evidence was not. An earlier case, *Woodson v. North Carolina*, had set out the importance of such sympathetic emotion in an eloquent way, insisting on the connection between sympathy and being treated as a unique person with one's own narrative history:

> A process that accords no significance to relevant facets of the character and record of the individual offender or the circumstances of the partic-

---

26. *California v. Brown*, 479 U.S. 538, 538 (1990).

ular offense excludes from consideration in fixing the ultimate punishment of death the possibility of compassionate or mitigating factors stemming from the diverse frailties of humankind. It treats all persons convicted of a designated offense not as uniquely individual human beings, but as members of a faceless, undifferentiated mass to be subjected to the blind infliction of the penalty of death.[27]

All the opinions in *California v. Brown* acknowledge this precedent, thus validating the role of the norm of judicious spectatorship and also its connection with following the entirety of a complex narrative history. They differ only about whether the instruction as stated (which asks jurors to disregard "mere" sympathy) would naturally be interpreted to demand the exclusion of appropriate sympathy. The majority opinion holds that jurors would readily see that they were being asked only to disregard "untethered" sympathy, while the dissenters argue that the jurors would not be clear about this, given the way in which prosecutors standardly represent the instruction. My argument indicates that the dissenters are correct: there is great confusion in many people's thought on this point, and a corresponding need to clarify the boundaries of appropriate and inappropriate sympathy. Sympathetic emotion that is tethered to the evidence, institutionally constrained in appropriate ways, and free from reference to one's own situation appears to be not only acceptable but actually essential to public judgment. It is this sort of emotion, the emotion of the judicious spectator, that literary works construct in their readers, who learn what it is to have emotion, not for a "faceless undifferentiated mass," but for the "uniquely individual human being." This means, I believe, that literary works are what Smith thought they were: artificial constructions of some crucial elements in a norm of public rationality and valuable guides to correct response.

---

27. *Woodson v. North Carolina*, 428 U.S. 280, 304 (1976).

Chapter Five

Elizabeth George, Cantor's Theorem, and the Admissibility of Scientific Evidence

Lief Carter

> The earth and the sand are burning. Put your face on the burning sand and on the earth of the road, since all those who are wounded by love must have the imprint on their face, and the scar must be seen.
>
> Farid al-Din 'Attar, *The Conference of the Birds*
> (only epigraph for Elizabeth George's *Playing for the Ashes*)

> Can our stories be solidly factual? I think not. At law we are not allowed the luxury of refusing to come to a decision because we do not have enough facts. We have to fill in the gaps...
>
> L.H. LaRue, *Constitutional Law as Fiction* 41 (1995).

I. Elizabeth

Kenneth Fleming is dead. He died of carbon monoxide inhalation on the bed in the cottage of Gabriella Patten, his mistress, a woman of great beauty. Several hours before Ken died, a neighbor had seen and heard the two shouting angrily at each other outside the cottage. Gabriella then abruptly drove off in Ken's Lotus.

The investigators classified Ken's death as murder. In the living room of the floor below the bedroom where he died, they found the burned remains of an overstuffed chair. Its smoldering had filled the cottage with carbon monoxide. The same smoldering so thoroughly consumed the oxygen in the cottage as to kill itself rather than burst into flame.

New Scotland Yard's Detective Inspector Thomas Lynley and his assistant, Detective Sergeant Barbara Havers, on arriving at the scene, discovered the non-combusted remains of a primitive incendiary device: a cigarette with wooden matches taped, heads up, around the bottom half of the cigarette. When the lit cigarette reached the matches, they burst into flame. Such preparations hardly seemed necessary in order to commit suicide. Unless, of course, the suicide's dying wish is to frame an enemy for murder.

II. Cantor's Theorem and Murder Mysteries

According to Quine, "Georg Cantor proved in 1890 that the classes of objects of any sort outnumber the objects."[1] Here is a simple illustration: Take the numbers 0 through 9. There are more than ten ways to classify these ten positive integers: odds, evens, pairs (0 & 1, 2 & 3, etc.), triplets, quartets, and quintets, classes of numbers that double (1 & 2, 2 & 4, 3 & 6, etc.), classes that triple (1 & 3, 2 & 6, 3 & 9), quadruple (1 & 4, 2 & 8) quintuple (1 & 5), sextuple, septuple, etc. Note we are at thirteen classifications of ten objects and still counting the ways.

Returning to Quine, who reaches Cantor in the course of his discussion of infinite numbers:

> [Cantor] shows there are a multitude of infinities, indeed an infinity of them. When the objects in the above reasoning are integers, the argument shows there are more classes of integers then integers. But there are infinitely many integers; so the number of classes of integers is a higher infinite number. The same reasoning shows that there are more classes of classes of integers than classes of integers; so here we have a still higher infinity. The argument can be repeated without end...[2]

Effective writers of mysteries at least intuitively build on Cantor's truth. The good mystery unfolds in a way that compounds the classifications of events, motives, emotional conditions, and so on. We delight in the author's skill at compounding the number of competing plausible explanations of the murder. And yet the author of the well-crafted mystery eventually provides a solution that seems most right. How does she do this?

Since I belong to the school of pragmatic post-modernists, I cannot help but believe that what counts as a satisfying solution to a mystery is contingent and socially constructed. I do believe, however, that this construction has deep and strong foundations in liberal political beliefs and practices. The satisfying solution avoids, or gives the appearance of avoiding, arbitrary, dictatorial, authoritarian choices. It appears to follow from some experience that author and reader (ruler and ruled) share.

---

1. Quine, *Quiddities: An Intermittently Philosophical Dictionary* 96 (Cambridge: Belknap Press, 1987).
   2. *Id.* at 97.

In liberal politics we claim to avoid the arbitrary by submitting political choices to some form of deliberation and justification. We expect to participate in the solution. Judges write opinions; in liberal polities we are empowered to criticize them. We also expect to participate in the mystery novel, to try to solve the puzzle before the author dictates it to us. The author treats the reader in authoritarian rather than liberal fashion when she introduces a *deus ex machina*,[3] a solution based on facts so improbable or so unknowable as to discredit our participation in and connection to the author and her world.

The words "author" and "authority" both derive from the Latin word for "creator" — "auctor." Another way of explaining our resistance to the *deus ex machina* solution is that we want to believe in the author, and the judge, as the true creator. We want to trust the integrity and coherence of their creation in order, in turn, to trust that we share a community with them.

The mystery author constructs a confluence of people — their actions and their timings, their motives, and other objects in the set — to create a "better fit" of objects within some classifications than within others. We may call this "good fit" test, in a generic sense, an aesthetic test. Close encounters with good fits somehow satisfy us. We variously call this experience of satisfaction truth, or justice, or beauty, or, perhaps less frequently, love.

III. *William Daubert, et al., v. Merrell Dow Pharmaceuticals, Inc.*[4]

Two minors suffered birth defects known as "limb reduction," a condition associated historically with the drug thalidomide. Through their parents as guardians, they brought suit against Merrell Dow, the manufacturer of the drug Bendectin, which was prescribed to their mothers for prenatal morning sickness. About 17.5 million women received the drug

---

3. The term originates from the use in early theater of an actual device lowered over the stage that represented God's divine intervention and resolution of the conflicts presented in the play. The term is now used metaphorically to describe the cheap and easy resolution of dramatic tension by the introduction of an unexpected character or event at the end of the play. A more recent example might by the appearance of the king's messenger at the end of Molière's *Tartuffe*.

4. 509 U.S. 579 (1993).

between 1957 and 1982. The *Daubert* litigation examines an evidentiary question: What standard of scientific validity justifies placing before a jury the argument that Bendectin caused the plaintiffs' birth defects?

Prior to this litigation the accepted answer to this question derived from *Frye v. United States*[5] which rejected the admissibility of the results of a primitive form of lie detector test. *Frye* stated that "the thing from which the deduction is made must be sufficiently established to have gained general acceptance in the particular field in which it belongs."[6] Defendant Merrell Dow in summary judgment proceedings convinced the trial court that plaintiffs' expert testimony, read in the light most favorable to the plaintiffs, could not meet the *Frye* test. Plaintiffs appealed to the Supreme Court. The Court's 1993 decision in *Daubert* abandoned the *Frye* test. The Court adopted a more flexible standard, emphasizing the traditional touchstones of relevance and reliability.

In reversing the Ninth Circuit, the Supreme Court explained that lower courts should engage in a two-part analysis. First, trial courts must determine whether an expert's testimony reflects "scientific knowledge," whether the findings are "derived by the scientific method," and whether it amounts to "good science." Second, the court must ensure that the expert testimony would logically advance a material aspect of the case. The Supreme Court referred to this as the "fit" requirement.[7]

On remand to the Ninth Circuit, Judge Alex Kozinski announced for a unanimous three-judge panel that he would not remand back to the trial court. Instead, the panel applied the new test to its rereading of the original record. Judge Kozinski stated that appellate courts should review trial court findings made pursuant to the new test under the deferential abuse of discretion standard; however, since the trial record was developed under the old test, he wrote that "the interests of justice and judicial economy will best be served by deciding those issues that are properly before us and, in the process, offering guidance on the application of the *Daubert* standard in this circuit."[8]

The question I would like to pose is whether the process of coming to confident conclusions in murder mysteries is a useful model for assessing the process of determining evidentiary accuracy in litigation. More specifically, does the mystery model as described here assist our ability to analyze the adequacy of two legal moves: 1) Did the Supreme Court justly

---

5. 293 F. 1013 (D.C. Cir. 1923).
6. *Id.* at 1014.
7. 509 U.S. at 588–92.
8. 43 F.3d 1311, 1315 (1995).

substitute the *Daubert* test for the *Frye* test; 2) Did Judge Kozinski justly resolve the claims of the *Daubert* plaintiffs?

IV. Elizabeth

Elizabeth George structures her novel *Playing for the Ashes*[9] by weaving together two perspectives. The story begins with the first of many entries titled simply "Olivia":

> Chris has taken the dogs for a run along the canal…Beans is loping along on the right, flirting with falling into the water. Toast is on the left. About every ten strides, Toast forgets he only has three legs and he starts to go down on his shoulder.
>
> Chris said he wouldn't be gone for long, because he knows how I'm feeling about writing this. But he likes the exercise and once he gets going, the sun and the breeze will make him forget…I'll try not to be cheesed off about this. I need Chris more than ever right now, so I'll tell myself he always means well and I'll try to believe it.[10]

Readers soon conclude that Olivia's entries are a journal, written to a specific but unnamed person for some specific but mysterious purpose. And Olivia notes early on that she is writing as "the trial" begins. Readers get hints in her early journal entries (though it is revealed much later) that Olivia has contracted ALS ("Hawking's Disease"). She has a projected two-to-five-year life expectancy.

These entries intersperse with ordinary numbered chapters, written from the normal authorial third party perspective, that lay out the circumstances of Kenneth Fleming's death and the investigation of it by the independently wealthy Detective Inspector Lord Thomas Lynley and the working-class Detective Sergeant Barbara Havers, the principal characters whose lives Ms. George carries from one novel to her next.

Thus, after Olivia's first entry, Chapter 1 begins: "Less than a quarter of an hour before Martin Snell discovered the crime scene, he was delivering milk." Save for the fact that Ken lived with and was supported strongly by Olivia's mother while Ken (separated from his own wife and family) pursued his career as one of England's greatest cricket players, the bulk of Olivia's entries (which make perhaps a quarter of this long book) have no apparent points of contact with the ordinary narrative. Olivia's audience

9. Elizabeth George, *Playing for the Ashes* (New York: Bantam Books, 1994).
10. *Id.* at 1.

and purpose for writing become one of the many mysteries Ms. George layers together. Because Olivia's journal seems so disconnected from the murder narrative, we expect Ms. George to make the final fit between the two especially convincing.

V. Kozinski's Problem

If we live in a world of infinitely infinite possibilities, academics must make some hard choices: We can redefine a trial as a virtually pure form of play, as a game structured by purely procedural rules where winning one game has no bearing on who should win the next. Or judges can authoritatively impose, for the sake of efficiency, arbitrary limits on how we can classify, and hence what we can legally know, rather like the author who arbitrarily appeals to *deus ex machina* to resolve a plot conflict or mystery. Or we can believe that, despite the infinity of infinities, we can structure the rules to find satisfyingly true and just answers. I argue here that the Supreme Court's majority opinion in *Daubert* affirms the possibility of the third and most optimistic choice.

What caused Jason Daubert's birth defects? Judge Kozinski's opinion on remand nicely sets up the case's mystery:

1. Some chemicals, known as "teratogens," are statistically associated with limb reduction defects when pregnant mothers consume them, e.g., the valid and reliable statistical connection between thalidomide and limb reduction.

2. No scientific model explains a causal relation between the ingestion of these compounds and the defect. No one knows what chemical characteristics of a known teratogen travel along what causal pathways to produce limb reduction defects.

3. A plaintiff may successfully recover damages in spite of this scientific ignorance of actual causal paths if the correlational evidence is sufficiently compelling.

4. No published study has shown a correlation between Bendectin and limb reduction.

5. All published studies show that Bendectin is not a teratogen.

6. None of plaintiffs' proposed experts had done any research on this question prior to being hired by plaintiffs to testify in this case.

7. One group of proposed experts has analyzed previous studies done by others that show no statistically significant correlation. These experts will testify that these studies, reanalyzed, do show a causal connection. They have done no original research on the subject themselves, however.

8. Another group of experts is willing to testify that Bendectin causes limb reduction in humans because it has been shown to cause such defects in laboratory animals.

9. A third group of experts is willing to testify that Bendectin has a chemical structure similar to other suspected teratogens.

10. The Food and Drug Administration continued to approve Bendectin long past the plaintiffs' gestations.

11. Plaintiffs' witness Dr. Palmer would testify, based on his review of the mothers' medical records which reveal the timing and quantities of Bendectin ingested, that Bendectin did in fact cause the limb reduction in these plaintiffs.

12. Something does not become "scientific knowledge" or "derived by the scientific method" simply because a scientist says so. The opposite conclusion could not fit with the substantive standards of review that the Supreme Court set in *Daubert*.

13. The courts, including the appellate courts, properly play a "gatekeeping" role by defining some forms of evidence as inadmissible in spite of its potentially persuasive value.

And so Judge Kozinski wrote:

> Our responsibility . . . is to resolve disputes among respected, well-credentialed scientists about matters squarely within their expertise, in areas where there is no scientific consensus as to what is and what is not "good science," and occasionally to reject such expert testimony because it was not "derived by the scientific method." Mindful of our position in the hierarchy of the federal judiciary, we take a deep breath and proceed with this heady task.[11]

VI. Elizabeth

Who caused Kenneth Fleming's death? *Playing for the Ashes*, like any good mystery, makes its readers continuously conscious of—indeed marvel and reflect upon—the numerous plausible but often mutually inconsistent ways of fitting the objects in the story together. The effect is expansive, cumulative, so that at the peak of suspense we read virtually every sentence as pregnant with potential clues, pushing us simultaneously toward the infinite and toward the most likely killer. This push does not propel us in opposite directions. Our

---

11. 43 F.3d at 1316.

very sensitization to the possibilities increases our need for, our valuing of, the drive to solve the puzzle, to achieve a classification that coheres. To show how this book illustrates the point, let me offer a plot synopsis.

Kenneth Fleming, a promising working-class student and an even more promising cricket player, impregnated Jean in his late teens. He dropped out of school, quit his sport, married her, and fell back into the working class lifestyle to support his family. Jean and Ken had three children: Jimmy (whom we meet as a sixteen-year-old, chain-smoking, juvenile delinquent, a rebel who skips school and refuses to wear his glasses); his younger sister Sharon (Jimmy's virtual opposite—a quiet, thoughtful student and an amateur ornithologist), and his younger brother, Stan (whose frequent "wanking" Jimmy disdainfully describes to his mother).

One of Ken's teachers at the time he dropped out of school, Miriam Whitelaw, now a wealthy widow, did everything to convince Ken not to marry Jean at the expense of his education and career. Years later, she intervened in Ken's life and financed his return to professional cricket. He quickly became a superstar. In the cricket world's fast lane, Ken met and fell in love with the glamorous Gabriella Patten, separated from her husband, Hugh, a wealthy cricket sponsor. Hugh refers to Gabriella as a "fluffy tart." She had convinced Hugh to divorce his first wife. Later, pretending outrage at Hugh's admitted later infidelities and denying her own, she demanded a big divorce settlement from Hugh until he had her tracked to her cottage and photographed while she made love to Ken in the cottage yard.

Ken left his wife and children several years before his death. Pending Gabriella's long-delayed divorce, he has lived, at her urging, with Olivia's mother, Miriam Whitelaw. Miriam, well more than twice Ken's age, denies rumors and allegations of a sexual liaison with Ken at every opportunity throughout the book. Indeed, Miriam leased her country cottage in Kent to Gabriella. There, Gabriella and Ken frequently met, and Ken died.

In the weeks prior to the murder, Ken had, for the first time in the dilatory years of their separation, resolved to end his marriage immediately. He had therefore pushed his wife, Jean, to accelerate their divorce proceedings. Ms. George portrays Jean as virtually consumed by her maternal commitment to her children. Readers suspect that she had hoped Ken would eventually return to her.

On the night of the murder we know that Ken had, earlier the same day, suddenly cancelled plans to take Jimmy on a short vacation to Greece. Ken had learned less than two days before his death of Gabriella's recent casual affairs with some of his own teammates. Ken suddenly cancelled his trip to Greece and returned on the night of his death to the cottage to sever his relationship with Gabriella.

The mystery also compels readers to classify coherently the following objects, revealed in both the investigation and Olivia's journal:

1. That the cottage doors were locked from the outside at the time of the fire.
2. That a key to the cottage, hidden in a specific place in the potting shed, was missing.
3. That Miriam, Jean, Jimmy, and countless others (including perhaps Gabriella's other liaisons) knew the location of the key, and that Hugh knew the location of the cottage, if not the key.
4. That a large number of cigarette butts were found in some bushes along a fence at the edge of the cottage grounds, where someone might have waited, smoking for some time; that the cigarette butts matched the brand that both Jimmy and Jean smoked; that a set of fresh footprints that exactly match Jimmy's set of Doc Martens shoes were found in the mud by the fence.
5. That Gabriella's litter of barely weaned kittens was not found in the cottage with Ken's body, a surprise since the kittens were too young to leave the house on their own.
6. That Miriam Whitelaw, estranged for nearly a decade from her daughter Olivia, had changed her will to leave all her assets to Ken.
7. That at the time of the murder Olivia's disease had seriously debilitated her; that she had lived for a number of years on a houseboat with a man, Chris, who lacked the financial means to care for her properly once her illness progressed to the point of upper-body paralysis; that Olivia would have no place to turn other than to her mother (or her mother's assets, should she inherit them); that Olivia was beginning the process of reconciling with her mother; that Miriam Whitelaw would not have emotional and physical room to care for both Ken and Olivia.
8. That Chris, Olivia's mate, had always refused Olivia's sexual advances; that Chris is the underground leader of the London chapter of "ARM," an animal rights guerilla group that systematically raids laboratories to release (or kill, if they are in great pain), cats, rabbits, and other experimental animals; that in Chris's mind his love for Olivia arises from the same instincts as does his love of animals, an irresistible commitment to give care.
9. That Olivia, who was barely mobile, left the houseboat with Chris's assistance early on the night of the murder and that neither returned until well after dawn.

VII. Cantor Revisited

Thus far in my story, the Supreme Court, Judge Kozinski, and Elizabeth George have each left us pushing outward toward multiple possibilities.

Doing so seems to prevent closure, to perpetuate indecision. One scientist wishes the chance to persuade a jury that Bendectin is chemically so similar to known teratogens that the jury can plausibly find a causal relation in this case. Another asks for the chance to persuade a jury that causation in lab animals is similar enough to human causation to reach that conclusion. Another insists that he can demonstrate an actual physiological cause of damage to these two children while *in utero*. All experts claim to possess valid scientific knowledge. All claim to meet the *Daubert* test. Yet no published results support their assertions. Indeed all published analysis concludes that Bendectin is not a teratogen. Experts can classify data in an infinite number of ways. If we allow anyone who calls herself a scientist to put any classification she chooses before a jury, will trials therefore inevitably become pure play, perhaps little more than legal food fights?

Jimmy's footprints were found by the cottage fence, so fresh as to date from close to the time of Ken's death. His father has bitterly disappointed him, doubly abandoned him by cancelling their trip to Greece and moving swiftly to divorce Jimmy's mother. Jean's hopes for a reconciliation have been seemingly ended forever. Kenneth stands in the way of Olivia's reconciliation with her mother and her chance to die peacefully (or at least Chris, who has demonstrated his willingness to kill animals out of kindness, believes that is so). And the kittens are missing. Ken's impending wedding to Gabriella (unknown to Olivia due to her estrangement from her mother) means the end of Miriam Whitelaw's unique friendship with Ken. Gabriella has just been jilted.

Author and judge must eschew LaRue's "luxury of refusing to come to a decision." They must persuade us that one classification of the objects is so much a better fit than the others as to deserve the labels of true and just. Thus we return to the central problem, how to avoid the *deus ex machina*. If objects are infinitely classifiable, are all choices necessarily arbitrary? If so, classic liberalism has a serious problem.

Wittgenstein once wrote that "what a thing really is depends on the fictions I surround it with." We are coherence seekers. We continuously create theories that interact with experience not to expand classifications but to choose which classification best satisfies. It is a primary way we affirm life. Thus the milkman, Martin Snell:

> He lifted the top of the milk box. He started to place his delivery inside. He stopped. He frowned. Something wasn't right.
>
> Yesterday's milk hadn't been fetched. The bottle was warm. Whatever condensation had gathered on the glass and dripped to the bottle's base had long since evaporated.
>
> Well, he thought at first, she's a flighty one, is Miss Gabriella. She's gone off somewhere without leaving a note about her milk. He picked up

yesterday's bottle and tucked it under his arm. He'd stop delivering till he heard from her again.

He started back towards the gate, but then he remembered. The gate, the gate. Off the latch, he thought, and he felt a flutter of trepidation.

Slowly, he retraced his steps to the milk box. He stood in front of the garden gate. Her newspapers hadn't been fetched either, he saw. Yesterday's and today's—one copy each of the Daily Mail and The Times—were in their respective holders. And when he squinted at the front door with its iron slot for the post, he saw a small triangle of white resting against the weathered oak and he thought, She's not fetched the post either; she must be gone. But the curtains were opened at the windows, which didn't seem practical or wise if she'd taken off. Not that Miss Gabriella appeared to be either practical or wise by nature, but she'd know enough not to leave the cottage so obviously unoccupied. Wouldn't she?

He wasn't certain. He looked over his shoulder at the garage, a brick and clapboard structure at the top of the drive. Best to check, he decided. He wouldn't need to go in or even to open the door all the way. He'd just need a peek to make sure she'd gone. Then he'd take away the milk, he'd carry the newspapers off to the rubbish, and he'd be on his way. After a peek.

The garage was big enough for two cars and the doors to it opened in the centre. They usually had a padlock, but Martin could see without a close inspection that the lock wasn't currently being used. One of the doors stood open a good three inches. Martin went to the door and with an indrawn breath and a glance in the direction of the cottage, he eased it open one inch more and pressed his face to the crack.

He saw a glimmer of chrome as the light struck the bumper of the silver Aston Martin that he'd seen her spinning along the lanes in, a dozen times or more. Martin felt a peculiar buzzing in his head at the sight of it. He looked back at the cottage.

If the car was here and she was here, then why had she not taken in her milk?

Perhaps she'd been gone all day yesterday from early morning, he answered himself. Perhaps she got home late and forgotten about the milk altogether.

But what about the newspapers? Unlike the milk, they were in plain sight in their holders. She'd have had to walk right past them to go into the cottage. Why wouldn't she have taken them with her?

Because she'd been shopping in London and her arms were filled with packages and she'd simply forgotten to fetch the newspapers later, once she'd set the packages down.

And the post? It would be lying right inside the front door. Why would she have left it there?

Because it was late, she was tired, she wanted to go to bed, and she hadn't gone in the front door anyway. She'd gone in through the kitchen so she hadn't seen the post. She had walked right by it and gone up to bed where even now she was still asleep.

Asleep, asleep. Sweet Gabriella. In a black silk gown with her hair curled against it and her lashes like buttercup filaments against her skin.

It wouldn't hurt to check, Martin thought. Most definitely, it wouldn't hurt to check. She wouldn't be miffed. That wasn't her way. She'd be touched that he thought of her, a woman alone out here in the country without a man to see to her welfare. She'd likely ask him in.

He settled his shoulders, took the newspapers, and pushed open the gate. He made his way along the path. The sun hadn't struck this part of the garden yet, so the dew still lay like a beaded shawl on the bricks and the lawn. Against both sides of the old front door, lavender and wall-flowers were planted. Buds on the first sent up a sharp fragrance. Flowers on the second nodded with the weight of the morning's moisture.

Martin reached for the bell-pull and heard its jangle just inside the door. He waited for the sound of her footsteps or her voice calling out or the whirl and clank of the key in the lock. But none of that happened.

Perhaps, he thought, she was having her bath, or perhaps she was in the kitchen where, perhaps again, she couldn't hear the bell. It would be wise to check.

He did so, going round to thump on the back door and wondering how people managed to use it without knocking themselves senseless on the lintel, which hung only five feet from the ground. Which then made him think . . . Could she have been in a rush to get in or get out? Could she have rendered her sweet self unconscious? There was neither answer nor movement behind the white panels. Could she be lying this very moment on the cold kitchen floor, waiting for someone to find her?

To the right of the door, beneath an arbour, a casement window looked into the kitchen. And Martin looked into the window. But he couldn't see anything beyond a small linen-covered table, the work top, the Aga, the sink, and the closed door to the dining room. He'd have to find another window. And one preferably on this side of the house because he was feel-ing decidedly uneasy about peering through the windows like a Peeping Tom. It wouldn't do to be seen from the road. God alone knew what it would do to business if someone drove by and saw Martin Snell, milk-man and monarchist, having a peek where he oughtn't.

He had to climb through a flower-bed to get to the dining room win-dow on this same side of the house. He did his best not to trample the violets. He squeezed behind a lilac bush and gained the glass.

Odd, he thought. He couldn't see through it. He could see the shape of curtains against it, open like the others but nothing more. It seemed to be dirty, filthy in fact, which was even stranger because the kitchen win-dow had been clean as brook water and the cottage itself was as white as a lamb. He rubbed his fingers against the glass. Strangest of all. The glass wasn't dirty. At least, not on the outside.

Something jangled in his mind, some sort of warning that he couldn't identify. It sounded like a flock of snow buntings in flight, soft then loud then louder again. The noise in his head made his arms feel weak.

> He climbed out of the flower bed. He retraced his steps. He tried the back door. Locked. He hurried to the front door. Locked as well. He strode round the south side of the house where wisteria grew against the exposed black timbers. He turned the corner and made his way along the gladstone path that bordered the structure's west wall. At the far end, he found the other dining room window.
>
> This one wasn't dirty, either outside or in. He grasped onto its sill. He took a breath. He looked.[12]

Martin Snell moves toward a truth by constantly applying a coherence test to an unfolding set of evidence. As if to underscore the life-affirming appeal of this construction of "truth by coherence" (the same appeal of the murder mystery itself!), Ms. George gives us an Olivia who affirms death. Prior to meeting Chris, Olivia had lived the viciously nihilistic life of a strung-out, punk prostitute. Olivia's father died suddenly of heart failure minutes after a chance public encounter with Olivia. She, drugged and drunk, let two men stimulate her genitals before him and propositioned him crudely while he and Miriam waited for a car at night near Covent Garden. Olivia never saw her mother again until the night, more than a decade later, that Ken died.

Seeking good classifications, i.e., seeking justice and truth, affirms life. We properly react to those who do justice at any level of classifying and choosing—fact finding and rule making—by asking whether we trust the sincerity of their efforts to make things fit. Mysteries left unsolved imply nihilism's triumph, a triumph of life's meaninglessness and incoherence apart from raw acts of will and power.

One confusion I need to forestall is this: I have deliberately imbedded mysteries in this essay, but I am not thereby trying to tease my readers. I have not said, perhaps via an abstract, either who killed Kenneth Fleming or how Judge Kozinski disposed of *Daubert* or how I connect the two. But let me reiterate that, in spite of Cantor's theorem, I have claimed throughout this paper that the power of the judge and the power of the author need not ultimately reach arbitrary and authoritarian conclusions. Just the contrary. We all know that in a mystery (but not necessarily all books, e.g., the Holy Bible), a plot whose solution depends on the intervention of *deus ex machina* disappoints. When we read mysteries we experience standards of coherence and fit as strong constraints on arbitrary authority. I've structured this essay to present mysteries to solve so that readers can participate in the construction of its truth. Just like jurors at trial.

If we are on to something accurate and attractive here, then both the mystery novel and the law, done well, pose powerful refutations of various charges levelled against post-modern thought, for example that it is nec-

---

12. *Playing for the Ashes* at 13–15.

essarily nihilistic, or self-refuting, or conservative. Without resorting to Dworkin's Hercules, we may refute the proposition that we live in a world in which the powerful merely construct and enforce the frames of discourse. Truth depends on its framing, but some frames are more coherent than others. Especially so when we participate in the framing rather than having them dictated to us at the outset. So the good mystery framer would have us believe.

So, we should not treat mystery stories, or their writers, as teases. They earn our trust first by reminding us of what we already know—that the objects in our lives mean many, often mutually contradictory, things and that life, including the life of science, is profoundly mysterious. The mystery, sometimes almost brutally, exposes us to the infinite possibilities of classification. It impels us, like Martin the milkman, to make the connections that in turn affirm our capacity to trust the goodness of the meanings we collectively create.

VIII. Elizabeth

Playing for Ashes does not disappoint. We come to delight in and then be moved by the connections and meanings that George's mystery compels us to make. For example, we get to know Kenneth Fleming's complexities primarily through the characters of his three children. When Jean asks Jimmy—the street-tough, gritty competitor and rebellious loner— to tell her how his dad explained the sudden cancellation of their trip, Jimmy only lights a match and, showing no sign of pain, lets it burn down until it sears his finger. The act implicates Jimmy in the murder, but it simultaneously teaches us about Ken. We meet Jimmy side-by-side with his caring and responsible sister, an avid student of birds, and know Ken's observant, scholarly side better. Stan's "wanking" underscores Ken's sexual attraction to Gabriella Patten.

More central to my theme here, Ms. George's solution to the mystery of Ken's death does not disappoint because, while it inevitably involves many authorial choices, these choices cohere. Only readers of the novel can fully appreciate this, but I can suggest enough. The coherence that avoids the *deus ex machina* disappointment at the novel's conclusion solves the novel's first mystery: Why did Ms. George choose her one epigraph? Why must we, and how can we, see the scars of love's wounds?

Somewhere past the middle of the book, readers, if I can project my own reading experience, will begin tentatively deciding "who did it," and why. That choice may change (indeed a reader who doggedly defends her earliest solution will miss much of the fun), but we cannot help experiencing our capacity to arrive at the truth, to make our own best fits. And we experience a liberal desire to do so *with* the author, the authority, rather than wait for the authority to dictate the truth to us. Let me try to hint at that experience.

When Detectives Lynley and Havers questioned Jimmy, he soon confessed to the crime and produced the key missing from the potting shed. However, Jimmy refused at first to report any details of the crime. In part because he was a juvenile and in part because Lynley's instincts told him something in Jimmy's story didn't fit, Lynley did not arrest Jimmy in spite of the footprint match. The murder made front-page news across England. Reporters hounded Lynley and Havers, knew of their repeated questioning of Jimmy both at his home and at headquarters, and generated great pressure on New Scotland Yard to arrest him. But by the time forensics showed the cigarettes used in the incendiary device and Jimmy's cigarette brand did not match (though Jimmy's brand did match the pile of butts near the fence), Lynley had goaded Jimmy into telling the "facts" about the killing that absolutely did not fit with other corroborated statements. For example, Jimmy said that he saw Ken and Gabriella making love, impulsively grabbed the key from the potting shed and started the fire. But Jimmy would not (and presumably could not) have said whether the doors were locked, or how the fire had started. He knew nothing about the kittens.

Readers thus know by midpoint in the book that Jimmy was at the cottage very near the time of the killing but did not start the fire. Did he see the killer? Was he in league with the killer? Has he been protecting the killer? Did he hate his father so much that he wants to think of himself as the killer? Has he been so wounded that he merely wants to end it all? (And, if they have mused earlier about the sins of the fathers and sons, readers might briefly reopen the possibility that Ken *did* commit suicide.)

The climactic confrontation between Lynley and Jimmy follows a long foot chase ending with Lynley, rather implausibly, pulling a wild and exhausted Jimmy from the River Thames shortly before they both would have drowned. Jimmy, defeated and exhausted, then gasps to his worried mother, who has just arrived at his side, "Saw.... Saw you there. That night.... Dad.... It was dark but I saw." Jimmy has throughout protected his mother, and thereby himself from the loss of his remaining parent. He had burned the match down until it seared his finger as if to say, "I'll never tell."

But Jimmy was mistaken. Jean did not kill Ken. Readers have already eliminated this woman, preoccupied by her care for her children, as a killer who would deprive the children of their father or the financial support his athletic career promised. While still gasping and coughing on the banks of the Thames, Lynley, who knows Jimmy's nearsightedness, asks him whether he was wearing his glasses. Jimmy shakes his head in the negative. He saw someone, but whom?

Presumably a woman, but Olivia was in no shape to commit the crime. Miriam Whitelaw? What motive would she have to kill the only man left in her life, her most favored protegee whom she dearly loved? Besides, we know she fainted dead away when Lynley told her Kenneth had died.

Lynley convinces Jimmy that his mother is not the killer and they come to an understanding. The only way to flush out the real killer would be to put Jimmy on trial. Only the inspectors, Jean, Jimmy, and the true killer know he is innocent. Will the threat of a miscarriage of justice force the actual killer to come forward?

And now Ms. George fits her pieces together. On the evening of the killing, Chris had driven the debilitated Olivia to her mother's house to begin the reconciliation that would assure Olivia adequate care in her dying years. Olivia from her youth had a key to her mother's house. She saw lights, heard music, got no response, and tired, let herself in. But her mother wasn't there. Olivia waited for hours. Near midnight the lights, on an automatic timer, suddenly went out. She eventually fell asleep. Her mother's arrival at 3:00 a.m. awakened her. Her mother's flustering seemed natural, since she had not seen Olivia since her husband had died, and had not known of Olivia's illness. Miriam Whitelaw, after taking what seemed to Olivia an excessively long time to change, returned, smelling a bit of gin, whereupon Miriam, somewhat excitedly, seemed eager to reconcile. She fully sympathized with Olivia's plight. She promised to help. They talked until Chris retrieved Olivia after dawn.

Two days later the papers carry the surprising news of Ken's death. Hearing nothing from her mother, but knowing how the news must have devastated her, Olivia returns to her mother's home, this a few hours after Miriam has finished giving all the evidence she can to the police. Miriam had tried to kill Gabriella and had chosen Ken's trip to Greece as the safest time to do so. This night she has prepared the warm bath and the razors for her suicide. But when Olivia arrives the second time, Miriam emerges, dazed from the bathroom. Knowing Olivia's plight, she says, "I could not cut. I could not leave you in your condition." And, for the same reason, she would not confess to the murder.

If Ms. George had limited her mystery to the question of who killed Kenneth Fleming and why, she would disappoint her readers. Within that frame, the coincidental return of the prodigal Olivia on the night of the murder *is* a disappointing *deus ex machina*. It would conflict with my coherence thesis. Her return the next night, when she learns her mother killed Kenneth by mistake, follows fittingly from the first visit. But the first visit is too coincidental.

The creator thus presents us with another puzzle. Ms. George crafts her book so that virtually every detail—Jimmy produces the key; Miriam smells of gin—plausibly fits in mutually inconsistent categories. Why would she throw in such a coincidence? The original epigraph gives us a strong clue. (Indeed, all three of the George novels that I have read give, in retrospect, powerful revelations about their deepest mysteries at the very outset.) This is not a murder mystery; it is a love mystery. "Playing for the ashes," a term derived from an event in the history of cricket competition between England and Australia, refers to love's wounds and scars, and to the nearly infinite number of forms that love can take as it both wounds and heals:

1. Olivia's many casual sexual encounters, motivated by the satisfactions of rebellion and pay, kill her father.
2. Ken's adult lusts lead to the end of his marriage and, indeed, his death.
3. Ken and Jean's puppy love, a childhood friendship, creates an unwanted pregnancy.
4. Ken's love of and sense of duty to family leads to a mismatched marriage and, for a time, a wasted talent.
5. Olivia interprets Chris's chaste caring and support for her, based on pure friendship and simple gifts, as physical rejection of her.
6. Miriam's chaste love of Ken's beauty and excellence induces her to attempt to kill the "fluffy tart," Gabriella Patten, in order to preserve the beautiful, to prevent Ken from making the same mistake twice. Instead she kills what she most loves.
7. Chris's leadership of ARM illustrates a love of animals—or is it a love of justice?—blind enough to risk human life.
8. Jean's devotion to her children deprives her of any evident external happiness. She is constantly tired and frazzled. For a time she suspects Jimmy is the killer and is willing to protect him from the law.
9. Jimmy, convinced that his mother killed his father, loves his mother enough not only to go to prison but to accept for the rest of his life the false identity as his own father's killer. He becomes again his father's son, the man willing in his teens to make sacrifices for his family that border on suicide.
10. Ken's love of honesty, his impulse to confront Gabriella's dishonesty, leads him to break off a trip with his son that could have brought father and son closer together.

Note that I've derived ten classifications of love's two edges in this book. I'm still counting the ways. To complete the coherent reading of this book as love mystery, we need two more examples that tell why, in this revised frame, Olivia's coincidental return home was no mere *deus ex machina*.

11. Miriam now faces a deep dilemma. Will her love for her own flesh, her sympathy for her only daughter who is now dying, and the

powerful act of reconciliation itself, lead her to remain silent, silent while the son of the man she has loved most goes to prison unjustly accused? Recall that this love led her *not* to take her own life when she, of all the wounded and scarred people in the novel, had the best reason to commit suicide. Only Olivia, Miriam decides, should have the power to resolve the dilemma of love.

12. Will Olivia, a destructive self-lover and a cynical liar for the better part of her life, now abandon her own mother and her own source of security for the sake of justice to a boy she has never met and knows only as the son of a man Miriam had openly preferred to Olivia when Olivia and Kenneth were children? Olivia's journal, written specifically to Inspector Lynley, answers affirmatively. For justice's sake she reports her mother's guilt. Olivia thus cuts herself off from her mother's reconciliation and love in her dying months. But has Olivia acted selfishly? Has she simply chosen to affirm life rather than death now that she faces it? Or does she do it for Chris's security, and ultimately her own? By telling all, including the alibis only afforded by ARM's illegal raids on and destructions of animal research sites, she creates an implicit bargain with Lynley and New Scotland Yard not to arrest Chris for his part in ARM. But there is more, and it strongly suggests Olivia's selflessness. Olivia knows Chris has a long-time girl friend, Amanda. As she finishes her journal, Olivia asks Chris to make the final decision whether to send it to Lynley. Here is the passage:

> "So I've done it," I say. I feel his fingers tighten on mine. I say, "If I send this to him, Chris, I can't go home. I'm here. We're stuck. You and I. Me. The mess that I am. You can't... You and... You won't be able to..." I can't quite say the rest. The words are so easy — You and Amanda can't be together the way you'd like to be while I'm still here and I'm still alive, Chris. Have you thought of that? — but I can't say them. I can't say her name. I can't put her name with his.
>
> He doesn't move. He watches me. Outside the light is growing steadily. I hear a duck flap on the surface of the canal, taking off or landing, impossible to tell.
>
> "It's not easy," Chris says evenly. "But it's right, Livie. I do believe that."

Readers of mysteries, like triers of fact in cases that depend on complex and inconclusive scientific evidence (and like Martin, the milkman), read and listen and look for ways to make judgments. They (we all) make judgments by choosing which truth claim, among competing claims inherent in the material, makes the elements of the problem fit together. Ms. George models how we do that. She might say, "I hereby give you a choice: You can read this book as a murder mystery, but I want you, more deeply, to read it as a meditation on the double-edged nature of love. So, I present to you, quite deliberately, Olivia's first encounter with her mother. Precisely because, as a device for solving the 'whodunit,' it cheapens the internal coherence of the mystery—in a story where all the other pieces fit so tightly—I hope this device will move you in a different direction. Olivia's encounter with her mother on the night of the murder fits far better if we see it as a necessary event. Miriam, Olivia, and Chris have suffered love's most heart-wrenching wounds, and my story must give you a way to see them, indeed to see my entire story not as a murder to be solved but as a way of seeing love's inevitable wounding, and simultaneously its healing."

IX. The Supreme Court's Decision in *Daubert*

In a world in which we now acknowledge multiple possible but mutually inconsistent realities (a world ushered in in part by the official acknowledgment of the scientific community that falsifiability is the essence of scientific theorizing), does it make sense to abandon the 70-year-old *Frye* test requiring evidence be generally accepted in the scientific community? Yes. Application of the *Frye* test in the sixteenth century would presumably have upheld the Church's condemnation of Galileo. Just as in the mystery genre, we know that mysteries cannot be solved by wholesale rules about general acceptability. Mysteries, like whether Bendectin is a teratogen, get solved at retail, one at a time, where facing the infinity of possibilities allows us to choose the best one confidently.

Note that I really make two separate claims here. First, I suggest that mysteries of the quality of *Playing for the Ashes* suggest generic standards, standards of good fit, that apply to all liberal legal reasoning. This attempt to rescue liberalism does not, however, link the novel to the particular problem posed by *Daubert*. My second claim holds that this novel gives specific additional help in deciding on the potential rules governing the admissibility of scientific evidence.

The Supreme Court's opinion fares well under both my claims, but let me analyze it primarily in terms of the first claim. How coherently did the Court state and justify its alternative? Charles Fried, former U. S. Solicitor General, represented the losing party, Merrell Dow. Not incidentally, he had written in 1981:

> [Philosophy proposes] an elaborate structure of argument and considerations which descend from on high but stop some twenty feet above the ground... [Lawyers and judges] are the masters of the "artificial Reason of the Law." There really is a distinct and special subject matter for our profession. And there is an distinct method down there in the last twenty feet. It is the method of analogy and precedent. Analogy and prece-

dent...are the *only* form of reasoning left to the law when general philosophical structures and deductive reasoning give out, overwhelmed by a mass of particular details...[13]

One might read this passage to argue that judges necessarily assert raw arbitrary power, masked in the artificial and technical language of a unique profession, to avoid the overwhelming and paralyzing effects of particular details. Is Fried right?

Justice Blackmun's opinion for the unanimous court held that nothing in either the language or the history of the adoption of Federal Rule of Evidence 702 necessarily mandated application of the *Frye* test. Rule 702 states in part:

> If scientific, technical, or other specialized knowledge will assist the trier of fact to understand the evidence or to determine a fact in issue, a witness qualified as an expert by knowledge, skill, experience, training, or education, may testify thereto in the form of an opinion or otherwise.

Justices Rehnquist and Stevens would at this point have simply remanded and allowed lower courts the first crack at interpreting Rule 702 in the light of *Frye*'s demise. But for a seven-person majority, Blackmun reached additional substantive conclusions:[14]

1. Trial judges remain responsible for insuring that admitted evidence is both reliable and relevant.
2. In order to qualify as scientific knowledge, an inference or assertion must be derived by the scientific method. Proposed testimony must be supported by appropriate validation, i.e., "good grounds," based on what is known.
3. Blackmun next describes the "fit" test. He uses a simple example: An analysis of the phases of the moon to show potential lunar illumination on a given night would presumably be accepted, but arguments that full moons cause irrational behavior would not be absent some "scientific" verification of a fit between moon phases and behavior.
4. In order to decide whether knowledge is both scientific and fitted to the task at hand, judges should ordinarily consider:
   a. Whether a theory or technique can be (and has been) tested and subjected to falsification;
   b. Whether a theory or technique has been subjected to peer review, though not necessarily publication, since "[s]ome

---

13. Charles Fried, "The Artificial Reason of the Law or: What Lawyers Know," 60 *Tex. L. Rev.* 35, 57 (1982).

14. See *Daubert*, 509 U.S. at 587–95.

propositions...are too particular, too new, or of too limited interest to be published."

c. The known or potential error rate in any particular technique.

d. That a limited version of *Frye*'s general acceptance concept still may play a role, e.g., suggesting that "'A known technique that has been able to attract only minimal support within the community' [citation omitted] may properly be viewed with skepticism."

e. That abandoning an absolute general acceptance test need not result in a free-for-all fight before "befuddled" juries and powerless judges. Judges may still grant summary judgment. They may also direct verdicts if after cross-examination the reasonable juror could not conclude that plaintiff's position was more likely true than not.

The majority's final point is worth quoting at length:

> [T]here are differences between the quest for truth in the courtroom and the quest for truth in the laboratory. Scientific conclusions are subject to perpetual revision. Law, on the other hand, must resolve disputes finally and quickly. The scientific project is advanced by broad and wide-ranging consideration of a multitude of hypotheses, for those that are incorrect will eventually be shown to be so, and that in itself is an advance. Conjectures that are probably wrong are of little use, however, in the project of reaching a quick, final, and binding legal judgment—often of great consequence—about a particular set of events in the past. We recognize that in practice a gatekeeping role for the judge, no matter how flexible, inevitably on occasion will prevent the jury from learning of authentic insights and innovations. That nevertheless, is the balance that is struck by the Rules of Evidence designed not for the exhaustive search for the cosmic understanding but for the particularized resolution of legal disputes.[15]

How well does Blackmun's opinion stand up to my general claim that we can solve legal mysteries without *deus ex machina* solutions? Very well, I think. I find it coherent and fitting (with the exception of the full moon example, which strikes me as an example not of fit but of reliability) at virtually every level. Should and could the Court have been more specific? Not without incoherently violating its very justification—*Frye*'s premise that scientists generate general agreement about truth is false—for abandoning *Frye* in the first place.

More important, by acknowledging that we live in the same evidentiary world of Cantor's Theorem, Russell's Paradox, and mysteries of the kind

---

15. *Id.* at 597.

Elizabeth George gives us, the Court builds connections to us, not just to we who call ourselves scholars but to us as we sit as jurors, and to trial judges. Just as Elizabeth George makes connections by ranging far beyond the techniques of forensics and sleuthing, the majority repeatedly goes beyond Fried's "artificial reason of the law." Blackmun's opinion relies on Karl Popper's endorsement of falsifiability as science's sine qua non. It is not ashamed to take definitions of basic terms from Webster's Third International Dictionary. It quotes us briefs from individuals, from the National Academy of Sciences, and from the American Association for the Advancement of Science to affirm a community broader than "the law."

> Indeed, scientists do not assert that they know what is immutably "true" — they are committed to searching for new, temporary theories to explain as best they can, phenomena. [And] Science is not an encyclopedic body of knowledge about the universe. Instead, it represents a *process* for proposing and refining theoretical explanations about the world that are subject to further testing and refinement.[16]

Blackmun's opinion explores Hempel's *Philosophy of Natural Science* and essays from *The New England Journal of Medicine* and *The Journal of the American Medical Association* with titles like "How Good is Peer Review?" and "The Philosophical Basis for Peer Review."[17] And the opinion, by quoting Cardozo, concludes with a hint that law can achieve beauty:

> The work of a judge is in one sense enduring and in another ephemeral...
> In the endless process of testing and retesting, there is a constant rejection of the dross and a constant retention of whatever is pure and sound and fine.[18]

Post-modernist thought may redefine what is pure and sound and fine, but it does not abandon Cardozo's aspiration. More important, as *Playing for the Ashes* illustrates, we continue to believe we achieve it. Blackmun helps us participate by fitting together objects from well beyond the boundaries that the artificial reason of the law sets, just as Ms. George empowers our participation with her by fitting together not technical forensics, but the ways love connects life and death.

By contrast, in dissent Chief Justice Rehnquist disconnects from us by writing:

---

16. *Id.* at 590 (emphasis in original).
17. *Id.* at 593–94.
18. *Id.* at 597 n.13.

I defer to no one in my confidence in federal judges; but I am at a loss to know what is meant when it is said that the scientific status of a theory depends on its "falsifiability," and I suspect some of them will be, too.[19]

X. Kozinski's Solution

Blackmun's majority opinion satisfies internal coherence tests. It avoids *deus ex machina*, and thus enhances its authority and trustworthiness. It goes beyond itself to connect with and build on beliefs and constructions in a larger community. Just as Ms. George trusts her readers to construct the mystery story with her, so the Blackmun opinion trusts us to construct our appreciation of evidentiary uncertainty with him. More important, his opinion trusts judges to do the same as they grapple with the mysteries of scientific knowledge introduced in specific cases. This trust is a form of love.

Now let us put Judge Kozinski's subsequent opinion to this test. Ms. George's novel implies three conclusions:

1. If we believe that mysteries are solved at retail, confident conclusions in a liberal culture require that those with final power to decide must, like her readers, have the chance to grapple with the infinite range of possible conclusions.
2. Confident participation in truth-finding—deciding what to believe and why—involves rejecting possibilities, narrowing, of saying what does not fit as much as what does. (We put each of Ken's possible killers to a test very much like scientific falsifiability.)
3. We make confident sense of the immediate by placing it in a larger theoretical frame. Ken's death makes sense in the larger context of love's emotions and motives. Whether Bendectin causes birth defects becomes knowable only when we place it in the larger frame that defines what testable knowledge is.

I read the Supreme Court's majority opinion as consistent with these specific lessons. I cannot read Judge Kozinski's opinion on remand that way. His opinion, to be sure, structures his solution to the Bendectin mystery very much as Elizabeth George structures the solution to the mystery of Kenneth's death. We can connect with it rhetorically. Both authors first construct the many different ways the problem might be resolved and then taper back to a choice, something Blackmun's rhetoric does not do. Both authors acknowl-

---

19. *Id.* at 600.

edge, directly in Kozinski's case, indirectly in George's, that their highest task is to persuade us that no *deus ex machina* drives their conclusion.

Judge Kozinski, having taken the deep breath quoted above, immediately moves to apply the first half of the *Daubert* test. Having titled the preceding section "Brave New World," he titles this section of his opinion "Deus ex Machina." Because he draws our attention so explicitly to the problem of arbitrary judicial power, he heightens our expectation that he will make no arbitrary moves. But he makes them.

Ultimately, Judge Kozinski forecloses the option of remanding to the District Court, even though no one in the litigation has challenged either the scientific credentials of plaintiffs' witnesses nor the conventionality of the research techniques they used. This is not a case in which a murderer wants to plead innocent by reason of insanity because the moon was full. Justice Blackmun's opinion at no point suggests that appellate courts are in a better position than either the Supreme Court or the original trier of fact to apply the new test to the admissibility of Daubert's evidence.

When Judge Kozinski evaluates plaintiffs' claims in light of various indicators of scientific validity, he cavalierly dismisses some that the Court states and relies heavily on others Blackmun never mentioned. He first considers whether the theory or technique employed by plaintiffs' experts is generally accepted in the scientific community and whether the rate of error reported by both is acceptable. He notes that the only expert who claims that he "specifically performed studies" on Bendectin never reported the methodology or technique he used, so there is no way of assessing its general acceptability. He then points out that all of the re-analyzed data presumably used valid tests of acceptability and rates of error but the authors do not explain why old and new results directly conflict. But is this not a matter to be resolved at trial, or at the very least by the trier of fact in summary judgment under the new *Daubert* standard? Kozinski does not say. In a footnote he dismissively writes: "As to such derivative analytical work, it makes little sense to ask whether the technique employed " 'can be or has been tested'... or what its 'known rate of error' might be."[20] Why not?

Citing Huber's *Galileo's Revenge: Junk Science in the Courtroom*, Kozinski's opinion emphasizes the fact that none of the experts had done any research on Bendectin prior to being hired by plaintiffs in this case. Here Kozinski addresses the pragmatics of independent versus hired gun research:

> [I]ndependent research carries its own indicia of reliability, as it is conducted, so to speak, in the usual course of business and must normally

---

20. 43 F.3d at 1317 n. 4 (book describes how the prevalent practice of expert-shopping leads to bad science) (citations omitted).

satisfy a variety of standards to attract funding and institutional support. Finally, there is usually a limited number of scientists actively conducting research on the very subject that is germane to a particular case, which provides a natural constraint on parties' ability to shop for experts who will come to the desired conclusion.[21]

Kozinski's allusions to the evils of junk science here make perhaps the most persuasive part of his opinion. But Blackmun's controlling opinion had made no mention of the importance of independent prior research whatsoever.

Having taken some pains to say all this, Judge Kozinski then reverses his field 180 degrees and concedes that, under part one of *Daubert*, he should remand to the District Court to give plaintiffs a chance to reargue their positions and that the actual basis for his holding rests on the conclusions that plaintiffs fail to meet part two of the *Daubert* test. We might quibble by asking why he did not say so at the outset, but the real problem is that in this critical part of the opinion Kozinski becomes narrowly legalistic, unlike Elizabeth George and Blackmun, who satisfy by expanding the kinds of connections we can make as we read. Because this is a diversity case, he turns to California's evidentiary rules. According to Kozinski, California would require that, if the background rate of limb reduction defects is one per thousand, Bendectin be proved to at least double that rate to two per thousand. "None of plaintiffs' epidemiological experts claims that ingestion of Bendectin during pregnancy more than doubles the risk of birth defects."[22] True, but more than double is not what California law says.[23]

California law also requires proof of causation in the specific litigated case. But plaintiffs' experts had not testified to such causation. Well, not exactly: Dr. Palmer would, but Judge Kozinski would forbid his testimony under part one of *Daubert*. But Kozinski has already said he would not decide the summary judgment issue under part one. Moreover, it is not clear that Kozinski is properly applying the part two "fit" test at all. Plaintiffs claim that their experts deserve the opportunity to try to show via accepted scientific techniques that Bendectin caused these defects. They thus claim that their testimony will "assist the trier of fact to understand the evidence or to determine a fact in issue." That is all the fit component requires.

---

21. *Id.*

22. *Id.* at 1320–21.

23. Kozinski relies on a federal case from the Third Circuit interpreting California law. See *id.*, citing *DeLuca v. Merrell Dow Pharmaceuticals, Inc.*, 911 F.2d 941, 958 (3d Cir. 1990).

Kozinski leaves us to conclude that, behind his cute section titles (for example, "No Visible Means of Support"), he invokes only the artificial reason of the law. Like Jimmy, who confesses but refuses at first to talk, and then says things that do not fit in order to wall himself off from those who could help him, Judge Kozinski's opinion frustrates our participation with him. His artificial world, unique to lawyers and judges, not only excludes us, but seems authoritarian, stale, arbitrary and out of touch with egalitarian ways of connecting and knowing and believing. Both his style and his conclusions deny the wisdom that complexity and contradiction and pain give birth to meanings that we variously call love, truth, beauty, and justice.

XI. Conclusion

Critical readers can tell a good mystery novel from a bad mystery novel, even though they are not novelists or experts in criminology or detective work. A familiarity with the pre-existing norms and conventions of the genre, a discerning and attentive disposition, and a sensitivity to the fit between the story and what readers know to be true in their own lives, provide them with all the critical tools they need. Likewise, competent judges need not be experts in biotechnology, medicine, or chemistry in order to evaluate the relevance and reliability of the competing stories they must listen to in the course of complex tort litigation.

Chapter Six

Saul and David, and Corporate Takeover Law

David A. Skeel, Jr.

I.

Delaware has long been the state of choice for the country's largest and most prominent corporations. No other state comes close to matching its roster of publicly held firms. One of the effects of this, and of Delaware's commitment to retaining its preeminence, is that Delaware has by far the most expert and experienced state judiciary with respect to corporate law issues.[1] The expertise of Delaware's judges gives Delaware corporate law decisions a level of certainty and predictability that would-be competitors would have difficulty matching.

Or so the story goes. A great irony of the frequently noted dependability of Delaware decision making is that the case law in one of the most important and prominent areas of corporate law — directors' responsibilities in the context of a hostile takeover bid — is notorious for its *un*certainty, and for what appear to be baffling inconsistencies in the cases. In some of the takeover cases, Delaware courts have scrutinized directorial conduct quite aggressively, yet in others they appear to defer to directors' discretion.[2] At times, the courts have carefully articulated standards for directorial

I am grateful to Jane Baron, Jeff Dunoff, Tom Grey, Max Harris, Paul Heald, Judith Koffler, Geoff Miller, Max Stearns and the participants at the "Literature and Legal Problem Solving" conference at the University of Georgia School of Law for helpful comments on earlier drafts; to Christine Taran for excellent research assistance; and to Temple Law School for generous funding.

1. See, e.g., Roberta Romano, *The Genius of American Corporate Law* (Washington, D.C.: AEI Press, 1993). For a discussion of Delaware's chancery court system, which contributes in significant respects to the quality of Delaware's corporate law decision making by providing a special court for business disputes, see, e.g., David A. Skeel, Jr., "The Unanimity Norm in Delaware Corporate Law," 83 *Va. L. Rev.* 127, 132–36 (1997) and William H. Rehnquist, "The Prominence of the Delaware Court of Chancery in the State-Federal Joint Venture of Providing Justice," 48 *Bus. L.* 351 (1992).

2. Compare *Paramount Communications, Inc. v. QVC Network*, 637 A.2d 34 (Del. 1993) (holding that directors' failure to consider third party bid violated their fiduciary

conduct, but on other occasions they seem to pay little attention to their own standards.[3]

What are we to make of the takeover cases? The response of many commentators has been either to develop Byzantine theories about Delaware doctrine in an effort to fit the divergent outcomes within a single, all-encompassing conceptual scheme, or to simply dismiss the cases as hopelessly incoherent.

In this essay, I would like to propose another way of looking at the Delaware cases that emphasizes a striking aspect of the courts' opinions: their tendency to portray the parties in vividly critical terms and to describe the events of the case as if it were a story.[4] In emphasizing the narrative form of the courts' opinions, I do not suggest that Delaware's doctrinal pronouncements are irrelevant. Instead, I will argue that, while the cases do take corporate law doctrine into account, the principal concern in the decisions is not whether the directors' action technically complies with the mechanical elements of existing doctrine but whether they have faithfully responded to the relevant doctrine.

Much of the analysis will focus on Delaware's two most important recent corporate law cases, *Paramount Communications, Inc. v. Time, Inc.* ("*Time-Warner*")[5] and *Paramount Communications, Inc. v. QVC Network* ("*QVC*").[6] The same corporation, Paramount Communications, was both the bidder who was thwarted in *Time-Warner* and the target corporation who resisted a disfavored bidder in *QVC*. Paramount lost its case in the Delaware Supreme Court on each occasion. In each case, and in others raising similar issues, the directors of the target corporation proceeded with actual knowledge of prior judicial articulations of Delaware takeover law. The directors' response to the formal legal doctrine, and the subsequent judicial evaluation of their performance, provides a particularly valuable perspective on a difficult set of Delaware decisions.

---

duties); with *Paramount Communications, Inc. v. Time, Inc.*, 571 A.2d 1140 (Del. 1989) (deferring to target directors' resistance to unwanted offer).

3. Compare *Unocal Corp. v. Mesa Petroleum Co.*, 493 A.2d 946 (Del. 1985) (establishing two-prong test for scrutinizing directors' use of defensive measures); with *Unitrin v. American General Corp.*, 651 A.2d 1361 (1995) (lenient application of *Unocal* test).

4. For a brief but fascinating description of this aspect of the Delaware case law, see Edward B. Rock, "Preaching to Managers," 17 *J. Corp. L.* 605 (1992) (review of Louis Lowenstein, *Sense and Nonsense in Corporate Finance* (Reading, Mass.: Addison-Wesley, 1991)). See also Edward B. Rock, "Saints and Sinners: The Peculiar Mechanisms of Delaware Corporate Law," 44 *UCLA L. Rev.* 1009 (1997).

5. 571 A.2d 1140 (Del. 1989).

6. 637 A.2d 34 (Del. 1993).

In the spirit of this volume of essays, rather than examining the nature of this conversation between Delaware courts and corporate directors by reference to the cases alone, I will begin in a quite different context: the Biblical narrative of Saul and David. I will look most closely at the events leading to God's rejection of Saul, then complete the analysis with a briefer discussion of, and contrast to, David.

Even at a superficial level, the Biblical narrative bears an intriguing resemblance to the Delaware cases. As with Saul and David, many of the Delaware cases involve opposing personalities. It is hard to resist the comparison between Saul and Paramount's hard luck directors, for instance, and between David and the directors of Time. More important than outcome similarities are the narrative details that highlight the differences between Saul's and David's response to divine commandments, and Paramount's and Time's response to Delaware legal commandments. Examining Saul's plight not only sheds light on why he was rejected while David was not,[7] but also on why the actions of some but not other directors in Delaware corporate law takeover cases constitute breaches of fiduciary duty.[8] Both Saul and David, and the directors in the Delaware cases, are responding to texts they view as authoritative (the Hebrew scriptures and God's instructions to Saul and David, and Delaware's cases and statutory law for the directors).

Before giving a brief overview of the Delaware fiduciary duty case law and describing the *Time-Warner* and *QVC* cases, let me detail relevant aspects of the biblical narrative.

II.

Saul and David are perhaps the most widely known of the Bible's numerous pairs of individuals whose lives are inextricably intertwined. Unlike Cain and Abel or Jacob and Esau, they are not brothers; yet, their lives parallel one another in striking and often uncanny ways. Both are plucked from obscurity and chosen to rule Israel as its king and both establish their

---

7. My analysis of this aspect of the comparison draws on, and has interesting similarities to, the literature on the "Constitution as Scripture," that I discuss at greater length in Part IV.

8. I should mention a caveat that will become obvious as we discuss the Biblical accounts of Saul and David: the narratives are complex and have been subject to a wide range of often conflicting interpretations. I adopt a particular approach, one which inevitably reflects the influence of my own evangelical Christian perspective, but I recognize that this is not the only plausible way to interpret the passages in question.

authority through military prowess. As often is the case in such pairings, however, they meet quite different fates, Saul ending his life as an outcast and David reigning as the most beloved king of Israel.

For present purposes, I would like to focus on the incident that causes God to withdraw his favor from Saul for good, Saul's behavior after his victory over the Amalekites.[9] Samuel, Israel's judge and prophet, had instructed Saul on behalf of God to "attack the Amalekites and totally destroy everything that belongs to them," not sparing any of the people or their livestock.[10] Saul did defeat the Amalekites and destroyed much of the population, but he spared the Amalekite king and kept the best of its sheep and cattle. By the end of the chapter, Saul has been rejected, beginning a downward spiral that concludes with his suicide.

This passage is so puzzling and gripping that I vividly remember when and where I first read it. What struck me on that initial reading was how reasonable, even merciful, Saul's actions seemed, in contrast to the harsh literal instructions God had given him through Samuel. Why not spare a defeated nation and preserve the best of its livestock? The severity and permanence of God's rebuke seemed particularly draconian given Saul's stated intention of offering the unblemished livestock as a sacrifice to God.[11] Moreover, as David replaces Saul, David seems just as flawed himself, as evidenced by his adultery with Bathsheba and the apparent dissembling in his exchange with the priest at Nob.[12]

Some years later I reread this account and was struck by the tension between the account of God's sovereignty, on the one hand, and free will and human accountability on the other. From this perspective, Saul's fall and David's rise illustrate the completeness of God's control over his people.[13]

---

9. The Amalekite incident appears in 1 *Samuel* 15:1–34. The account of Saul's life begins in 1 *Samuel* 13:1, and continues to 1 *Samuel* 31, the conclusion of the first book of Samuel. After the Amalekite incident, David becomes the focus of Samuel's narrative. In addition to *First* and *Second Samuel*, the events of David's life also are described, from a somewhat different perspective, in *First Chronicles*. All Biblical references and quotations are from the New International Version, unless otherwise noted.

10. 1 *Samuel* 15:2–3.

11. 1 *Samuel* 15:15.

12. After David saw Bathsheba taking a bath, he committed adultery with her and when he learned she was pregnant, he had her husband Uriah sent to the front lines to certain death. 2 *Samuel* 11:2–26. In the earlier incident at Nob, David had told the priest that he was carrying out a secret mission for King Saul in order to persuade the priest to feed him and his men, although in reality he was fleeing from Saul rather than carrying out Saul's business. 1 *Samuel* 21:1–6.

13. Jacob and Esau can be seen in these terms, and to a lesser extent, Cain and Abel. The divergent fates of Isaac and Ishmael are an additional example. When Abraham's wife

My intention here is to come at this remarkable and complex narrative by examining Saul's and David's respective responses to divine instruction. While the discussion will center on Saul's and David's individual motives, it is important to keep in mind that the narrative also recounts Israel's collective performance as a nation. The narrative begins with Israel's insistence that it be given a king, so that they can be like the nations around them, despite Samuel's warning to them that the king will mistreat the nation and take much of its wealth for himself.[14]

The obvious difficulty in assessing a Biblical character's response to God is that a primary concern is his faithfulness or unfaithfulness to God, which is a quality of his heart rather than simply of his actions. Thus, it may not be clear from a list of an individual's actions whether his or her performance is one of loyalty and obedience. At times the Biblical narrative simply tells us whether or not an individual's performance, whatever its vicissitudes, is faithful. *Kings* and *Chronicles* frequently do just this, often concluding a brief description of a king with the pronouncement that he did or did not "walk in the ways of the Lord."[15]

The chronicler of Saul and David adopts a much more elaborate approach, employing a variety of narrative strategies whose effect is to produce a vivid and instructive portrayal (one which itself enacts some of the complexity of human life).[16] Perhaps most importantly, the writer uses a careful selection of narrative details, and of focal incidents, to develop a general theme about the character of Saul's and David's performances. One can easily miss this cumulative picture if one focuses on an isolated aspect of the narrative, such as God's rejection of Saul after he spares the king and best livestock of the Amalekites. The Amalekite incident is the cul-

---

Sarah despaired of ever giving birth to the child God had promised Abraham and her, she encouraged Abraham to have a child with her servant Hagar instead. Hagar did bear a son, Ishmael, but both she and Ishmael were banished after Sarah gave birth to Isaac. *Genesis* 21:1–21. For a New Testament account of the story, emphasizing the symbolic distinction between Isaac as heir and Ishmael as servant, see *Galatians* 4:1–31.

14. 1 *Samuel* 8:5–22. Israel's particular concern was that it have "a king to lead us and to go out before us and fight our battles." 1 *Samuel* 8:20.

15. See, e.g., 2 *Chronicles* 17:3–4 (Jehoshaphat "did not seek the Baals, but sought the God of his father and walked in his commandments").

16. For an insightful analysis of Biblical narrative generally, and one that discusses aspects of the accounts of Saul and David as well as numerous other biblical narratives, see Robert Alter, *The Art of Biblical Narrative* (New York: Basic Books, 1981). In addition to drawing on Alter's insights, the discussion that follows can be seen as paralleling in many respects Martha Nussbaum's arguments for a particularized approach to philosophy and reading. See Martha C. Nussbaum, *Love's Knowledge* (New York: Oxford Univ. Press, 1992).

mination of a series of narrative events that suggest a much different perspective on Saul's treatment of the Amalekites.

The first of these incidents took place at Gilgal, after Saul summoned the Nation of Israel to fight the Philistines. Samuel had instructed Saul to wait for him there for seven days, at which time Samuel would arrive to sacrifice burnt and fellowship offerings.[17] In the face of widespread terror among his troops at the end of the seven days, Saul himself made the burnt offering that Samuel had described. As with the Amalekite incident, it is hard not to feel sympathy for Saul's plight, particularly given the apparent tardiness of Samuel. Understandably, Saul defends his disobedience by blaming Samuel for arriving late and argues pragmatically that he needed to seek God's favor because the troops where beginning to scatter. Yet in the brief compass of this incident, we see the beginnings of a general, recurrent theme: the perceptions of those around Saul will divert his obedience to God in a time of crisis, and, more importantly, Saul's own status is in many respects his primary concern.

An incident involving Saul's son Jonathan reinforces this theme. During a subsequent siege of the Philistines, Saul swore to God that anyone who ate anything before he had defeated the Philistines would be cursed.[18] Jonathan, who had left camp on a private foray with his arms bearer, was not aware of the oath and violated the fast by eating honey. Although Saul suggests that Jonathan must die in accordance with the curse, the troops rush to Jonathan's defense and Saul does not have him put to death.[19]

In these details, we see the character traits that surfaced at Gilgal. As at Gilgal, Saul has acted rashly, here by imposing a debilitating fast on his army in the midst of a battle—a dangerous command that seems far less understandable than his call for sacrifices at Gilgal. The writer also gives subtle hints that Saul is interested not in honoring God but in his own glory. In making his oath, for instance, Saul calls for a curse on anyone who eats "before I have avenged myself on my enemies," suggesting that

---

17. 1 *Samuel* 10:8. The Pentateuch (the first five books of the Bible) sets forth the specifications for various kinds of offerings in great detail. Burnt offerings, for instance, were made twice daily and at other times as an expression of devotion to God. *Leviticus* 1:3–17 outlines how the offering must be prepared and requires that the entire offering be burned at the altar. By contrast, because fellowship offerings symbolized peace between God and his people, the offerer ate part of this offering. See *Leviticus* 3:1–17; 7:14–15; 7:31–14.

18. 1 *Samuel* 14:24. The curse occurs after Saul's initial failure to wait for Samuel at Gilgal and prior to his disobeying of the instructions Samuel gives him in connection with Israel's battle with the Amalekites.

19. Saul's treatment of his son Jonathan is complicated by his jealousy of the close relationship between Jonathan and David. Jonathan subsequently helps David to escape when Saul turns against David and attempts to kill him. 1 *Samuel* 20:1–42.

he has his own vendetta and program in mind rather than God.[20] The writer also pointedly notes, when Saul later builds an altar to God, that "it was the first time he had done this"[21] — once more indicating where Saul's focus has and has not been. Finally, in deciding to spare Jonathan, Saul does not admit that his oath was misguided; the narrative suggests instead that he based his decision on his desire to maintain the loyalty of his troops.

Against the backdrop of these previous incidents, Saul's decisions remain understandable, but so does God's rejection of him. We notice, for instance, a narrative detail that the writer has been careful to include: when he goes out to look for Saul, Samuel is told that Saul went to Carmel, where "he has set up a monument in his own honor."[22] Saul lies to Samuel when they meet, insisting that he has dutifully carried out the Lord's instructions to destroy the Amalekites and their livestock. When Samuel exposes the lie, Saul blames his troops, saying that they spared the livestock, claiming that they did so in order to sacrifice the best sheep and cattle to God. Saul finally admits that he has sinned, but even then he does not quite accept full responsibility, saying "I was afraid of the people and so I gave into them,"[23] and begs Samuel to return with him in order to preserve his status among the people.

Saul's contention that the sheep and cattle were spared so that they could be sacrificed to God warrants special mention. This is the second time that Saul attempts to disguise his unfaithful response to God's commandments as faithful, in each case invoking the specific instructions that God had given Israel in order to indicate their dependence on Him and to ask His blessing and mercy. At Gilgal, he had in fact made a burnt offering to God, but he did so in desperation, disobeying the instruction that Samuel was to be the one to make the offering. Here, Saul contends that the livestock would be given as a sacrifice, but as we have already seen, Saul's more immediate concern was probably self-interest.

Just as attending to the narrative details of Saul's behavior helps to explain his rejection, a similar inquiry sheds light on David's success. David was far from perfect himself, as evidenced most spectacularly by his adultery with Bathsheba. Yet, even in his sinfulness, David's performance is characterized by a faithfulness of spirit, in marked contrast to Saul. For instance, after Saul refuses to admit that he has sinned in connection with his victory over the Amalekites, Samuel tells him that God requires obedience, not the cynical resort to sacrifices that Saul has in mind.[24] By con-

---

20. 1 *Samuel* 14:24.

21. 1 *Samuel* 14:35.

22. 1 *Samuel* 15:12.

23. 1 *Samuel* 15:24.

24. 1 *Samuel* 22.

trast, once he is confronted, David immediately admits to his sin with Bathsheba. In fact, in striking counterpoint to Saul's weaseling, David recognizes that the only sacrifice acceptable to God in the face of such a sin is a contrite heart.[25]

III.

From Saul and David, let's shift now to Delaware's two most important corporation law decisions of recent years, *Paramount v. Time*[26] and *Paramount v. QVC*.[27] These cases involve the special fiduciary duties that the directors of a corporation owe to its shareholders in the context of an attempted takeover of the corporation. Before considering the opinions themselves and what commentators have had to say about them, we first should briefly consider the case law that led up to the two decisions.

Delaware courts have traditionally applied two different standards to evaluate directors' performance of their fiduciary duties. Under ordinary circumstances, courts apply the extremely deferential "business judgment rule" standard when shareholders complain about directorial decision making. If a director has a personal interest in the challenged transaction, on the other hand, courts scrutinize the transaction far more aggressively.[28]

The surge of takeover activity in the 1980s posed a conceptual difficulty for the Delaware courts. Directors' resistance to unwanted takeover

---

25. David expresses his repentance in poetic form in Psalm 51, which is worth quoting directly: "O Lord, open my lips,/and my mouth will declare your praise./You do not delight in sacrifice, or I would bring it;/you do not take pleasure in burnt offerings./The sacrifices of God are a broken spirit;/a broken and contrite heart,/O God, you will not despise." *Psalm* 51: 15–17.

26. 571 A.2d 1140 (Del. 1989).

27. 637 A.2d 34 (Del. 1993).

28. See, e.g., *Sinclair Oil Corp. v. Levien*, 280 A.2d 717 (Del. 1971) (contrasting the two standards in the context of a parent corporation's dealings with its subsidiaries). In addition, whereas Delaware's corporation law statute permits a corporation to opt out of the duty of care, corporations cannot waive their directors' duty of loyalty. Del. Code Ann. tit. 8, § 102(b)(7) (1988). And Delaware's statute, like that of most states, has a special provision dealing with duty of loyalty issues, whereas Delaware has left the duty of care to common law. Del. Code Ann. tit. 8, § 144 (1988) (dealing with self-interested transactions).

As with all things in the fiduciary duty context, the relationship between the duties of care and loyalty in the Delaware cases is somewhat more complex and confusing than this overview portrays. See, e.g., *CEDE v. Technicolor, Inc.*, 634 A.2d 345 (Del. 1993) (suggesting that the intrinsic fairness standard applies in the duty of care context once a violation has been shown).

overtures often did not stem from personal greed, yet considering a tender offer was hardly an ordinary business decision, especially given the likelihood that a takeover would cost the directors their jobs. Delaware responded by developing a set of intermediate standards to apply in these cases. In *Unocal Corp. v. Mesa Petroleum Co.*,[29] its Supreme Court announced that directors can use defensive measures to resist a takeover only if the directors reasonably believe that the takeover involves a financial threat to the target corporation and if the scope of the defense is proportionate to the threat. Thereafter, in *Revlon, Inc. v. MacAndrews & Forbes Holding Co.*,[30] the court made clear that directors' options are far more limited once a "sale or breakup" of the corporation becomes inevitable. If the corporation is in the "*Revlon* mode," its directors must focus exclusively on obtaining the highest possible price for their shareholders.[31]

The Delaware Supreme Court's decisions in *Unocal* and *Revlon* have led to frequent speculation by commentators and Delaware's Chancery Court as to how strictly *Unocal* is to be applied and when the special *Revlon* duties require a corporation's directors simply to sell it to the highest bidder. The Delaware Supreme Court addressed these issues in its two most important cases in recent years, *Time-Warner* and *QVC*. Despite broad similarities, however, the two cases seem to reach dramatically different conclusions. Once we have considered the cases and commentators' attempts to make sense of the court's reasoning, we can consider the insights that Saul and David may offer for this difficult corner of corporate law.

A.

In *Time-Warner*, Time's directors began discussing the pros and cons of merging with various possible partners, including both Warner and Paramount, nearly six years before their combination with Warner.[32] Time's directors eventually gravitated toward Warner and after extensive negotiations, much of which concerned managerial responsibilities,[33] the two

---

29. 493 A.2d 946 (Del. 1985).

30. 506 A.2d 173 (Del. 1986).

31. The Delaware Supreme Court put this point a bit more colorfully, holding that the directors' responsibility changes from "defenders of the corporate bastion to auctioneers charged with getting the best price for stockholders at a sale of the company" once a sale or breakup becomes inevitable. 506 A.2d at 182.

32. 571 A.2d at 1143.

33. The chief managerial obstacle was the question of how to give both Time's Nick Nicholas and Warner's Steven Ross a stake in running the combined company. Negotiations initially broke down when Steven Ross refused to agree to step down after five years as co-chief executive, as Time's directors insisted. 571 A.2d at 1145.

companies agreed to engage in a stock-for-stock merger. The original transaction was thwarted, however, when Paramount made a tender offer directly to Time's shareholders shortly before Time's shareholders would have voted on the proposed merger.[34] Fearful that Time's shareholders would prefer the Paramount offer, which offered significantly more value on its face, Time and Warner restructured their deal as a tender offer by Time to the shareholders of Warner in order to eliminate the need for a vote by Time shareholders. Time's directors denounced the Paramount bid as an eleventh hour effort to derail Time's carefully planned merger with Warner.

The Delaware Supreme Court largely agreed and rejected Paramount's request to force Time's directors to remove the defensive measures that stood in the way of Paramount's tender offer. Despite the fact that Warner's shareholders would have controlled 62% of Time-Warner under the original transaction, the Court held that neither this nor the restructured deal amounted to a change in control transaction. Thus, Time's directors never became subject to the stringent *Revlon* duties. Because the Time and Warner directors' decision to restructure their transaction effectively thwarted Paramount's bid, the Court characterized it as a defensive measure subject to scrutiny under *Unocal*. Yet the court defined the "threat" for the purposes of this inquiry quite broadly, suggesting that both the Time directors' ostensible concern that a takeover by Paramount would jeopardize the unique "Time Culture," and the directors' fear that Time's shareholders might "mistakenly" prefer Paramount's bid to a deal with Warner, could be seen as threats to Time that justified defensive action.[35] The Court went on to conclude that Time's response to the threat was reasonable and thus that the directors did not need to make room for the Paramount bid. The Court repeatedly emphasized that the combination with Warner was a carefully thought-out component of Time's long-term business plan and

---

34. Unlike a merger proposal, which is a corporate transaction that requires not only directorial approval, but also (ordinarily) an affirmative vote of the shareholders of both corporations, a tender offer is in form simply an offer by the offeror to buy a given amount of stock from the holders of the stock at a given price. The initial transaction in *Time-Warner* was a bit more complicated than a ordinary merger, but the ultimate effect was the same for present purposes.

35. Many observers saw the emphasis on preserving the "Time Culture" as ironic, given that the Time directors who had most vigorously asserted the need to protect this culture viewed the proposed combination with an entertainment company such as Warner as a devastating blow to Time's journalistic purity. For a fascinating discussion of this, and of the developments in *Time-Warner* generally, see Connie Bruck, "Deal of the Year," *New Yorker*, Jan. 8, 1990, at 66.

that Time's directors were the ones who should be determining what was best for the company.

Many observers concluded that *Time-Warner* greatly watered down Delaware's *Revlon* and *Unocal* duties and that the decision gave the directors of a target corporation nearly complete discretion whether to consider or reject an unsolicited takeover bid. The opinion in *QVC* cast significant doubt on these observations. In *QVC*, Paramount's directors had, like Time in the *Time-Warner* case, concluded that a merger was likely to be in the firm's long-term best interests. By 1990, Paramount had entered into serious discussions with Viacom that eventually resulted in a proposal to combine the two corporations through a two-step transaction structured as an acquisition of Paramount by Viacom. Paramount's Marty Davis had spoken with Barry Diller of QVC on various occasions throughout this time, but consistently discouraged QVC from making a bid. QVC nevertheless decided to enter the bidding, and when Paramount's directors refused to remove the defensive mechanisms that stood in the way of QVC's attempted tender offer, QVC, as a shareholder of Paramount, sued to enjoin Paramount's continued use of the defenses.

In many respects, the factual background of *QVC* bears an uncanny resemblance to that of the *Time-Warner* case. Like Time's directors in the earlier decision, Paramount's directors credibly argued that they had carefully concluded that combining with Viacom was in Paramount's long term best interests and had consistently acted in furtherance of this plan. Yet, the Delaware Supreme Court rejected these efforts to analogize the two cases. Noting that Viacom was controlled by a single individual, Sumner Redstone, who would also control the combined Viacom-Paramount entity once the dust had settled, the Court held that the proposed transaction constituted a change of control which triggered the special *Revlon* duties.[36] In contrast to *Time-Warner*, which showed relatively little solicitude for the shareholders of Time, the Court in *QVC* repeatedly emphasized the precarious status that Paramount's shareholders would have if the transaction with Viacom went through. The Delaware Supreme Court also was troubled that Paramount had rebuffed QVC throughout the process.[37] As a result, rather than showing great deference to directorial decision making as it had in *Time-Warner*, the Court held that Paramount's directors had

---

36. As noted in *Time-Warner*, although Warner's shareholders would have held 62% of the stock of the combined Time-Warner entity had the initial merger gone through, the Delaware Supreme Court concluded that this did not amount to a change in control of Time for the purposes of triggering *Revlon*.

37. See, e.g., 637 A.2d at 49–50 (noting that "QVC persistently demonstrated its intention to meet and exceed the Viacom offers" but was rebuffed nonetheless).

violated their fiduciary duties, and effectively forced the directors to conduct an auction for control of the company.

B.

From the moment the Delaware Supreme Court issued its decision in *QVC*, lawyers and commentators have struggled to reconcile the apparently inconsistent tenor of the two decisions. What do the cases suggest about the current direction of Delaware corporate law?

The most skeptical approach to Delaware's corporation law jurisprudence suggests that the Supreme Court's doctrinal pronouncements in the takeover cases are largely irrelevant. On one view, the Court simply applies a "smell test" to the cases.[38] Thus, in *Time-Warner* the Court may have been impressed with Time's directors' apparent good intentions, seeing Paramount as an eleventh hour interloper determined to torpedo the Time-Warner deal. With respect to *QVC*, this perspective might suggest the Court concluded that Paramount had unfairly thwarted QVC's overtures due to its chief executive officer Martin Davis' widely reported hostility toward Barry Diller of QVC.[39]

Perceptions such as these do play a role in the Court's decision making process, as we shall see. Yet, the Court has spent more than a decade developing and attempting to define the *Unocal* and *Revlon* standards, sending subtle and not-so-subtle messages about appropriate approaches to directorial decision making in the takeover context. Given the Court's longstanding commitment to this doctrinal project, it is hard to believe that the elaborate structure that has emerged is just window dressing.

In contrast to those who conclude that the Delaware cases involve little more than a smell test, other commentators have offered elaborate justifications to explain how Delaware doctrine appears to play out. One of the most recent and convincing doctrinal accounts is Marcel Kahan's contention that both *Time-Warner* and *QVC* reflect Delaware's emphasis on a "contingent allocation of authority" to the directors of a corporation.[40]

---

38. See, e.g., Dennis J. Block, Nancy E. Barton & Stephen A. Radin, "The Business Judgment Rule," in *Twentieth Annual Institute on Securities Regulation* 173, 180–81 (C. Nathan et al. eds. 1989); Douglas M. Branson, "The Chancellor's Foot in Delaware: *Schnell* and its Progeny," 14 *J. Corp. L.* 515 (1989).

39. See, e.g., Susan Antilla, "Hard Lessons of Paramount's Saga," *N.Y. Times*, Dec. 26, 1993, at F11 (widely known that Martin Davis "hates Barry Diller").

40. Marcel Kahan, "Paramount or Paradox: The Delaware Supreme Court's Takeover Jurisprudence," 19 *J. Corp. L.* 583 (1994). An earlier article by Ronald Gilson and Reinier Kraakman arguably has been the most influential doctrinal account of the Delaware takeover cases. Gilson and Kraakman argue that even if the scrutiny called for by *Unocal* and *Revlon* is difficult to apply, it forces target directors who wish to defend

On this view, Delaware law imposes heightened *Unocal* duties in the takeover context due to the target directors' inevitable conflict of interest. But as long as shareholders retain their power to reverse their directors' actions—by electing different directors who will chart a different course, for example—the Court will uphold the directors' use of defensive measures (as in *Time-Warner*) if a majority of the directors are independent and the board employs a thorough decision making process.[41] On the other hand, some transactions, such as sales and changes in control, eliminate shareholders' chance to have the final say. The Delaware Supreme Court invokes *Revlon* in these contexts (as in *QVC*) and engages in a particularly stringent review of the transaction in question.[42]

If we apply this framework to *Time-Warner* and *QVC*, we can quickly see both its explanatory power and its limitations. Recall that in *Time-Warner* the Delaware Court applied the *Unocal* standard and concluded that Time's directors had satisfied their obligations. The "contingent allocation" approach suggests that the Court appropriately declined to invoke its *Revlon* duties, because the shareholders of Time never lost the capacity to change its direction. They never lost their ability to receive a takeover premium comparable to the value Paramount was offering, since Paramount or another firm could make a takeover offer for the combined Time-Warner company even after its merger.[43] In *QVC*, on the other hand, Sumner Redstone would have had complete control of Viacom and Paramount after their merger, thereby canceling the voting power of Paramount's shareholders and eliminating the possibility they would ever receive a takeover offer. This is why *Revlon* applied, and the Paramount-Viacom transaction was struck down.

Kahan's "contingent allocation" approach is an insightful doctrinal explanation of *Time-Warner* and *QVC*, and of Delaware's takeover jurisprudence in general; yet, it fails to completely satisfy. The suggestion that Paramount could make an offer for Time-Warner, thereby maintaining Time's shareholders' ability to receive a takeover premium, seems a bit far-fetched. To be sure, a third party could have made an offer for the combined Time-Warner entity after the companies were combined. But the size of Time-

---

against a takeover effort to articulate how an alternative strategy will offer greater benefits to shareholders. Ronald J. Gilson & Reinier Kraakman, "Delaware's Intermediate Standard for Defensive Tactics: Is There Substance to Proportionality Review?," 44 *Bus. L.* 247 (1989).

41. Kahan, supra note 40, at 586–88.

42. *Id.* at 588.

43. *Id.* at 596. This possibility was emphasized by both the Supreme Court and the chancery court in *Time-Warner.* 571 A.2d at 1151; *Paramount Communications, Inc. v. Time, Inc.* [1989 Transfer Binder] Fed. Sec. L. Rep. (CCH) § 94,514 at 93,280.

Warner and the significant amount of new debt it incurred made such a possibility very unlikely.

A quite different explanation suggests that, rather than reflecting a coherent doctrinal framework, the Delaware case law is deliberately opaque, but that this is a virtue rather than a dilemma.[44] By injecting an element of uncertainty into the cases, proponents of this view contend, the Delaware courts encourage the parties to settle, since neither side will wish to litigate given the unpredictability of the outcome.[45] An obvious problem with this explanation of the case law is that it is not at all clear that the cases reduce litigation;[46] on the contrary, litigation rather than settlement seems to be the norm in the takeover context.[47]

What makes the Delaware case law so fascinating and perplexing is that, while each of these perspectives offers important insights, no single account fully explains what the Delaware Supreme Court is up to. Doctrine matters, both as a means the Court uses to give guidance on appropriate decision making and as the Court's articulation of its own role in scruti-

---

44. Charles M. Yablon, "Poison Pills and Litigation Uncertainty," 1989 *Duke L. J.* 54 (1989). Yablon's specific focus was on the Delaware Supreme Court's response to use by the directors of a target corporation of "poison pill" takeover defenses, but the argument can be seen as applicable to the takeover cases generally, as I suggest in the text that follows.

45. *Id.* at 65–71. For other views of how uncertainty can have beneficial effects, see Robert A. Burt, "Constitutional Law and the Teaching of the Parables," 93 *Yale L. J.* 455, 469 (1984) (arguing that Christ's parables raise doubts that heighten their listeners' vulnerability, thus counteracting a we-they mentality, and that the Supreme Court's race and institutionalization cases may serve a similar purpose).

46. Yablon's argument that uncertainty increases the likelihood of settlement conflicts with extensive law-and-economics literature that reaches precisely the opposite conclusion, contending that parties tend to litigate if the outcome is uncertain and settle only when it is clear. See, e.g., George C. Priest & Benjamin Klein, "The Selection of Disputes for Litigation," 13 *J. Leg. Stud.* 1 (1984). In the takeover context, the effect of uncertainty in Delaware law seems more consistent with the Priest and Klein view, as I note in the text below.

47. In addition to the approaches I have discussed, other commentators have argued that Delaware decision making is influenced by external pressures, such as the fear that Congress will federalize corporate law; see, e.g., Victor Brudney & Marvin A. Chirelstein, "A Restatement of Corporate Freezeouts," 87 *Yale L. J.* 1354, 1354 n.2 (1978) (discussing *Singer v. Magnavox*, 380 A.2d 969 (Del. 1977)); or concerns about the market for corporate control; Jeffrey N. Gordon, "Corporations, Markets, and Courts," 91 *Colum. L. Rev.* 1931 (1991) (characterizing the outcome in *Time-Warner* as a reaction by the Delaware Supreme Court to the perceived excesses of the 1980s takeover boom). An obvious limitation of these approaches is that they explain only of a few isolated cases. Nevertheless, external pressures do appear to affect Delaware decision making, as I note in my analysis below.

nizing directors' exercise of their duties. Yet, so does the Court's perception of the parties—there quite often are "white knights" and "scoundrels" in a Delaware takeover case.[48] The discussion of Saul and David offers a surprisingly useful perspective on how these seemingly diverse threads can come together in any given case.

IV.

Even apart from their substantive assessments of the *Time-Warner* and *QVC* cases, many observers were struck by a fascinating irony about the parties: the same corporation, Paramount, was a key player in both of these crucial Delaware decisions. Although it was a bidder in *Time-Warner* and the target corporation in *QVC*, Paramount lost both times. In one sense, the story of the cases is a story about how Paramount lost one case, switched sides, and lost again.

To understand why Paramount and its star-crossed chief executive, Martin Davis, fared so poorly, we should compare their response to the commands of the Delaware corporate law text with the similarly ill-considered response of Saul to the divine mandate communicated to him by Samuel. This mode of inquiry can be seen as stemming in some respects from a recent literature characterizing constitutional law and the Constitution in theological terms. Starting in the 1970s, several constitutional law scholars began to explore in detail the increasingly frequent suggestion that the Constitution is the source of a secular "theology" in this country. These scholars analogized the Constitution to religious texts such as the Bible or Koran and suggested that the debates over how to interpret the Constitution parallel theological debates as to the proper mode of interpretation of a central religious text.[49]

As the Constitution does for the United States, Delaware provides the central, authoritative text for corporations.[50] Like constitutional law,

---

48. See Rock, supra note 4 (describing Delaware's tendency to characterize the parties in moralistic terms).

49. Thomas Grey contrasted the general Catholic view of the Bible as supplemented by tradition, with the Protestant emphasis on scripture alone and argued that constitutional interpretation divides into roughly analogous "supplementer" and "textualist" camps. Thomas C. Grey, "The Constitution as Scripture," 37 *Stan. L. Rev.* 1 (1984); see also Thomas C. Grey, "Do We Have an Unwritten Constitution?," 27 *Stan. L. Rev.* 703 (1975). Sanford Levinson has also explored the analogy between theology and constitutional law. See Sanford Levinson, *Constitutional Faith* (1988).

50. Delaware corporation law is the de facto national state corporation law because of the large percentage of publicly held corporations that have chosen to incorporate in Delaware. For an analysis of the reasons for Delaware's continued preeminence, see Romano, *The Genius of American Corporate Law*, supra note 1; see also David A. Skeel,

Delaware corporate law continues to unfold. Corporate law can be seen as the existing statutory framework and case law, together with the elaborations that Delaware makes each time it amends its corporate law statute or the Supreme Court decides a case. From this perspective, the narrative structures of Delaware corporate law and the Bible are parallel. The actions of both Saul and Paramount were subject to an existing text; and the Biblical account of Saul and the Delaware Supreme Court decisions in *Time-Warner* and *QVC* can be seen as records of their respective responses to a text that now are themselves a part of that text.

The starting point in each situation, then, is an existing text. For Saul, two aspects of the Biblical text were particularly important. First, in addition to the general Biblical record that preceded him, Saul was given explicit instructions both at Gilgal, where he was to wait for Samuel to arrive and provide a burnt offering, and with the Amalekites, whom Saul was to destroy utterly.[51] Second, the Pentateuch prescribed in great detail the nature and occasions for the burnt offerings and other sacrifices that Saul should make.

Similarly, in Delaware corporate law, the statutory framework calls for a corporation to be managed "by or under the direction of" its directors,[52] but gives shareholders the right to vote on fundamental transactions such as the mergers that were proposed initially in both *Time-Warner* and *QVC*.[53] Delaware law also includes an extensive common law in the takeover context, some of which we have already seen. For example, in *Unocal*, *Revlon* and subsequent cases, the Delaware Supreme Court has made clear that it will apply a heightened standard of review due to the conflicts of interest that undermine directorial decision making in this context. The cases also provide more specific instructions for directors who face a takeover bid, emphasizing the importance of vesting decision making authority in outside, independent directors, rather than those most likely to have a conflict of interest.[54] The Court has suggested the desirability of

Jr., "Rethinking the Line Between Corporate Law and Corporate Bankruptcy," 72 *Tex. L. Rev.* 471 (1994) (considering various views as to whether or not the charter competition that has led to Delaware's preeminence is desirable).

The moral authority of the Delaware case law is powerfully reinforced by the remarkable frequency with which the Delaware Supreme Court speaks with a unified voice. I have considered this facet of the Delaware cases in detail elsewhere. See Skeel, supra note 1.

51. See supra notes 22–23 and accompanying text (Gilgal); notes 12–13 and accompanying text (Amalekites).

52. Del. Code Ann. tit. 8, § 141(a) (1994).

53. Del. Code Ann. tit. 8, § 251 (1994).

54. The Delaware courts have emphasized the importance of independent directors in numerous cases. Frequently cited examples include *Ivanhoe Partners v. Newmont Mining Corp.*, 535 A.2d 1334 (Del. 1987); *Unocal Corporation v. Mesa Petroleum*, 493 A.2d 946 (Del. 1985).

consulting outside experts such as investment bankers to review the fairness of a proposed transaction.[55] The Delaware text gives both general guidance and specific instructions for the directors of bidder or target corporations.

Much as we saw in our discussion of Saul and David, actors' technical adherence or non-adherence to the literal terms of the controlling texts does not seem to be the key factor in explaining the relevant authority's rejection or acceptance of their behavior. As with Saul and David, the players in Delaware's corporate law narratives in *Time Warner* and *QVC* seem to have responded similarly to the relevant prior texts. Both corporations had a majority of outside directors on their boards, and both relied on investment bankers' expertise in making their decisions as to the best transaction for the corporation. While the directors of Paramount refused to negotiate seriously with QVC after they had reached an agreement with Viacom, Time's directors acted quite similarly, stonewalling Paramount so that they could complete their existing transaction with Warner.

In the Biblical context, the faithlessness of Saul's response to divine command proved crucial to understanding why God rejected him. The infidelity of Saul's performance is emphasized in several recurrent characterizations of his actions (solipsism, fear, disingenuousness). Underscoring the importance of faithful performance and developing themes to assist a reader in drawing inferences about the performance is a technique similarly employed in the Delaware cases. Whereas the prior Delaware corporate law text itself did not dictate the outcome in *Time-Warner*, the opinion gives a sense of why the court decided the case by focusing on the faithfulness of Time's directors' performance. Several themes appear again and again in the opinion. The first is the extensive and lengthy planning that ultimately led to Time's agreement to combine with Warner. The court points out, for instance, that Time's directors began considering a strategic merger as early as 1983, and that they selected Warner as a better partner than any of the other obvious candidates, including Paramount.[56] The second is the directors' obsessive concern that the unique Time "culture" be preserved—a concern they emphasized throughout their negotiations

---

55. The most widely cited example of this is *Smith v. Van Gorkum*, 488 A.2d 858 (Del. 1985), which found the directors of Trans Union liable for breaching their duty of care due to serious flaws in the decision making process, including the directors' failure to get expert advice on the merger in question. Although the Court explicitly stated that directors do not necessarily need to engage an outside investment banker—expert advice from an insider may suffice—many observers have construed *Van Gorkum* as strongly suggesting that directors should get an outside opinion.

56. 571 A.2d at 1143–44.

with Warner.[57] Although Time's directors rebuffed the last minute bid by Paramount for Time in violation of an important aspect of the Delaware text, the opinion makes clear that the directors' performance as a whole was a faithful one.

Despite the facial similarities in the cases, the themes that emerge in the QVC decision reveal a strikingly different kind of performance by Paramount's directors in their negotiations with the potential bidders. Whereas Time's directors carefully pursued a rational long-term strategy, Paramount's directors are portrayed as notably insensitive to the interests of the Paramount shareholders. The Paramount directors' transaction with Viacom would have eliminated the Paramount shareholders' voting power since Sumner Redstone would control the combined Viacom-Paramount corporation; yet, Paramount's directors moved forward without fully taking this into account. The directors never seriously considered the possibility of an alternative transaction, blindly acceding to their chief executive officer's insistence on joining forces with Viacom.[58]

As with Saul, Paramount's directors are portrayed as having cynically attempted to disguise their unfaithful performance as a faithful one. Thus, they characterized their merger with Viacom as part of a long term plan, yet it appeared to have been of recent vintage, and Paramount's directors had refused to consider a QVC offer from the very beginning.[59] Similarly, Paramount purported to rely on outside directors and expert investment banking advice; yet, its chief executive consistently kept the other directors in the dark and its investment bankers' endorsement of the Viacom offer was equivocal in some respects and probably overly optimistic.[60]

Delaware case law focuses closely on how the directors of a target corporation like Time or Paramount have responded to prior Delaware decisions. In this sense, the narrative emphasis found in the opinions is more important than their doctrinal pronouncements. As Nussbaum suggests, attending to particulars situates the reader as a participant in the drama, better able to comprehend the unique situation confronted by the characters. One discovers in the facts the admirable or dishonorable qualities of director behavior rather than a laundry list of prescribed actions. Being a faithful director is complex business; only by focusing on the facts rather

---

57. By my count, the Delaware Supreme Court refers to the "Time Culture," and the directors' concern to preserve it, on seven different occasions in its fifteen page opinion.

58. See, e.g., 637 A.2d at 41 (Paramount board given report that focused almost exclusively on the "conditions and uncertainties" of the QVC offer and made no effort to discuss the conditions with QVC).

59. 637 A.2d at 38 (describing how Martin Davis of Paramount learned of QVC's interest and told Barry Diller of QVC that Paramount was not for sale).

60. 637 A.2d at 41.

than the dogma can a reader best understand the ethical dimension of directorial behavior.

This explanation casts doubt on the skeptical view that Delaware's courts simply dress up the facts to support an under-reasoned conclusion. If the Court merely enjoyed exercising its power, it could easily do so with a brief, selective presentation of facts together with an application of takeover doctrine. The Delaware opinions take a far more didactic approach. Particularly at the chancery court level, the decisions provide remarkably detailed accounts of the facts, so that the case centers on the extensive story of the parties' interactions.[61]

These extensive descriptions of who the parties are and what they did can be seen as a response to the vexing problem of providing guidance for directors. When a court's principal concern is the faithfulness of a performance—a species of ethics—narrative may be the best teacher. Once again, the Biblical account of Saul's life offers an instructive comparison. Had the writer simply described the events of Saul's life in brief outline, noting his disobedience, we would not gain much insight into why God rejected him, especially given God's failure to reject the disobedient David. Through the more extended account and the use of various narrative devices, the writer presents a much more complex picture of Saul, one that suggests the actual "feel" of a particular kind of performance.[62] Doctrinal expositions, like the Ten Commandments or the Delaware statute, have their place; but difficult questions of good faith demand the particularities that only narrative structure can provide.

Both *Time-Warner* and *QVC* can be seen in similar terms. In each case, the court suggests the feel of a faithful or unfaithful performance through narrative. The clear implication is that the story of the case is important, and is intended to be instructive, just as the Biblical record of Saul's and

---

61. This tendency in the case law seems to be more pronounced in the takeover cases we have been considering than in other areas and can be traced in many respects to the proliferation of these cases in the mid-1980s and thereafter. For speculation as to why this might be so, see Skeel, "The Unanimity Norm," supra note 1, at 171–72 (precariousness of Delaware's status in the face of repeated calls for federalization of corporate law).

62. This characterization of the Delaware cases suggests obvious parallels to Martha Nussbaum's arguments for a "literary" mode of judging (and by implication, of reading cases) that emphasizes a particularized assessment of the parties and their circumstances. See, e.g., Martha C. Nussbaum, "Equity and Mercy," Chapter One of this volume. In many contexts, institutional and other constraints make it unrealistic to expect judges to give the kind of particularized attention that "literary" judging envisions. Yet one of the unique aspects of Delaware's specialized chancery court system is that Delaware judges can and do give such attention to the important corporation law cases that come before them.

David's "performances" is instructive. The courts do go on to apply exist-ing doctrine and to articulate rules, but Delaware's corporate directors and their attorneys must learn to read how earlier cases have played out.

The didactic purpose of Delaware narratives becomes even more appar-ent once we consider who the primary readers of the cases are. Despite the national implications of Delaware decision making, the litigants in the cases are represented by a remarkably small number of lawyers, whose firms appear in case after case. These lawyers know one another and the Delaware courts intimately and act as a discrete community of interpreters of Delaware law.[63] The expert advice these lawyers offer their clients must go well beyond a recitation of Delaware doctrine; they must develop a feel for the narratives of Delaware's previous cases and thus of the Supreme Court's likely response to a board of directors' decision making in any new context.[64]

---

63. To begin to appreciate the extent to which this is true, one need only compare the law firms representing the principal players in *Time-Warner* to those in *QVC*:

—Simpson, Thatcher & Bartlett (NY) represented Paramount in *Time-Warner* and in *QVC*.

—Wachtell, Lipton, Rosen & Katz (NY) represented Warner in *Time-Warner*, and QVC in *QVC*.

—Cravath, Swaine & Moore (NY) represented Time in *Time-Warner*, and did not appear in *QVC*.

—Sherman & Sterling (NY) did not appear in *Time-Warner*, and represented Viacom in *QVC*.

—Morris, Nichols, Arsht & Tunnell (Del) represented Time in *Time-Warner*, and Via-com in *QVC*.

—Richards, Layton & Finger (Del) represented Warner in *Time-Warner*, and Para-mount in *QVC*.

The parties have Delaware council in each case, as is required in Delaware, and often have outside council as well.

Many of the law firms also appeared in one or more of the other five prominent Delaware Supreme Court hostile takeover cases. Wachtell, Lipton appeared in two of the other five cases, for instance, and the Delaware firm Morris, Nichols, Arsht & Tunnell appeared in all five. (The five cases are *Unocal Corporation v. Mesa Petroleum Co.*, 493 A.2d 946 (Del. 1985); *Revlon Inc. v. MacAndrews & Forbes Holdings, Inc.*, 506 A.2d 173 (Del. 1986); *Ivanhoe Partners v. Newmont Mining Corp.*, 535 A.2d 1334 (Del. 1987); *Mills Acquisition Co. v. Macmillan, Inc.*, 559 A.2d 1261 (Del. 1988); and *Unitrin v. American General Corp.*, 651 A.2d 1361 (Del. 1995)).

64. To be sure, even a lawyer who had not participated in previous takeover cases could read the earlier decisions, just as lawyers do in other contexts, and acquire a sense of Delaware's expectations for corporate directors as a result. What makes Delaware's cor-porate takeover bar unique is that its practitioners not only read the takeover decisions, but they also have actively participated in the previous cases, often as advisors prior to liti-gation as well as representing the litigants. Because of this involvement and their having

V.

The objective of this essay is not to determine whether the Delaware Supreme Court's resolution of one or more of its takeover cases is "right" or "wrong" or to provide a complete theory of Delaware's corporate takeover jurisprudence. Instead, the Biblical account of Saul and David has been used to suggest a new way to understand what the Delaware courts do when they decide a takeover case. Delaware case law, like the Biblical accounts of Saul and David, places crucial emphasis on the faithfulness or unfaithfulness of the parties' performance of an authoritative text. In order for an opinion to do this well, narrative form, rather than doctrinal pronouncement, seems to offer the most effective method of communication. Narratives can offer positive exemplars, such as David and the directors of Time, and negative ones, such as Saul and Paramount, and invite those who follow to inform their subsequent choices in light of their own participation in the narrative as readers.

---

observed the reactions of the Delaware judges firsthand over a series of cases, they are likely to have an unparalleled appreciation of the nuances of the opinions the Supreme Court eventually writes.

Chapter Seven

Don Juan and the Tort of Seduction

Paul J. Heald

> Imagine creating from the unique circumstances of women and men and
> the *sui generis* character of sex its own original and unique legal category.[1]

Consider the following scenarios: 1) A therapist uses confidential information revealed within the counseling relationship to seduce a client; 2) A
college student lies about his or her marital status to get a classmate into
bed; 3) An employer exploits confidential information obtained from a friend
to seduce an employee; 4) Same employer is rebuffed, yet persists unsuc-
cessfully in the attempted seduction; 5) A worker lies about his or her religious affiliation in the process of seducing a co-worker; 6) Same worker lies
instead about whether he or she is HIV positive; and 7) A chemistry teacher
makes no misrepresentations, but seduces an immature high school junior.

Two reactions to the above hypotheticals are predictable. First, the
moral sense of most readers is likely to be offended by all of them. Second, most readers would be unlikely to argue for liability in all seven cases.[2]
In fact, under a diverse set of common law and statutory rules only some
of the above scenarios present actionable behavior.[3] Although these obser-

---

1. Lea VanderVelde, "The Legal Ways of Seduction," 48 *Stan. L. Rev.* 817, 901
(1996).

2. See Dan Subotnik, " 'Sue Me, Sue, What Can You Do Me? I Love You': A Disquisi-
tion on Law, Sex, and Talk," 47 *Fla. L. Rev.* 311 (1995). Subotnik reports two surveys
asking questions about scenarios similar to those presented above. In answer to the question whether victims should be able to recover for emotional damages caused by sexual
lies, fifty percent answered "yes" and fifty percent answered "no." *Id.* at 394. The
response was similar to the question whether lies about marital status should be actionable. *Id.* at 398–99.

3. Example One likely presents a violation of a common law fiduciary duty. See infra
note 32. The seduction in Example Two is almost certainly not actionable. See infra note
7. The seduction in Example Three, which evidences no breach of common law fiduciary
relationship, is probably not actionable. *Id.* The employee's willingness will also likely bar
an action under federal sexual discrimination law. The unwelcome nature of the employer's advances in Example Four may constitute actionable sexual harassment under federal
law. See infra note 34. Example Five presents no actionable conduct, see infra note 6,

vations can be offered with relative confidence, an answer to the general question underlying my seven examples is quite elusive: When should persuading, or attempting to persuade, the object of one's sexual desire to say "yes" be considered to be actionable?

This issue is very much alive in state legislatures,[4] in between the covers of the regional reporters,[5] in the law reviews,[6] in the popular media,[7] and in the news.[8] While commentators uniformly view seduction with a mixture of revulsion and fascination, they remain widely divided on the extent to which the law should intervene in intimate relationships. For example, the notorious Nashville "fantasy lover" stimulated debate about the legal bounds of seductive conduct. This Don Juan-a-be phoned women at night and told them to unlock their doors, take off their clothes, blindfold themselves, and wait for him in bed.[9] A surprising number of victims complied with his requests. Many complained later that they erroneously presumed that the voice on the phone came from a husband or lover, and not from the married, successful businessman whom they later discovered had been their mystery partner. Although we can probably agree on the moral impropri-

---

while the nature of the lie in Example Six and its consequences to the physical health of the victim result in liability in some jurisdictions. See infra note 33. The behavior of the teacher in Example Seven probably is not wrongful at common law, see infra note 18, but a cause of action may lie against the school or school district if it should have anticipated, yet failed to take adequate steps, to prevent the wrong. See infra note 31.

4. See, for example, Comment, "Loss of Consortium and Intentional Infliction of Emotional Distress: Alternative Theories to Alienation of Affections," 67 *Iowa L. Rev.* 859 fn.4 (1982) (listing states that have recently abolished the tort of alienation of affections by statute).

5. See cases cited in notes 18, 26, and 32.

6. See, Jane Larsen, " 'Women Understand So Little, They Call my Good Nature "Deceit" ': A Feminist Rethinking of Seduction," 93 *Colum. L. Rev.* 374 (1993) (discussing the confused state of seduction law and proposing a new comprehensive tort for sexual fraud); Subotnik, supra note 2; Linda Lacey, "Introducing Feminist Jurisprudence: An Analysis of Oklahoma's Seduction Statute," 25 *Tulsa L. J.* 775 (1990); M.B.W. Sinclair, "Seduction and the Myth of the Ideal Woman," 5 *J. of Law & Inequality* 33 (1987).

7. See "Should the Law Punish Lovers Who Lie? 84% Say Yes," *Glamour*, June, 1994, at 133.

8. See, for example, Kenneth Jost, "Questionable Conduct," 80 *ABA Journal* 70 (November 1994); Martin Fox, "Judge Rejects RICO Claim for Seduction: No Basis for Legal Redress in Lawyer's Relationship," 210 *New York Law Journal* (July 2, 1993); Sulamith Gold, "Don Juan in Court: Would Reviving Seduction Suits Keep Lovers Honest?", *Chic. Trib.* sec. 5 at 1 (Jan. 5, 1993); and "Best Man Takes Wife," 93 *Los Angeles Daily Journal* 3 (Dec. 3, 1980).

9. "Blindfolded Women Seek Charges Against Fantasy Man," *Tampa Trib.*, Feb. 3, 1995, at 2.

ety of the mystery Tennessean's behavior, attorneys, judges, and scholars have a much harder time agreeing whether such a seduction is tortious.[10]

Recent interdisciplinary perspectives on the issue from economists,[11] feminists,[12] and others[13] leads me to consider the possibility that a literary perspective might enrich the debate. If the premise underlying this collection of essays is correct, that "certain truths about human life can only be fittingly and accurately stated in the language and forms characteristic of the narrative artist,"[14] then literature may, in fact, be uniquely able to inform our judgment.

In spite of the enormous number of fictional works that explore the theme of seduction, I have decided to choose the obvious: Don Juan in his numerous manifestations. Given that Don Juan is the single most frequently recurring character in Western fiction,[15] even that task is overwhelming. Nevertheless, the canon of the most famous works is fairly digestible, and examining these works provides valuable and unexpected insight into the appropriate parameters of the seduction tort. Before we discuss Don Juan, however, we must take a brief look at the legal issue we hope to clarify.

I. Seduction Law

Although a direct[16] tort action for seduction may still be brought by a victim or by a parent or a spouse (under the guise of an action for alienation of affections), in several jurisdictions,[17] recent opinions have reject-

---

10. Compare Larsen, supra note 6, with Subotnik, supra note 2.

11. See, for example, Richard A. Posner, *Sex and Reason* 392–95 (1992); see also Larsen, supra note 6, at 419–24.

12. See Larsen, supra note 6; Lacey, supra note 6.

13. See Subotnik, supra note 2.

14. Martha C. Nussbaum, *Love's Knowledge* 5 (New York: Oxford Univ. Press, 1990).

15. See Armand E. Singer, *The Don Juan Theme, Versions and Criticism: A Bibliography* (Morgantown: West Virginia Univ. Press, 1965) (191-page bibliography, listing 1,941 versions of the Don Juan story).

16. By "direct" I mean the express tort action. Cf. Ala. Code sec. 419 (1940) (repealed 1977). See, for example, O.C.G.A. § 51-1-16 ("The seduction of a daughter, unmarried and living with her parent, whether followed by pregnancy or not, shall give right of action to the father or to the mother if the father is dead, or absent permanently, or refuses to bring an action. No loss of services need be alleged or proved. The seduction is the gist of the action, and in well-defined cases exemplary damages shall be granted").

17. See Larsen, supra note 6, at 401 fn.118 (listing eighteen jurisdictions).

ed the action, casting aspersions on its offensive proprietary origins. For example, in 1994, in *Franklin v. Hill*,[18] the Georgia Supreme Court declared the state's seduction statute[19] unconstitutional on the grounds that it provided for compensation only if a daughter, but not a son, was seduced. The court was so dismayed by the pedigree of the action in Georgia that it did not seriously consider saving the statute's constitutionality by expanding it to cover the seduction of boys as well.[20] It noted that the statute was "passed in 1863 at a time when women and children were the legal property of their husbands or fathers [and] vindicates the outraged feelings of the father whose daughter's virtue has been ruined."[21] The court unearthed an ancient opinion of the Georgia Supreme Court to demonstrate the irrelevance of the tort to modern values.[22] In 1856, Justice Lumpkin spoke of "the dishonor and disgrace thus cast upon his family [by the seduction]; for this atrocious invasion of his household peace. There is nothing like it, since the entrance of Sin and Death into this lower world."[23]

The *Franklin* opinion does a good job of putting a historical perspective on the tort.[24] It has its origins in property law and patriarchical notions of the family, although by the late 19th century the victim herself had been provided with a cause of action in many jurisdictions.[25] The court failed, however, to devote more than a single sentence to the facts of the case which involved an attempt by Nancy Franklin to obtain redress for the seduction of her eleventh-grade daughter by one of her high school teachers, Andrew Hill. When the local prosecutor did not charge the teacher with statutory rape, the age of consent in Georgia being fourteen at the time,[26] the upset mother (we are not told the mental state of the daughter) had little option under state law but to plead the archaic cause of action.

Although the Fulton County Daily Report declared the seduction action dead in Georgia after *Hill*,[27] just four months later the same court was willing to provide a remedy for seduction in different context. In *Tante v. Her-*

---

18. 264 Ga. 302, 444 S.E.2d 778 (1994).

19. See supra note 16.

20. When Alabama was confronted with the unconstitutionality of its alimony statute that provided relief only to divorced women, but not men, it saved the statute by interpreting it to provide a remedy for men also. See *Orr v. Orr*, 374 So. 2d 895 (1979).

21. 444 S.E.2d at 781.

22. See *Kendrick v. McCrary*, 11 Ga. 603 (1852).

23. *Id.* at 606.

24. As does VanderVelde, see supra note 1.

25. See Larsen, supra note 6, at 382–412 (tracing the history of the seduction tort).

26. See *Drake v. State*, 239 Ga. 232, 236 S.E.2d 748 (1977).

27. See Emily Heller, "Justices Make Seduction Law a Thing of the Past," *Fulton County Daily Report* (Wednesday, June 29, 1994).

ring,[28] the court confronted the case of an attorney who successfully represented a client in a social security disability appeal and also seduced her by exploiting confidential psychological and medical information he obtained in the course of his representation. The victim and her husband (also a victim himself—he contracted a venereal disease passed on from the lawyer), obtained a verdict against the attorney on the theory of breach of fiduciary duty.[29] According to the court, the lawyer had a legal duty not to exploit the confidential information to which his position made him privy. So, a civil action is not available under Georgia law against a teacher who abuses his[30] position to seduce a young student,[31] but an action is available against a lawyer (and by analogy against a doctor or psychiatrist or cleric) who similarly abuses his power.

This essay will refer to the sort of seduction action in *Herring* as "indirect," in the sense that an alternative legal form is used to provide a remedy to the victim of seduction. Several courts have used this strategy to recognize remedies for seduction in the context of professional/confidential/fiduciary relationships[32] and also in cases where the seducer has lied about his fertility or freedom from sexually transmitted disease.[33] In addition, a Title VII claim of sex discrimination[34] can provide a covert remedy for attempted seduction. In the workplace, would-be seducers may be guilty of sexual harassment when they offend their co-workers by attempting to develop intimate relationships.[35] Seduction as a tort, therefore, has retained some vitality in a number of different contexts, including as a seldom-invoked express cause of action in some jurisdictions.[36]

---

28. 264 Ga. 694, 453 S.E.2d 686 (1994).

29. *Id.* at 688 fn. 7.

30. Given the typical facts of these cases, and the focus on Don Juan, the masculine pronoun will be used throughout.

31. A remedy may be available under federal law for victims who attend schools receiving Title IX funding. See *Franklin v. Gwinnett County Public School Dist.*, 503 U.S. 60 (1992) (school district potentially liable for money damages if it did not take appropriate action to stop sexual harassment it knew or should have known about).

32. See, for example, *F.G. v. McDonell*, 65 U.S.L.W. 2010 (7-2-96) (cleric liable for seducing parishioner he was counseling); see also Larsen, supra note 6, at 410–11 (collecting cases).

33. See, Larsen, supra note 6, at 404–05 (collecting cases).

34. See 42 U.S.C. § 2000(e) et seq. (prohibiting sexual discrimination and harassment in the workplace).

35. Seduction law may have its roots in the ancient Roman cause of action for *inuria*. See Digest 47.10.15.15–24.

36. See Larsen, supra note 6, at 401 fn.118 (listing eighteen jurisdictions).

Obviously, no comprehensive legal principle clearly identifies when seduction is actionable. In a long and well-written article, Jane Larsen makes a powerful argument for redefining the scope of the traditional action to include a comprehensive cause of action for sexual fraud. She asserts that obtaining consent to sex through express or implied material misrepresentations should be recognized as a way to unify the law in the area.[37] Rather than leaving other bodies of law to develop remedies in a piecemeal fashion, thereby leaving victims without redress, she argues that a new tort with well-defined parameters would be more appropriate. She is primarily concerned with the failure of the law to provide a remedy for the first and third examples that began this essay. She does an excellent job detailing the very real damage done when a victim discovers that consent to intimacy has been obtained through reasonable belief in an intentional lie.

The counter-arguments that Larsen deals with come from both economists and feminists, all of whom she answers on their own terms. Economists analyzing a cause of action for sexual fraud are concerned with the effect of the tort on the sexual marketplace.[38] Might not fear of litigation lead to less sex, probably a bad thing given the utility most people derive from having it? Might the introduction of suspicion diminish the quality of sex for those willing to brave it under the new rule? Larsen makes economic arguments in return, suggesting that better sex and less trauma should be the result of the rule.[39] She also recognizes that many feminists question the need for a cause of action for sexual fraud. If women are equal to men, shouldn't they be able to protect themselves? Isn't the history of the tort steeped in male patriarchy? Shouldn't maximizing a woman's autonomy and freedom of choice be our dominate values? Larsen responds from a feminist perspective that asserts feminine difference does not mean inferiority and suggests that the special vulnerability of women, and very real differences in power between men and women, should not be ignored in considering a new tort for sexual fraud.[40]

Although Larsen subtitles her paper with a quote from Mozart's opera "Don Giovanni" and uses some literary examples to trace historically the plight of the seduction victim, she does not explore the possibility that literature may add more to the debate than economics or feminist jurisprudence.[41] If an exploration of the various manifestations of Don Juan Tenorio does not contribute to an understanding of seduction law, then perhaps the assertion that literature can help us address legal problems needs to

---

37. *Id.*
38. See Larsen, *supra* note 6, at 418–25, 443–45.
39. *Id.*
40. *Id.* at 425–43.
41. *Id.* at 375–79.

be reconsidered. Even a brief discussion of Don Juan's checkered past, however, can help us reframe the debate over the proper parameters of liability for seduction, although the path down which Don Juan leads us is not the path we might expect.

II. Don Juan and the Spirit of Abstraction

After exposing the students in my law and literature course to various incarnations of Don Juan in the works of Tirso de Molina, Molière, Mozart, Hoffman, Byron, Pushkin, Kierkegaard, Shaw, de Montherlant, and Frisch, I asked them whether they had learned anything about how to seduce someone. The unanimous response was "NO." Did the plays, operas, poems, and short stories teach them anything about the nature of the sex act? Again, the answer was "NO." What we learn from the literary evolution of Don Juan turns out to be far removed from the bedroom antics and swordplay of his popular reputation.

A. Don Juan from Tirso to Mozart

Although bits and pieces of the Don Juan legend appear before the appearance of *El burlador de Sevilla*,[42] Tirso de Molina's 1630 work is generally credited as being the first complete play about Don Juan Tenorio. Most works, up to and including Mozart's "Don Giovanni," follow the basic plot established in Tirso's play: Don Juan beds women of a wide variety of social classes through impersonation, intimidation, and smooth-talking; the fallout of his seductions is flight and swordplay, usually resulting in the death of the father of one of his victims; after encountering the statue of the slain father, he blasphemously invites it to a dinner which concludes in his being dragged down to hell; comic relief is provided by his fearful servant, who has acted as an accomplice to his crimes.

J.W. Smeed comments that in Tirso's play, "Don Juan's fate is to serve as an awful warning."[43] Indeed, the play is quite didactic: Don Juan is a primarily deceitful and blasphemous character; he and those like him will burn in Hell if they do not repent. This is the story of a sinner, and later treatments prior to Mozart, especially in Italy, Germany, and England display Don Juan in increasingly more wicked and violent terms.[44] In some versions his father dies of a broken heart; in others, Don Juan commits patri-

---

42. Gabriel Tellez [Tirso de Molina, pseud.], *El burlador de Sevilla y convidado de piedra* (1630). The play is usually translated as "The Trickster of Seville."

43. J.W. Smeed, *Don Juan* 1 (London: Routledge, 1990).

44. *Id.* at 17–19.

cide.[45] In all versions, Don Juan pays dearly for offending God and prevailing social norms.

French plays of the period portray an increasingly fatalistic Don Juan who justifies his behavior in reference to his "nature." Molière's work, *Don Juan ou le festin de pierre*,[46] called by George Bernard Shaw one of the two greatest comedies of all time,[47] shows significant development in the motivations of the character. In this preview of the Nietzschean Don Juans of the turn of the last century, Molière portrays the title character as an archrationalist free-thinker. Although the plot is very similar to Tirso's, Molière's Don Juan spends much of his time besting his servant Sganarelle in their frequent arguments over the nature of morality and reason. Despite Sganarelle's failure to out-reason his master, Don Juan still ends burning in Hell, and Sganarelle, the unsophisticated but repentant servant, survives.

Although most early Don Juan dramas are morality plays on the surface, some modern critics see these versions of the story as:

> a volatile mix of cultural tensions, pitting nature against culture, man against woman, individual against community, and liberty against order. The opposition of these forces marks Don Juan and the seduction narrative as products of classical liberalism, for which these dualities are definitional.[48]

Although these tensions clearly exist in many versions of the story both before and after Mozart, the early works resolve them in the same way: Don Juan burns for his sins. His story is primarily a tale of the triumph of conventional morality.

But only until Mozart, asserts E.T.A. Hoffmann. Mozart's opera "Don Giovanni," which has obsessed virtually every author writing about Don Juan since its first performance in 1787, marks a turning point in the career of the famous seducer. Hoffmann, inventor of the science fiction/fantasy tale, early romantic composer, attorney, member of the Prussian supreme court, and the most respected music critic of his time, heard in "Don Giovanni" a fundamental subversion of the old morality play.[49]

B. From Mozart to Frisch, with Homage to Hoffmann

Even before Mozart's "Don Giovanni," there are hints that Don Juan is more than he appears, not just a pleasure seeker, but rather a rebel. After

---

45. *Id.* at 18.

46. Molière, *Don Juan ou le Festin de Pierre*, in W.D. Howarth (ed.), *Blackwell's French Texts* (Oxford: Blackwell, 1958).

47. See Smeed, supra note 43, at 13.

48. Larsen, supra note 6, at 376 n.3.

49. See Smeed, supra note 43, at 45–63.

Mozart he is almost always portrayed as longing for something more than physical pleasure. In the words of de Montherlant, his character becomes an "empty sack"[50] in which one discovers a multiplicity of attempts to attain transcendence. A brief glance at the most famous modern versions reveals an astounding variety of Don Juans.

1. Mozart and Hoffman

As lyric, Lorenzo da Ponte's libretto to "Don Giovanni" is sonorous and pleasing, deftly mixing irony and passion. In the story, however, we see little variation from the traditional plot first popularized by Tirso. Nothing in the libretto alone suggested that the opera would be one of the most influential works of art ever created. E.T.A. Hoffman, however, heard something extraordinary in the music. In the context of a fantastic tale of a traveler who witnesses a performance of "Don Giovanni" in a theater attached to his hotel, Hoffman offered a radical interpretation of the work.[51] During the opera, Hoffman's traveler senses a beautiful woman in his box. It is Donna Anna, simultaneously sitting and talking to him and performing on stage! She leaves during intermission, and he spends much of the night writing a letter explaining his ideas about the opera to the beautiful actress. In the wee hours of the morning, he smells her perfume, but she is not there. At breakfast, he learns in the common room of the hotel that the actress has died during the night, precisely at the time he sensed her presence.

The bulk of the story, the letter, ponders the success of the opera in light of its somewhat undistinguished plot. Why should audiences around Europe be so entranced by a horny old man? For that matter, why should the powers of Hell bother to concern themselves with a petty lecher, no matter how good he is with a sword? For Hoffman, the success of the opera lies in Mozart's musical subversion of the traditional morality tale. The Don Juan of the musical score is a heroic seeker of transcendence, an idealist reaching in vain for the eternal. He is not just looking for sexual stimulation; he is looking for God. For Hoffman, the music tells a radically different story than the libretto.[52]

Hoffman's impressions are well-grounded in the score. One of the most famous duets in opera history, and possibly the most lyrical piece in the opera itself, is sung by Don Giovanni and Zerlina, an innocent peasant girl he is trying to seduce on the eve of her marriage. The song, "La ci

---

50. Henri de Montherlant, *Don Juan* 133–34 (Paris: Editions Gallimard, 1958) ("[N]ous puissions mettre en lui tout ce qui ne s'y trouve pas. Don Juan, c'est une défroque, un sac vide.").

51. E.T.A. Hoffman, "Don Juan," in 1 *Poetische Werke* 73–88 (1957).

52. See Smeed, supra note 43, at 45–53.

darem la mano," is far more harmonious and memorable than the solos given to Don Octavio, the moralistic avenger of Donna Anna, Don Giovanni's first seduction victim in the opera. The tension between the subject matter (dirty old aristocrat abusing his position to deflower young virgin) and the sweetness of the music should be distracting, yet the music prevails so completely that our awareness of the essential sordidness of Don Juan's character is suspended.

By the end of the opera, one feels like cheering for Don Giovanni as he heroically sings his way down to hell. The surviving characters conclude the opera with a "good riddance" aria praising the justness of his fate; however, the memory that lingers is not of the triumph of virtue, but rather the aesthetic appeal of Don Giovanni's truthfulness to his striving nature even to the bitter end. According to Hoffman, Mozart's character has much more in common with Faust than with Casanova. In fact, Franz Horn asserts that "Faust and Don Juan are the peaks of modern Christian poetic mythology."[53] After Mozart and Hoffman, some German versions of Don Juan depict him as saved; in one version salvation is promised by the statue itself.[54] In France, for Gautier, Don Juan is seeking not Aphrodite in the guise of Donna Anna, but Eve, longing in vain for a return to the Garden of Eden.[55]

2. Byron

There seems to be no evidence that Byron was familiar, as many continental authors were, with Hoffman's tale, but Byron's epic poem *Don Juan* (1819–24) could have been written to fit Hoffman's new paradigm. Before Byron, the archetypical English version of the story was "Don Juan or the Libertine Destroyed."[56] Byron, however, creates a young romantic traveler who is sent away from home after being seduced by an older neighbor lady. In the poem, described by Goethe as "a work of boundless genius,"[57] the hero is shipwrecked, witnesses cannibalism, is marooned on an idyllic island with a beautiful girl, is sold into slavery, lives in a Turkish harem, escapes to aid the Russian army, becomes Catherine the Great's lover, and returns home to England to expose the hypocrisy of English morality. The poem demonstrates the superiority of nature to society (it even includes a mini-ode to Daniel Boone) and of democracy to monarchy. The Don Juan of Molière argued his nature caused his sinful impulse; for Byron, nature obviates the sin itself.

---

53. Franz Horn, *Luna, ein Taschenbuch* 322 (Leipzig 1805), quoted in Smeed, supra note 43, at 45.

54. See Smeed, supra note 43, at 46.

55. See *id.* at 56–57.

56. See, for example, Thomas Shadwell, *The Libertine*, in Summers & Montague (eds.), 3 *Complete Works* 19–93 (1927).

57. Quoted in Smeed, supra note 43, at 43.

As with Hoffman, Byron's Don Juan could hardly be described as merely searching for sex:

> Don Juan, who was real, or ideal,—
>> For both are much the same, since what
>> men think
> Exists when the once thinkers are less real
>> Than what they thought, for mind can
>> never sink,
> And 'gainst the body makes a strong appeal;
>> and yet 'tis very puzzling on the brink
> Of what is called eternity, to stare,
> And know no more of what is here, than
>> there;—[58]

He is a young man gloriously transcending his mortality and living the fullest expression of his creative impulse. Byron's death with his Don Juan only twenty years old (and yet the hero of 300 pages of verse) left unfinished his tribute to the natural virtue of Don Juan's spirit.

3. Pushkin

Whether Hoffman's and Byron's reinterpretations of the Don Juan character are satisfying or not, they have been enormously influential. After Mozart, Don Juan changes irrevocably. Pushkin's one act play illustrates the most famous Russian adaptation of the modern Don Juan.[59] Pushkin's Don Juan is an artist, an extemporaneous poet who at the end of his career has finally found the embodiment of the ideal woman in the grieving Donna Anna. He exults, "For, loving you, virtue herself I love." Unlike Don Juan prior to Mozart, he passes up the opportunity to lie and seduce Donna Anna; rather he lays his crimes at her feet. Although his conversion is too late to save him from fateful embrace of the statue of her dead husband, killed by Don Juan long before, Puskin gives us a glimpse of a transcendent vision at the end of Don Juan's debauched career.

4. Kierkegaard

Kierkegaard's Johannes, the protagonist in his powerful "Diary of the Seducer,"[60] is typical of the modern Don Juan. His obsession with seduction has absolutely nothing to do with physical pleasure, but rather with

---

58. Byron, *Don Juan*, Book XV, Canto XX.

59. Alexander Puskin, *The Stone Guest*, in 1 *Selected Works* 127–60 (1974) (Avril Pyman, Trans.).

60. See Soren Kierkegaard, "Diary of the Seducer," in 1 *Either/Or* 298–440 (David & Lillian Swenson, Trans., Princeton Univ. Press, 1971) (first published 1843).

his pursuit of the ultimate aesthetic experience. The key to that experience is "poetizing" himself into the heart of a young girl. He proclaims in
his diary:

> I am an aesthete, an eroticist, one who has understood the nature and
> meaning of love, who believes in love and knows it from the ground up,
> and only makes the private reservation that no love affair should last more
> than six months at the most, and that every erotic relationship should
> cease as soon as one has had the ultimate enjoyment....To poetize oneself
> into a young girl is an art, to poetize oneself out of her is a masterpiece.[61]

> I simply do not care to possess a girl in the mere external sense, but to
> enjoy her in an artistic sense. Therefore my approach must be as artistic
> as possible.[62]

> What am I doing? Do I fool her? Not at all; that would be of no use to
> me. Am I stealing her heart? By no means; I really prefer that the girl I love
> should retain her heart. Then what am I doing? I am creating for myself a
> heart in the likeness of her own. An artist paints his beloved; that gives
> him pleasure; a sculptor fashions his. I do this, too, but in a spiritual sense.
> She does not know that I possess this picture, and therein lies my real
> deception.[63]

Johannes's philosophy completely collapses the erotic and the aesthetic.
His striving is not a traditional search for God, but rather an attempt at transcendence through performance art.

5. Shaw

George Bernard Shaw's Don Juan, on the other hand, the hero of Act III
of *Man and Superman*,[64] is the dramatic embodiment of the philosophy of
Friedrich Nietzsche. Again, sex is not just sex. In Nietzsche's terms it is the
way humans partake in the totally amoral universal life force that renders all
conventional morality irrelevant. In the "sex relation the universal creative
energy, of which the parties are both helpless agents, overrides and sweeps
away all personal consideration, and dispenses with all personal relations."[65]
Don Juan's argument with the Devil as he exiles himself from Hell and ascends
into Heaven is one of the clearest explanations of Nietzschean moral philosophy found in fiction.

---

61. *Id.* at 362–63.
62. *Id.* at 368.
63. *Id.* at 384.
64. George Bernard Shaw, *Man and Superman* (New York: Penguin Books, 1946).
65. *Id.* at 161.

6. *De Montherlant*

After World War II, we begin to see a reaction to previous glorifications of Don Juan. In *Don Juan*,[66] Henri de Montherlant gives us an existential Don Juan headed nowhere but to his inevitable death. He is true to himself, acts in good faith and takes responsibility for all his actions. He does not believe in God and refuses to concoct anything else, be it art or human will, to take its place. De Montherlant tries to give us Don Juan in a world where God is dead, art cannot confer transcendence, and the Nietzschean alternative to God has just been proven manifestly unacceptable by the Third Reich. In one particularly absurd scene, an aging and obsessed victim of Don Juan presents three scholars who set forth their theories about him. One presents a veiled version of the position of Kierkegaard's Johannes, another expounds Mozart's Don Juan à la Hoffman, and the third provides the Freudian explanation of Otto Rank. Don Juan's servant demolishes all three theories and sends the scholars on their way with his sword. Don Juan is who he is; he does what he does.

7. *Frisch*

In *Don Juan or the Love of Geometry*,[67] Max Frisch's hero deconstructs himself. Rejecting passion in favor of mathematics, Don Juan fakes his death to avoid all the women who are lining up to sleep with a truly reluctant seducer. He winds up happily married, although somewhat henpecked, living in a castle where he can concentrate on his math. Although both de Montherlant and Frisch reject the notion that Don Juan is somehow a transcendent character, they definitely continue the modern trend of using him to make broader statements about the nature of reality. One could easily teach a course in the history of philosophy by tracing the literary career of Don Juan.

C. Abstraction as the Essence of Don Juan

After reading multiple versions of the Don Juan legend, one wants to shout, "Who is this guy?" Dirty old man? Arch-Romantic? Faust? Aesthete? Superman? Existential Man? Jacques Derrida? I would have to agree with my stu-

---

66. See supra note 50.

67. Max Frisch, *Don Juan or the Love of Geometry*, in *Four Plays* 87–160 (Michael Bullock, trans., Methuan, 1969).

dents that one learns little about the reality of the sex act or love or even how to seduce someone from these works. On the other hand, as the most popular character in western fiction, he is certainly a cultural icon. But of what? A Jungian literary critic might suggest that Don Juan represents some sort of masculine archetype. But an archetypical character arises out of common ground shared by its many manifestations. What commonalities exist here?

What pervades virtually every appearance of the post-Mozart Don Juan is the need to abstract, the impulse to generate theory from sensation, the movement from feeling to thinking—from fact to rationalization. The search for sex becomes the search for the meaning of life. Sexual encounters become the means of transcending reality, not just positive or negative experiences in themselves. This is a powerful observation because we all abstract sometimes. Consider my father who cannot eat in a French restaurant without drawing all sorts of connections between the food and the culture. The French philosophy of living itself apparently can be divined from its food. That's fine, but sometimes his dinner companions yearn for simple commentary on the flavor of the food. In Umberto Eco's *Foucault's Pendulum*,[68] the possible interpretations of an ancient message fragment obsess the protagonist and eventually cost him and his companion their lives. Toward the end of the book, the dogged academic hero shows the message to his wife, a scholar herself. After examining it for a moment, she convincingly concludes that it is a merely a shopping list penned by a medieval homemaker, not the key to unraveling the legend of the Knights Templar. Of course, it's a shopping list! Sometimes sex and good food are just sex and good food.

Whether one ascribes this impulse to abstract from everyday experience to a manifestation of a Jungian masculine archetype or not, it seems clearly entrenched in human nature. We do abstract; we do theorize; we do see connections with the eternal in the mundane. My suggestion is that the character of Don Juan is the literary embodiment of that impulse, not the impulse of the libido or, as suggested by Otto Rank, the drive to return to the lost security of the mother's womb. We do have libidinous impulses, and maybe we do yearn for those dimly remembered amniotic days, but the Don Juan motif seems concerned with a much different aspect of our human reality.

Surprisingly, this observation can help us think about seduction law, once we identify the counterbalance to the problems presented by the sort of Don Juanism described above.

---

68. Umberto Eco, *Foucault's Pendulum* (San Diego: Harcourt Brace Jovanovich, 1988).

III. The Particular and the Intimate

Without naming him as such, feminist authors seem very aware of the Don Juan described above. Commentators often describe as masculine the impulse to theorize and abstract away the real difficulties presented by particular human problems.[69] Others argue we should have less theory and more focus on human relationships.[70] Some even suggest that the rule of law is somehow masculine and often generates unjust results in its rigidity; equity is feminine and can do justice where general rules should be ignored.[71] Mediation is a feminine process where the actual parties sit down face to face and work on their problems; adversarial litigation is a masculine process where representatives of the real parties argue more about abstract law and procedure than the feelings that really concern their clients. Robin West writes about the role of autonomy in contract law in this way.[72] She points out that enforcing an abstract value like contractual autonomy will inevitably disadvantage women; therefore, feminists should rely less on broad autonomy arguments and focus more on individuals and the real impact of the law on their lives. The movement toward the acceptance of narrative as scholarship points consistently toward the primacy of the particular as opposed to theory.[73]

A powerful exploration of the dangers posed by the human impulse to abstraction is contained in Bessie Head's semi-autobiographical novel, *A Question of Power*.[74] Head's heroine is the illegitimate child of a white South African socialite and a black African stablehand. After a traumatic childhood in South Africa, and on the verge of a nervous breakdown, she exiles herself to Botswana to teach school and escape apartheid. Instead of finding refuge, she finds insanity. The novel is the graphic and powerful description of her breakdown and recovery. The critical theme of the

---

69. See, for example, Marijane Camilleri, "Lessons in Law from Literature: A Look at the Movement and a Peer at her Jury," 39 *Cath. L. Rev.* 557, 567 (1990) ("[S]ome feminists assert that the rule of law reflects the dominant masculine culture of equality, rights, and distance from others, and undervalues the feminine values of intimacy, nurturance, and care."); Jeanne Schroeder, "Feminism Historicized: Medieval Misogynist Stereotypes in Contemporary Feminist Jurisprudence," 75 *Iowa L. Rev.* 1135, 1188 (1990).

70. See, for example, Robin West, "Adjudication is not Interpretation," in *Narrative, Authority & Law* 176 (1993) ("The test of the morality of power in public life as in private may be neither compliance with community mores, as objectivists insist, nor political success, as subjectivists claim, but love.").

71. *Id.*

72. *Id.* at 27–88.

73. See, for example, Symposium, "Legal Storytelling," 87 *Mich. L. Rev.* 2073 (1989).

74. Bessie Head, *A Question of Power* (London: Heineman, 1974).

novel is that the recovery of her sanity is only made possible by her rejection of philosophy, of theory, of religion, of abstracting away from the reality of everyday life.[75] At the beginning of her breakdown she holds tight to abstract beliefs we all approve of: the brotherhood of humankind; non-violent political action; and universal love and salvation. Her understandable initial reaction to the violence of her childhood is to reach for the general values that stand against it, to embrace the political and philosophical movements that reject the evil that has been done to her. This impulse drives her insane. Theory has no power to save. She only recovers when she learns to embrace the particular: her friend Tom, her friend Kenoshi, her son, her garden, and her chores.

This focus on the particular, on relationship rather than theory, on love rather than law, stands in stark contrast to the transcendent themes in the modern depictions of Don Juan. This opposition is also presented in the debate over seduction outlined by Larsen. The core of the debate now focuses on the theoretical implications of rules expanding tort recovery for seduction, disputing what the effect will be on the sexual marketplace or considering whether the tort is consistent with classical liberal notions of autonomy. A different voice asks us to consider the fate of the individual victim who is lied to and relies to his or her very real emotional detriment. Our approach to the issue would be enriched by a principle that would mediate between the abstract considerations of market forces and classical liberalism, on the one hand, and the concreteness of individual pain, on the other. In other words, is there a legal principle that might mediate between the worlds of Don Juan and Bessie Head's heroine, Elizabeth?

IV. Mediating Rules in Contract Law

A brief look at contract law provides some examples of how doctrine develops to mediate between the impulse to abstraction and concern for the particular. For example, contract cases are filled with statements describing the sanctity of individual autonomy.[76] "Freedom of contract" is the byword for principles under which judges enforce harsh bargains. For example, courts that recognize surrogate mother contracts expressly remind us that competent adults are free to make binding deals, even regarding the most intimate aspects of their lives. This is not the whole story of contract law, however. The existence of a theory that justifies binding individuals to their

---

75. See Paul J. Heald, "Idealism and the Individual Woman: Madness and Humanity in Bessie Head's *A Question of Power*," 5 *Tex. J. of Women & Law* 83 (1995).

76. See *Schwenck v. Spitzer Marina*, 1994 WL 385972 (Ohio App. 1994) ("Ohio courts have held that freedom of contract is fundamental in our society.").

word has not prevented a host of doctrines that look to the particular facts of a case to mediate a harsh result. Any first-year student can point out that contracts are voidable for duress, unconscionability, impracticability, frustration of purpose, and failure to disclose a material fact, among many other reasons.

Section 2-302 of the Uniform Commercial Code is a good example of a mediating principle.[77] Contracts to sell goods are presumptively enforceable, but some contain terms so onerous as to be unconscionable, e.g., some limitations on consequential damages.[78] The arguments surrounding the proper scope of section 2-302 parallel issues raised in the comparison of Don Juan and Bessie Head. Our impulse to abstract prompts worries about a legal world without bright line rules:

> "We've got an autonomy theory—let's stick with it. The more exceptions one creates, the less good a theory it will be."
> "People who sign agreements should live with them."
> "We should not move away from general rules and get bogged down in the facts."
> "Rule of Law = Predictability = Justice."

Our impulse to the particular, on the other hand, prompts us to worry about Mrs. Williams in *Williams v. Walker Thomas Furniture*[79] and what will happen to other individuals if we let financing sellers bypass statutory safeguards in enforcing liens on collateral. We need exceptions to the autonomy principle in order to care for actual individuals in the marketplace.

Whether or not we denominate these conflicting impulses as masculine and feminine, they seem to exist in varying degrees in all of us. The history of section 2-302, and other contract policing doctrines that soften the hard application of the autonomy principle, shows that neither impulse truly carries the day. We have both a legal system that enforces agreements, generally recognizing the freedom of an individual to control his or her commercial fate, yet we also have a system that recognizes that these autonomous actors are not faceless and present special circumstances that may need to be considered.

Even though contract law is not perfect by any stretch of the imagination, mediation between the two impulses can be found there.

---

77. U.C.C. § 2-302 ("If the court as a matter of law finds the contract or any clause of the contract to have been unconscionable at the time it was made, the court may refuse to enforce the contract...").

78. See U.C.C. § 2-719(3) ("Consequential damages may be limited or excluded unless the limitation or exclusion is unconscionable.").

79. 350 F.2d 445 (D.C. Cir. 1965) (holding unconscionable various clauses in a retail installment sales agreement).

IV. Back to Seduction

Is a mediating principle at work in seduction law? The law seems to be struggling toward one. While generally rejecting the independent tort for sexual fraud advocated by Larsen, the law seems to be growing pockets of liability when special circumstances are present: the seducer is a doctor, lawyer, or minister; or the seducer has lied about his fertility or HIV status.[80] The ultimate question is whether these pockets are sufficient to mediate the legitimate worry that victims of seduction need more help and the legitimate worry that our love lives will become a snarl of litigation.

Following Larsen, a rule could be adopted that material misrepresentations of fact made to obtain sex are generally actionable when the victim's reliance is reasonable and damages result.[81] Her formulation, however, seems both underinclusive and overinclusive, a symptom of many attempts to formulate rules that draw lines to sort out cases before they happen. Her deception requirement creates two problems. First, a certain level of deception is clearly acceptable in our intimate relationships. Few lovers do not try to cast themselves in the best possible light. What the community regards as reasonable deception (make up? elevator shoes?) should not be actionable.[82] Second, the focus on deception leaves out the class of seductions where the seducer abuses his power, but does not lie, e.g. the opportunistic lawyer in *Tante v. Herring* or the sleazy teacher in *Franklin v. Hill*.

Rather than drawing bright line rules, one might borrow from the contract law principles discussed above and propose that seduction be actionable under an unconscionability standard. The use of deception can be unconscionable; the abuse of power can be unconscionable. A more flexible ad hoc standard would allow a factfinder to more directly assess the reasonableness of the seducer's behavior. Similar to negligence law, the focus would be directly on the seducer's behavior in light of what the community perceives to be reasonable. Importantly, the history of unconscionability demonstrates that the doctrine does not give judges free reign to indulge in emotionalism. The use of the standard has not resulted in judges voiding contracts simply because they are offended by the terms. Rather, the cases demonstrate an awareness of both the imbalance of power that one can find in contractual relationships and the potential damage done to our system of promising if judges were to void contracts without compelling reasons. Unconscionability may be a principle that can mediate between the pull toward bright line rules that abstract from actual cases

---

80. See supra notes 32–33.

81. Larsen, supra note 6, at 453.

82. Perhaps Larsen's requirement of reasonable reliance could be used to protect the seducer whose misrepresentations fall within accepted community norms.

and the pull toward a visceralism that would undermine the value of the rule of law.

Under this standard, *Tante v. Herring* is rightly decided. As a community, most people would probably agree that the abuse of confidential information by an attorney to seduce a needy client is unconscionable. What defense of reasonableness could the lawyer offer? On the other hand, the decision in *Franklin v. Hill* seems wholly unsatisfactory. It's not difficult to imagine situations where a high school teacher should be liable for sleeping with a seventeen-year-old student. Yet there may be different situations where the teacher should not be liable. The problem is that under the current law, a court need not discuss unconscionability or reasonableness at all. It need not acknowledge the conflict between the abstract and the particular we have identified. The broadest thesis of this essay is that the courts need to engage in such discussions, regardless of what substantive standard is adopted.

Conclusion

Literary sources suggest that the discussion of liability for seduction should focus on the search for doctrines that mediate our impulse to generalize away from real harm done to individuals and our impulse to try to remedy all the hurt we see in the world. Bright line rules designed to decide broad categories of cases before they arise will inevitably fail to mediate in this way, regardless of whether they are drawn by economists or feminists or libertarians. Although adopting flexible standards that make decision making more complex and agonizing is not always the answer to legal conundrums, the literature of seduction demonstrates fundamental tensions in ourselves and in our relationships that demand a different sort of conversation about seduction than we have yet enjoyed.

About the Authors

Lief Carter is McHugh Distinguished Professor of American Institutions and Leadership, Department of Political Science, Colorado College.

Paul J. Heald is Professor of Law, University of Georgia.

Susan Sage Heinzelman is Professor of English, University of Texas.

Martha C. Nussbaum is Professor and Ernst P. Freund Chair of Law & Ethics, University of Chicago.

David A. Skeel, Jr., is Professor of Law, University of Pennsylvania.